UNMASK YOUR
Brilliance

Thriving Beyond Workplaces Designed to Hide You

By

Michelle Mehrnoosh Bazargan

ISBN: 978-1-962202-24-4

Printed in the United States of America

Published by Ballast Books
www.ballastbooks.com
www.michellebazargan.com

For more information, bulk orders, appearances, or speaking requests,
please email: info@michellebazargan.com

To Lana Azadeh Black

May you always have the courage to be all of you and never let anyone dim your light and take away the infinite possibilities you possess deep in your heart. Remember this—no matter what dream you desire, the universe will have your back in making it a reality! Believe in and trust yourself!

Table of Contents

PART III

Introduction

*H*ow difficult can it be to approach the counter at McDonald's and request ketchup? In America, the answer might depend on your confidence in English.

For me, that simple act was sheer terror. Using my broken English and shyness in a country where I had landed not by choice but for survival felt like death repeating itself in my body.

So how on earth did I unintentionally go from that to landing on a TED Talk stage, presenting at board meetings, and giving keynote speeches around the world? The secret is not at all what you would think or the advice you are given in most "motivation" or "leadership" books.

My journey to becoming closer to authentically me started with some seriously deep soul-searching about what is unique and different about me, which enabled me to unearth profound truths and lies about myself and the life I was leading that most people never uncover. I finally asked myself a few key questions I'd like you to consider now.

How comfortable are you with the unknown? How willing are you to expose yourself, to be vulnerable and reveal your wounds? How ready are you to be seen as the real you and use your voice, even if it means being judged or rejected?

Now, imagine doing all of this in the place where we spend over 30% of our lifetime—that's over 10 years: the workplace.

Have you ever walked into your workplace, looked around, and wondered which parts of yourself you need to suppress to fit into the environment or "culture"?

Have you ever passionately offered suggestions on improving the business, only to hear "That's not how things work here," or "To succeed, you need to be like the top performers"?

Have you ever pondered why many organizations and environments have a uniform appearance, language, and adherence to outdated practices, almost as if they were cogs in the wheel of the matrix?

Whether it's a startup where everyone wears hoodies and speaks in hip slang or a Fortune 500 company where formality and buzzwords like "transformation" and "strategy" rule the day, these concepts often seem more complex than they need to be.

Regardless of your age, experience, or title, do you often question if the narratives spun by some organizations using words like "inclusion," "innovation," "sustainability," and being a "Best Company to Work For" are nothing but a façade?

Rest assured—you are not alone, and your suspicions hold true. We are often unconsciously encouraged to put on masks and hide, but what we fail to realize is the significant toll this takes on each one of us.

As a society, we're grappling with the highest rates of illness, depression, anxiety, suicide, and drug and alcohol addiction in history, and one contributing factor is the extent to which we hide and mask our true selves.

This is a very harsh reality to look at, so instead we distract ourselves and debate about things like "return to office" or "hybrid work." But the location you are in won't impact your creativity and brilliance if the real you is not welcomed. Unmasking unconscious truths and confronting unspoken lies designed to stifle us, that we rarely address in the workplace, will.

Throughout my professional journey spanning two decades, culminating in my current role as an executive business advisor, I've spent countless hours with thousands of diverse teams globally. These teams range from agile startups to Fortune 500 giants, and I've worked closely with executives, leaders, and managers across various industries and at all organizational levels. Over the years, I've observed leadership styles, cultural mindsets, and environments.

Regrettably, from an insider's perspective, your suspicions about the pressure for conformity and the prevalence of false narratives, misconceptions, and outright lies hold true in many (though not all) environments, departments, and organizations. There are those rare few that encourage visibility of what is truly unique about each of us, and then there are those that profess to champion innovation and creativity while intentionally or unintentionally stifling people by promoting conformity and uniformity.

All this, and yet we are not victims, and there is an uncomfortable challenge and reality we must face if we desire to change our world. As digital anthropologist and futurist Brian Solis tells us, "Environments become the sum total of what we all tolerate."

The collective tolerance within an environment shapes the overall culture and atmosphere of that environment, and we all have slowly contributed to this.

> *"Environments become the sum total of what
> we all tolerate."*

We tolerate masking ourselves and shutting off what is unique about us, we tolerate conformity, we tolerate giving away our power and shrinking, we tolerate shutting off our creativity and courage. We silence our voice when we know something is wrong.

We get programmed to give in to the judgment for fear of shame and rejection and make it our goal to be the same. We hide ourselves and slowly over time have no clue of our true power, brilliance, and capabilities.

From our first steps as toddlers, each of us is inherently aware of the infinite possibilities this beautiful world has to offer. Then something major happens. We begin to absorb the world around us.

We start collecting our family's, community's, and society's points of view. We go to the school system, where we learn that our inherent brilliance might not always receive applause.

We then enter the command-and-control workplace and corporate environment, and we are smothered by misconceptions like "We are family." We quickly drink the Kool-Aid and give up our unique identities and replace them with the identity of the organization. Under this illusion, we immediately receive constant "feedback" if we are not like everyone else, doing things the way everyone else does things, and we will quickly be rejected and told we're "not a cultural fit." If we don't change to fit in and be the same.

Instead of celebrating our unique gifts, we often let external projections and views dim our light. We allow the false shadow of shame to cloud our self-worth and start rejecting the very essence that makes us stand out.

In the workplace we throw around buzzwords like "empathy," "vulnerability," "trust," "gratitude"—yet 99% of most people have no idea what these words actually mean in the day-to-day application. How many times a day do we judge and reject ourselves with our own thoughts? Everything starts with self. If we are unable to have things like empathy and trust for ourselves, how then can we have empathy or trust for others?

Isn't it strange how our world's push for conformity and its narrow portrayal of success can cause us to ignore our own inherent talents and gifts? Yet this is the very thing that will differentiate us from machines and robots.

The greatest threat to humanity in this new era of rapid technological progress, exemplified by the swift advancements of generative AI, is the imperative to reconnect with our true nature as human beings. Our ability to foster self-awareness, walk a mile in someone else's shoes, get curious and ask questions to gain compassion, and genuinely see and include each other beyond a title and image—all which form the bedrock of creativity and innovation—is under threat as long as we continue to conceal our authentic selves.

> *"I aspire to empower individuals to rediscover the light within themselves, a bright radiance they may not even be aware they have dimmed."*

The call to action is clear: we must become aware and embrace our true selves to avoid the threat of being replaced by machines or having an unhealthy relationship with them. It's time to unmask, assert our uniqueness, reconnect as a collective, and shape a future where human brilliance reigns supreme.

Yet we still have a significant gap to close.

I aspire to empower individuals to rediscover the light within themselves, a bright radiance they may not even be aware they have dimmed.

How I Learned to Mask Myself

Like so many of us, the story of my life is a story of masking and unmasking.

At age 6, in the middle of a cold winter night, my mother and I boarded a bus. Bombs went off behind us. We lived in Iran, where overnight, war invaded the beautiful country and became our new daily lives. I still remember my mother's voice as she convinced my grandfather that she had to leave and that she could not raise a daughter in an oppressed country destroyed by the Islamic Revolution.

Deep inside, she knew my opportunities would be limited, if not deadly, if we stayed—and she was right. As recently as September 16, 2022, the world witnessed the brutal beating and killing of 22-year-old Mahsa Amini for exposing some hair through her hijab. And since then, the brutal killing of so many young women and men for using their voices to advance fundamental human rights like holding hands and riding bicycles in the streets.

We left everything behind, and with one bag, in the middle of the night during a winter storm, began our multi-year journey to arrive to the US.

Most Americans at the time had only the media's perspective of Iran, and because Iran's regime had taken Americans hostage, we were all viewed as terrorists. Kids would leave notes on my desk that said things like, "Go Home, Terrorist." This is why we hear Iranians calling themselves "Persian," as most people did not know that Iran was once called "Persia"—they thought it was another country. Oh, the small positives in lack of knowledge.

I felt forced into being shameful about where I was from and who I was, so what did I learn to do naturally? Hide and become invisible. For me it was life or death, I had to fit in, so I learned to wear a mask and keep aspects of my identity as closed off as possible.

I legally changed my name from Mehrnoosh to Michelle.

I changed my appearance and tried to look as "American" as possible.

I dyed my hair blonde. (It wasn't a good look.)

My parents even sent me to linguistics classes to make sure I would not have an accent and would not be bullied like my parents were. Little did I know back then that my accent was a sign of courage—a sign that I was bold enough to leave the unknown and seek greater possibilities. I should have never gotten rid of or hidden it.

I had no idea that my childhood experiences left me with severe complex post-traumatic stress disorder (CPTSD), which often results in children becoming shy, introverted, hypervigilant, overly aware, and extremely empathic. I also had zero idea that being an immigrant from another country, speaking another language, and having different cultural norms and experiences made me completely and totally different.

To make matters worse, entering a corporate environment only added to and exasperated this trauma and difference. As I quickly learned in many workplaces, being "different" was seen as a business liability. Unconsciously, I began to pull in people, leaders, friends, colleagues, and relationships that would replicate my past, all of which pushed me into darkness. (This is called "repetition syndrome" in psychology.)

By the time I was a fully seemingly successful adult, I had learned to wear a mask. Years spent hiding behind layers of shame had taught me to disconnect from my authentic self, and my work life reinforced this necessity. Eventually, I had the humility to look in the mirror and could not recognize the person I saw. I realized as a society we have been encouraged to be in survival mode, to disconnect from who we are and separate from each other. How generational trauma and wounding has caused all of us to become addicted to judgment, blame, shame, and division.

From within that darkness, I began EMDR therapy, which is one of the very few modalities that makes a connection between the mind and body and healing. During one session, my therapist asked me to write a letter to my younger self. I eagerly dug out a picture of myself as a child and gazed into her soulful eyes. What would she think of the stranger I had become? What would I tell her that would allow her to grow into her most authentic self? I put my pen to a blank page and began to write.

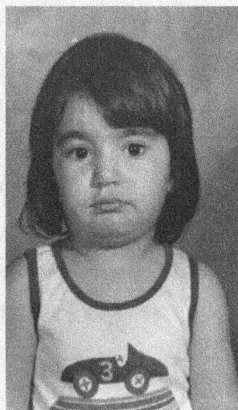

Dear Michelle Mehrnoosh Bazargan,

Hello, sweet, beautiful warrior. First of all, thank you for choosing to come to this weird planet. I know it seems like a strange land. I know you are highly sensitive and can "feel" everyone and everything and are a bit confused on what to do with the gift of being highly aware, having a 6th sense, and being an extreme empath and feeling so wrong.

You have been given a gift to see possibilities everywhere you go. This is why you look at people and desire to heal them and gift them everything you know they can have. You see their being and their souls and know they can be capable of creating anything they desire.

Please know that your awareness, your sensitivity, your passion, and your lens that anything and everything is possible in this abundant world is a strength, not a weakness.

You are different, you are here to create magic. You are powerful. Because of this, people may choose to be scared of you and scared that you can see them. The real them. The infinite being in them that is choosing to shrink and settle. They will hate that you see what they are capable of even though they are choosing limitation and lack for themselves.

They will judge you, fight you, abuse you, hurt you, shrink you, reject you, and try to tell you that you are wrong and to turn off your "light." It's a lie, it's not true. No matter how much you change and morph yourself, you will be seen as "too much" or "not enough." You will be too fat, too fit, too ugly, too pretty, too smart, too dumb, too tall . . .

Please don't change who you are, please don't lose you into the darkness of judgment. Whatever you do, please don't change your name to be accepted. Changing your name will become the beginning of hiding and masking your light, which is the essence of your real name. *Mehrnoosh* dates back to centuries of Persian origin, translated to mean "eternal light" or "everlasting light."

Mehr means "sun" or "love," and *noosh* translates to "eternal" or "everlasting." This name is quite poetic in its meaning and is reflective of the richness of Persian linguistic and cultural nuances.

You will eventually enter the corporate and workplace environment; you will be exposed to survival and lack mindsets and see outdated structures and methods that has turned many people into unconscious robots. You will see this right away and make it your job to save people and open their eyes to greater possibilities. You won't understand why they choose this life. You will try to convince them that the world is an abundant and big place, that there is so much to go around and it's not worth it to hate others for positions, titles, and money. They will hate you for it while secretly wishing they had your courage.

Don't separate, resist, react, or go into defense and fight. Definitely don't align and agree with them and make them right or prove them wrong. That will only give them more power and control over you. Don't step into their darkness. Keep your light and your power—it's the true essence of you.

I will write you a book and leave it for you. Please read it over and over! Don't buy the lies. Don't hide and mask up; it may feel good temporarily, yet it will come back to try to destroy you. Most of all, build your awareness, ask questions of everything and everyone. Use the tools in this book. Take absolutely nothing at face value.

Trust you, honor you, and be grateful for you. No one knows what they are doing or what is "true" for you; they are not you. Only you know, so don't pretend you don't. Don't make anyone else more important or powerful than you. They will try to convince you they have "more experience" and know more. It's a facade, and you are radically different.

You will most likely spend most of your time building a career in the business world or interacting with people in the workplace in some capacity. Make sure your career is aligned with who you are and what you desire to create in this world as your own legacy, not what is forced upon you.

True warrior status and legacy is not fitting in and not conforming; it's having the courage to be you and choose you. The rest is a lie. Have fun and laugh a lot!

Shine your light bright and inspire others to do the same. Now go have some ice cream and look up at the sky. It's filled with infinite possibilities and magic.

Love you to the moon!

It was a profound and eye-opening moment when I realized just how much I had been conditioned to suppress my true self, to wear masks, and to conceal and alter my authentic nature. This conditioning, ingrained in me by both the educational system and society, was later manipulated and misused by the corporations for which I worked. I later came to understand how deeply normalized this behavior had become, with many people conforming to the same pattern.

When my eyes turned from my own picture to the one framed on my desk of my 6-year-old niece, I had a revelation—it was my responsibility to break away from the mold of most people and take action to evolve our future generations and break the generational trauma we have accepted as normal.

I went on to change my legal name back to Mehrnoosh. Today I am a proud, strong, compassionate, and courageous Iranian American who knows that accents, pain, failing, learning, grit, curiosity, and resilience are all signs of courage.

We Recreate Our Childhoods in the Workplace

Revisiting my child self led me to another revelation, one that impacts each and every one of us. We are all walking, talking adults in big bodies in the workplace, unconsciously replaying our childhood dynamics, blind spots, and unconscious limitations.

We are disempowered and programmed as children to conform to certain belief systems and behaviors, or else face rejection. Here's the most disempowering lesson we're taught: what we *know* to be *true* for us and our own *awareness* doesn't matter—in schools, communities, and even families.

Remember that sinking "not good enough" feeling when you received your report card? That D or even B that made you feel less than? The shrinking feeling in your energy, body, and gut?

Consider that identical feeling when your manager gives you a performance review stating you're merely "meeting expectations" and gives you the canned list of "weaknesses" to improve. It's the same feeling, because the disempowerment continues, thanks to corporate programming.

How do we typically respond? We shrink. We change. We morph ourselves to fit in. We hide what's genuinely true for us and, in doing so, we slowly and unconsciously surrender our true selves.

This is because we have been sold a lie. Most modern-day workplaces and corporatized operating models, processes, and mindsets have not evolved since the industrial revolution. In the 1900s, Henry Ford created the assembly line to reduce risk and increase efficiency of vehicle production. And what have we done? We've modernized it to ensure that people are also part of the assembly line.

The workplace reinforces the message: we need everyone to be just like a car and be the "same" on the supply chain assembly line. Translation—what's true for you and about you doesn't matter here. Unconsciously, we're being programmed not to reveal our authentic selves. We fail to recognize that this form of hiding and unwillingness to be seen amounts to suppression of courage, creativity, and individuality.

With over 90,000 hours in our entire lifetime dedicated to work, we've grown accustomed to hiding our true, 360-degree, dynamic selves, cutting off all emotions, wearing tight masks by not sharing our thoughts, backgrounds, and stories, and conforming to the command-and-control constructs as normal behavior.

What has struck me as *most* disturbing is that, over time, we have normalized work environments that subtly abuse us, both emotionally and psychologically, by capitalizing on our unconscious programs and past traumas, and by creating additional trauma for us any time we dare to defy the corporate mold by being different.

Yes, I used a controversial word: *abuse*. What else would we call it when we're asked to cut off pieces of who we actually are? Would we dream of asking our children to do that?

Even though in some environments we have normalized this as a way of running a profitable business, it's not normal! It's our biggest threat and is slowly killing us.

This Book Is Not for Most People

In my professional journey, I've journaled and researched my interactions with executives and clients at all levels, looking for root behaviors beyond the surface, from 15-person startups to 24,000-employee, $70 billion enterprises, across all generations from boomers to Gen Z. Over the last few years, I gathered extensive research and surveys to understand people's core experiences and what they really think but hesitate to share in the workplace so they can *play the game* and avoid judgment, exclusion, and rejection in the form of *not being promoted*. Here is what I found that I thought was completely insane—**at the core, we're all the same!** Yes, even the toxic demon bitches and assholes.

Regardless of title, experience, or generation, we share similar unconscious limitations. We sacrifice our awareness, creativity, and courage. Meanwhile, deep down in our heart of hearts, we all just want to be seen, acknowledged, included, and heard. That is the core desire we are trying to fulfill from the surface behaviors.

For some, the pattern emerges through pleasing the board of directors. Others want to please their managers or colleagues. Then we distract ourselves by losing our minds over whether generative artificial intelligence, or a machine, will replace us. We obsess with understanding LLMs (large language models) and the best

ChatGPT "prompt" to use—forgetting that changing the world first starts with changing us.

Insights and research allowed me to connect the dots to a crucial missing piece we are not talking about: how, in our rapidly advancing era of technology and automation, the suppression of each person's unique human creativity and potential is not just a personal failure but a failure of our entire system.

"In our rapidly advancing era of technology and automation, the suppression of each person's unique human creativity and potential is not just a personal failure but a failure of our entire system."

The structures and mindsets of the industrial revolution persist, stifling innovation and individuality. The outdated command-and-control of most organizations, which capitalizes on past trauma to maintain conformity, has created a workforce that no longer serves us.

With this disconnect in mind, I conducted a search on Amazon for books on leadership, mindset, and achieving goals. I was flooded with over 20,000 to 40,000 results. Yet nearly none focused on a critical factor to being a human-centered conscious leader from any seat: becoming aware of and healing our generational unconscious programs, patterns, behaviors, and traumas.

Stepping into the strength of becoming aware of what is unique and true and reconnecting with the person looking back at us in the mirror. We cannot be great leaders in our new world order without reconnection with ourselves and then with each other. This book aims to address that gap.

This is why the clients I take on and coach are not "most people"—most people avoid tough conversations; most people don't have the courage to stop pointing the finger and look in the mirror and become who they are capable of becoming. To go deep and look at their values and purpose. Most people are unwilling to be uncomfortable by looking inside instead of outside.

This book is not about negotiating a higher salary, reaching your goals, how to get "confident," or how to get promoted. It's deeper!

How can we get confident if we are unaware of our uniqueness and our superpowers? Who cares if we achieve a status with more money at the cost of disconnection from ourselves and others?

This is not a "Boss in Heels," "Nice Girls Don't Get the Corner Office," or "How to Be Stoic" madness that has been misused to breed our culture of toxic femininity and masculinity.

So if that is what you were expecting, print the return label and send it back. But I highly suspect that if you are reading this, you are not like most people!

I wrote this book to challenge the status quo, to open our eyes to the mechanistic corporate environments and workforce cultures that often turn us into unconscious robotic participants.

Leadership is a behavior, not a title. Leaders have the insatiable courage to become aware and curious, and to connect and collaborate.

This book is an invitation to inspire you to un-hide, unmask all of you—not just the parts that are "acceptable"—and step up, revealing your unique self without needing a fancy title to do so. We must move beyond our professional facades, hiding behind company names we work for, and embrace our authentic selves, quirks, traumas, fears, and everything else, if we desire to thrive as a species.

In parts of this book, I am very direct about the lies we are accepting as truths, but this is not with the intention of shaming or judging anyone or making anyone or any environment right and wrong. It's to make us uncomfortable and shock us all into what we are accepting as completely normal, which is slowly killing us.

I will provide the tools to become more aware, curious, and courageous about who you are and remind you that you are more powerful than you are made to believe, especially in the workplace. These tools can also apply and be used to empower you in other areas of your life as well such as your relationship with money, friends, community, romantic partners, and more.

As Charlie Chaplin reminded us, "Life is a beautiful, magnificent thing, even to a jellyfish. The trouble is you won't fight. You've given up. But there's something just as inevitable as death. And that's life. Think of all the power that's in the universe, moving the earth, growing the trees. That's the same power within you if you only have the courage and the will to use it."

> *"Think of all the power that's in the universe, moving the earth, growing the trees. That's the same power within you if you only have courage and the will to use it."*
> *—Charlie Chaplin[1]*

In Part I, I critique and expose the lies and misconceptions that corporations and workplace culture programs lead us to believe. Why we are in the midst of a human revolution and why it's critical now more than ever in the age of technology automation to take back our creativity, boldness, and brilliance to prepare for the future. I explore how these misconceptions are programmed in us from childhood and how they limit our potential. How if we become aware of them, we can break the matrix programs and choose not to become a part of them.

In Part II, I share practical tools and insights that empower you to stop pointing the finger and start looking in the mirror at generational trauma and our identity crisis, which will help you become more conscious and aware in the workplace. We will explore how to question what you've been told, how to uncover survival programs, and how to discover your unique strengths and make empowering choices beyond those made on autopilot.

In Part III, we take a closer look at realigning with what you know; reconnecting with what is true for uniquely you; and unlocking the conscious leader that is hidden in each one of us— no title required.

I will offer tools and bring awareness to the things we do not talk about in the workplace, or really many parts of our lives. Things that are foundational to our joy, connection, and compassion, such as:

- The reenactment of our entire childhood and experiences in the workplace
- How corporate culture traumatizes us and capitalizes on your childhood programs
- How toxic femininity is a real issue, and why women do not support women
- How we are hiding the strength of our men
- Why being an immigrant in a foreign country changes your lens and entire trajectory
- Why corporate jargon and terms like "perception is reality" are a lie, and how we have the power to consciously choose

Drawing from my personal journey as an immigrant who has faced trauma in my personal life, which was further exacerbated while navigating the corporate world, I offer a unique perspective on the collective awareness we could foster. I share my path of self-discovery and the invaluable insights I lacked during my initial entry into the workforce. I wish someone had stressed that, without this foundational understanding of myself, acquiring skills, education, or new knowledge would be like building a skyscraper on unstable ground.

As you read, you will gain tools and *homeplay* instructions— our life should be a playful exploration of what is true for us, not *work*.

This is not about quitting your job, becoming an entrepreneur, or moving to an isolated mountaintop. My goal is to help people recognize what's holding us back as a collective, challenge the misconceptions we've all believed in, and inspire humans to harness their most significant strength—the courage to choose to be uniquely all of you!

Please take just one small nugget in this book that resonates with you, try it, use it, and share it.

> *"You are not a drop in the ocean.*
> *You are the entire ocean in a drop."*
> *—Rumi*

As you read along, remember Rumi's words: "You are not a drop in the ocean. You are the entire ocean in a drop." We all have the power to be a ripple of change. That is how we evolve our beautiful planet and leave it better for our children and future generations. Imagine if all 8 billion–plus of us became just 0.0001% consciously closer to who we are.

This is my invitation to step into the courageous, bold leader you are! Into your brilliance!

Let's do this together!

PART I

WHY NOW—THE GREATEST THREAT TO HUMANITY

CHAPTER 1

Corporate Machine: Understanding Misconceptions and Limitations

"You are part of our 'family' as long as you do as we say, dress the way we want you to, accept anything toxic and abusive as totally normal, spin our departments' numbers and performance . . . oh, and contribute to the PAC (the political action committee), and then you will be in my seat in no time!"

—Senior executive at a multi-billion-dollar organization, someone I naively called a mentor

I was 20 years old and walking into a massive auditorium for a town hall meeting. I remember feeling so warm and fuzzy when I read "We Are Family" on the PowerPoint. I felt like, *OMG, I have arrived, I am included and part of something greater than me.*

Young and naive, I bought into the concept of *we are family and we care about you* that many organizations shout in the headlines as something literal. I mean, everyone around me with "experience" in their 30s, 40s, 50s were all in.

Who could argue that they were on *Fortune*'s Best Companies to Work For list, that they had the highest Glassdoor reviews? Their list of extravagant perks never ended. Even better, everyone smiled and was so welcoming. Looking back, I can see myself in a movie scene from *Stepford Wives, Wall Street* or *The Matrix*. Watch these movies with a keen eye, and you'll realize they're not movies; they're documentaries of how things work.

It is in our DNA to want to be part of a tribe and belong, which is why community and being a part of something feels essential to us. Yet this innate human instinct is often used psychologically against us by many organizations. Statements like "we are family" and "we care about our people" are overused and often misleading.

Does family fire you if they over hired? Give you poor performance reviews because you don't fit in their box? Do they label you as *wrong*? Does family require you to "prove" your worth on the corporate hamster wheel for a title, promotion, or recognition?[2]

> *"This illusion of family in the workplace is a lie that we desperately want to believe."*

This illusion of family in the workplace is a lie that we desperately want to believe. It leads us to attach our self-worth and values to companies that are often symbolized by recognizable names. This is why we often see "Former (Insert Popular Company Name) employee" on LinkedIn headers, as if it is a badge of family honor. We unconsciously negate our unique individual value and give up our core identities. Our entire personal brand and identity becomes the name and brand color and logo of where we work. Why do we do this?

Corporate culture has long been committed to making sure everyone looks the same, works the same, and acts the same. Work structure still operates that way. We are sent into the defective pile like a widget if we don't perfectly fit into the cogwheel. This archaic leadership approach overlooks our inherent worth as individuals and slowly makes us feel wrong to the core.

Unfortunately, we've all been conditioned to think this is totally freaking normal. This happens because we fall for it. We all accept it. We even make each other wrong if we don't properly fit into the cog. It perpetuates not because of companies or abusive leaders and cultures. It happens because we allow it! We see it and ignore it.

Just as we accept the everyday culture of our own families as **normal** and **right**, so too do we accept the culture of our corporate "families."

I often get asked by my very senior leaders at organizations questions like, "How do I fix my lack of innovation problem?" Then, I look at their website and I straightforwardly tell them, "Your chamber is all the same—it's an echo of yourself." Their employees are all white males with the token female in HR or minority to check a box.

80% of the time if you ask the "token" if they are actually included and listened to, they will tell you "no."

There are countless individuals I coach who say they are tired and burned out and don't even know what their individual purpose is. Or they tell me that their purpose is being the VP of something at company XYZ, like that is a totally normal answer. That's not an identity or a purpose.

We have handed our identities, careers, and minds over to an entity that drives conformity in its people. What we don't realize is that it's easier to manage and control people who are the same. It's a lot harder to lead people when we encourage them to be uniquely themselves.

"It's easier to manage and control people who are the same. It's a lot harder to lead people when we encourage them to be uniquely themselves."

Day by day and little by little, we lose our passion, curiosity, creativity, courage, and so much more. We have unconsciously allowed this to happen. Then all of a sudden, we ask, "Will a machine or artificial intelligence replace me?" "Will my children's future be controlled by a machine?"

Yes! Keep disconnecting from who we are and separating from each other, and it definitely will! It's already in progress.

In many corporations or work environments, the minute we see someone ask questions or behave differently or evolve beyond this outdated madness, we say, "Yikes, you are not a good culture fit here."

Imagine bringing home a new romantic partner to meet your family for the first time. If that outsider can't easily meld into the typical family dynamic you are accustomed to, how often does it cause friction or even rejection in the relationship? The same thing happens in the workplace. When newcomers can't blend in or, worse, questions why things are done a certain way, they often get the cold shoulder or labeled as a "misfit."

Then we wonder why people are unhappy, checked out, depressed, burned out, lacking inspiration, and having low creativity. The threat of judgement, rejection, and being left out like we are at the high school lunch table makes people desperate to fit in, even when doing so limits our potential.

This unconscious autopilot survival program encourages people to mask and hide every aspect of themselves, becoming inauthentic, blocking their creativity, and sacrifice their entire lives, all to reach an image of success which is what the corporate system was designed to perpetuate.

"Let's be clear: waiting for the culture, others, or external approval is not an act of courageous leadership."

Extensive research affirms that people won't commit to inauthentic leaders for the long term. In our post-COVID-19 world, where everything often feels like an ongoing crisis, there's a growing awareness of what's genuinely authentic. Nonetheless, many leaders claim they'll be authentic and vulnerable only when the culture permits it. Let's be clear: waiting for the culture, others, or external approval is not an act of courageous leadership.

Companies often look for people who fit best with the existing culture when they should be looking for someone who can add something new to the business, help fill blind spots, push boundaries, and expand horizons in ways that will equip the organization for future success.

Frans Johansson is the founder and CEO of The Medici Group and advises Fortune 100 executives, startups, venture capital firms, and government agencies. He saw a theme with clients—his research showed that clients who hired for "qualifications on a résumé" and "culture fit" consistently had *lower* rates of innovation.

"Clients who hired for 'qualifications on a résumé' and 'culture fit' consistently had lower rates of innovation."

Research by London Business School colleague Dan Cable shows that employees who feel welcome to express their authentic selves at work exhibit higher levels of organizational commitment, individual performance, engagement, and tendency to help others.

Hay Group research insights found that companies with highly engaged people outperform their competition by 54% in employee retention, by 89% in customer satisfaction, and by fourfold in revenue growth.

We know the benefits, yet we still adopt and normalize outdated and toxic leadership behaviors and working methods that were brought up from the industrial revolution assembly line mindset. These methods were also made popular by former CEO of GE Jack Welch's and former Microsoft CEO Steve Ballmer's finite win-or-lose cutthroat ways, which had long-term impacts on the bottom lines of their companies. For example, Ballmer followed Welch's "Rank and Yank" model, which forced managers to organize their teams into bell curves whereby 20% of a team is cited as most productive, 70% are adequate, and 10% are bottom performers who are automatically fired.[3] Many organizations still to this day follow this outdated model in their employee ranking, promotion, and succession planning models.

These are the types of "normal" lies and limitations we have normalized about what makes a great leader, a high performer, or best practices which use outdated structures, mindsets, and methods.

Interestingly, in contrast, the number one question I get asked from executives at least ten times per week is this: how do we create a culture that has more inclusion, creativity, and innovation?

After thousands of conversations on "innovative cultures" with clients it boils down to this: If you're unwilling to let go of control and conformity, outdated leadership views, mindsets, and processes that are designed to limit people and teams, and instead embrace a level of chaos, no set of ideas or strategy decks will transform the culture. Your career, department, or organization will eventually face disruption.

It's a universal law: those courageous enough to be uncomfortable with the unknown possess the power to create.

Things are no longer working. Repetition of the past will no longer work to create the future. Reimagination is required. Giving up control is required. Getting uncomfortable is table stakes. Yet to reimagine means we must become present and aware and get off autopilot, or we will stop reimagination in its tracks.

We are in a never-seen-before era and inflection point that requires reimagination to move forward. Climate crises, global health issues, technological advancements, shifting political landscapes, and changes in social values are redefining how we live and work. Traditional organizational structures and mindsets, designed for stability and predictability, are ill-suited for these complex challenges.

The methods that got us here will not build the future. We may be technologically advanced, but in many ways, we have not evolved. If you look at an organizational chart from the 1800s or 1900s, around the time of the industrial revolution, you'll find it shockingly similar to today's structure. Worse still, we retain the same leadership mindsets, behaviors, and cultures. We have bought something completely broken as normal and even call it great leadership.

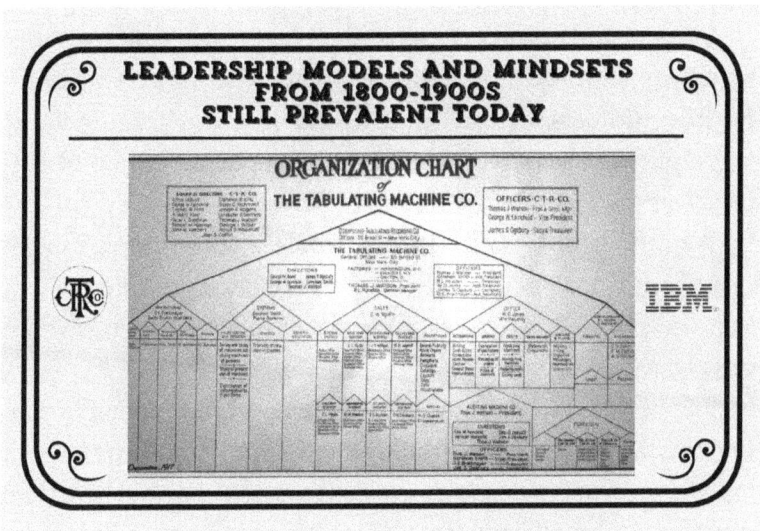

Pingboard: The Evolution of the Org Chart[4]

The industrial revolution was set up for command-and-control, reducing risk, and driving predictability by making everything, including people, cookie-cutter. It's no longer sustainable. Headlines reveal the failing systems, marked by the lowest employee engagement rates, significant skill gaps, stifled innovation, escalating mental health, and overall wellness challenges tied to the workplace.

We can't create the future and thrive with the same leadership behaviors and mindsets and the same commanding structures and limiting work models. We can't foster sustainable, inclusive growth if we're all trying to be the same, giving up our individual power and creativity.

"We can't foster sustainable, inclusive growth if we're all trying to be the same, giving up our individual power and creativity."

Leaders today must rethink their approach, shifting from immediate short-term shareholder focus to a broader perspective that considers societal demands and the ever-changing global environment. It requires a reimagination, not a repetition of outdated ways.

We can blame COVID-19 and people waking up. We can get scientific and analyze that the earth is spinning faster, and the universe is expanding. We can even say that generative AI is taking our jobs and will kill humanity.

The bottom line is that we are in the midst of a human revolution, and the collective is becoming more conscious that we have an imperative on our hands to go from unconscious survival behaviors to awareness that allows us to thrive and remember the core of who we are.

That's why marketing, branding, and lip service are no longer working. You can put words like "innovation," "inclusion," "transformation," and "family" in PowerPoints and websites and announce them at town halls. Yet people know that when they show up to work on Monday at 9:00 a.m., there will be no sign of any of it.

Awareness of the Unconscious Misconceptions and Lies

There's a fresh way of doing business. As *Harvard Business Review* and McKinsey research shows, companies like Allianz, Microsoft, Nucor, LVMH (the world's largest luxury goods company), and Arup (a creative engineering and design company) are already in on it. They're all about being open and adaptable, and tapping into the collective power of individuals. Their endgame? Sustainable, inclusive growth and benefits for all. They're forming collaborative networks with self-managing teams, creating value at lightning speed.[5]

These companies strive to have individual differences nurtured. Information is not suppressed or spun to sound good. The company adds value to employees, rather than merely extracting it from them. These organizations stand for something meaningful.

No matter what your title, you can contribute to changing the future of what we tolerate in the workplace and shift it to one where we are all empowered to be seen, be unique, and share our creativity. It is critical to remember that as individuals, we do have the power to choose our identity, values, and if where we desire to work is actually aligned from a place of awareness and not autopilot and survival.

In order to do this, first we must become aware of all the lies, myths, and misconceptions that do not contribute to this shift and evolution.

Here is a list of the top (definitely not all) myths and misconceptions that exist in many (not all) environments that limit our capabilities. I once was blindsided by many of these, and I watch so many buy into or follow these as true to this day.

Identifying and understanding these myths and misconceptions is the first step to becoming aware of what is a finite mindset and choosing wisely. In later chapters, we dive into tools to empower a more authentic you in the workplace and life.

1. Most People Do Not Know What They Are Doing, and Titles and Experience May Not Be as They Appear

Let's face it: in a world filled with constant change and evolution, it's nearly impossible for anyone to have all the answers. We find ourselves in a unique moment in time, where climate change, social transformations, economic pressures, looming threats of recession, and rapid technological advancements such as use of generative AI in everyday interactions have all converged. Given these circumstances, it's understandable that no one truly knows what they're doing.

To make matters worse, many organizations rely on outdated leadership principles and mindsets, promoting individuals based on irrelevant past performance. If a leader claims that they know everything, have all the answers, or are an expert, those are the number one red flags.

Yet there are those that have high levels of awareness and vulnerability and seek to collaborate to reimagine the future. For example, Roberto Marques is executive chairman and group CEO of Natura &Co, a multinational personal care and cosmetic company headquartered in Brazil, known in the United States for two of the brands it owns: The Body Shop, which began life in the United Kingdom in 1976, and Avon, founded 90 years earlier in New York.[6] Marques has been quoted saying, "Leadership today entails having the self-awareness to acknowledge you don't even know what you don't know, and the humility to listen to others."

"Leadership today entails having the self-awareness to acknowledge that you don't even know what you don't know, and the humility to listen to others."
—*Roberto Marques*

Unfortunately, few leaders as wise as Marques exist in the corporate sphere. Behind the facade of structure and hierarchy within corporations, decisions are often made on the fly, lacking clear direction or purpose. It's disheartening to see individuals promoted based on seniority or political maneuvering rather than actual competence or experience. This phenomenon, as written in the book *The Peter Principle*, articulates the research of how people tend to rise to their level of incompetence within a hierarchy. Recognizing this truth is crucial to awareness while navigating organizational success and planning your individual career and aspirations.

It's essential to be aware that everyone is grappling with these challenges. Simply holding a senior position or having a title does not automatically grant expertise or wisdom. Therefore, it's unwise to unquestioningly follow or mimic those who may not know what they're doing. Your time and career should not be placed in the hands of others based solely on their seniority and titles or whether the company is in the headlines.

2. Leadership Is Not a Title. It's a Behavior

One of the biggest misconceptions is that leadership is defined by one's title, position on an organizational chart, charisma, or number of successful KPIs executed. In reality, leadership is a behavior—the behavior of bravery. It involves the uncomfortable courage to let go of what is no longer relevant. Don't buy into the lie that a person with a "title" in a box on top of your box on an org chart is greater, more aware, or more powerful than you are! It's a box on a chart!

Leadership is not confined to those at the top; it can emerge at any level and in any role. It entails the courage and boldness to step up, take ownership, and make an impact. Let go of the outdated notion that leadership is granted solely by power and position. Embrace the idea that anyone can embody leadership through their actions and inspire others to reach their full potential.

As we navigate the new era of AI and automation, it's crucial to understand that the future of leadership hinges on transformative behaviors. These are in stark contrast to the outdated, finite, and very tactical management practices that have long been considered the norm but are rapidly becoming obsolete.

The harsh reality is that traditional management roles are increasingly viewed as irrelevant in meeting the complex demands of the future. Traditional tactical management roles face disruption from automation and evolving employee expectations that call for more value in all interactions including those with a manager.

3. Corporate Buzzwords Are Designed to Limit Us

I fell for this one hard! English was my second language, and I was never great at school. Blame it on my autism and ADHD. It didn't matter that I could build computer systems and engineer and design networks by the age of 12. What mattered was that I had no clue what the word "transformation" meant. Little did I know that the people with fancy titles, MBAs and PHDs, didn't either.

To this day when I ask a group of seasoned executives running multibillion-dollar organizations, with responsibility for thousands of people, to explain to me what "transformation" means to them, I get statements like this: "We're leveraging synergistic paradigms to disrupt the ecosystem through holistic, client-centric innovation and scalable agility."

Translation: they have no idea, but they sure feel impressed with avoiding it.

Don't let fancy, corporate buzzwords intimidate you or make you feel inadequate. These buzzwords are part of a program designed to make you feel inferior, wrong, and less capable.

The corporate world often employs such tactics, perplexing you and questioning your understanding. For years, I personally believed it was my fault. I was stupid, not good enough, and that theoretical knowledge and ability to "sound smart" trumped hands-on ability and capabilities.

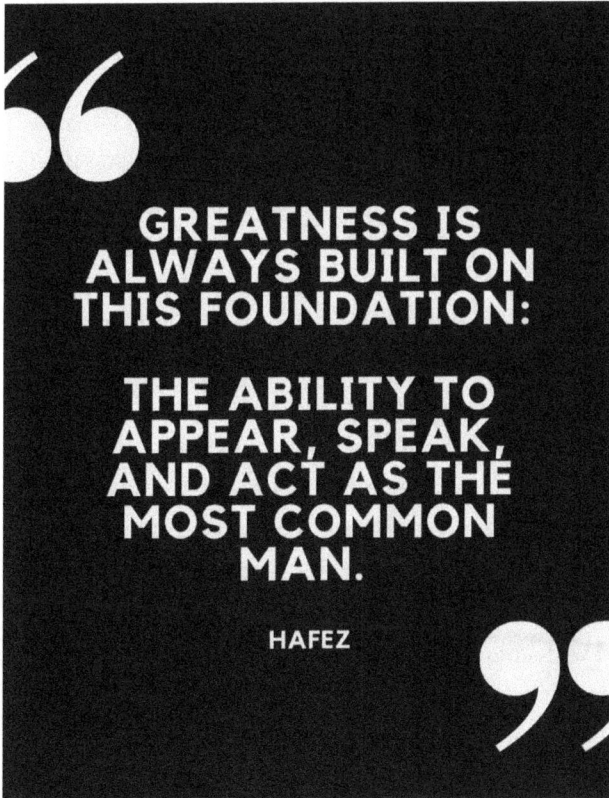

> **GREATNESS IS ALWAYS BUILT ON THIS FOUNDATION:**
>
> **THE ABILITY TO APPEAR, SPEAK, AND ACT AS THE MOST COMMON MAN.**
>
> HAFEZ

Coal miners and doctors and tennis instructors have specific jargon they use to get their points across, but "all-purpose business language is the language you use when you aren't really doing anything," says anthropologist David Graeber, the author of *Bullshit Jobs*.[7]

Jargon speak is not a sign of knowledge or intelligence.

4. Marketing and Branding Are Just That

Don't be captivated solely by the latest and greatest company brand names and marketing. Don't believe that merely associating yourself with these company names is a successful career path. Despite what is on the surface, it holds no intrinsic value in your overall life.

Let me share a secret: those "Greatest Places to Work," "Most Innovative," and "Most Diverse" lists can be easily manipulated and bought. I know this because, at one point, it was my responsibility to ensure our company secured a place on those lists. When marketing and media evaluates a company's worth, they often emphasize its perks, as if these perks, rather than genuinely exciting work, define a company's attractiveness as a career destination.

Questions about company value are relative. If questions in these surveys revolve solely around gym incentives without addressing leadership and management, their true worth comes into question. Such inquiries often overlook critical aspects, such as addressing individuals who, while working at some of these renowned companies, endured soul-crushing, abusive environments or had to contend with colleagues perpetuating limiting beliefs, leaving them feeling inadequate every day.

It's vital to scrutinize the hype and delve deeper than superficial images. Instead, seek genuine meaning, alignment with your values, and purpose when making career choices.

5. Become Aware of Who We Are Giving Our Time and Energy Away To

As insane as it sounds, we often take jobs at well-known companies for the image they give us because we care how others see us and what they will say. Why do we place such importance on what others say? Because we tie our identities and self-worth to a company name and whether they will view us as successful.

Are you identical to everyone else, sharing the same mindset, expectations, growth trajectory, and capabilities? The opinions of close friends, colleagues, or anyone else about a company should not dictate your decisions. You must conduct thorough research and assessment on your own. What matters most is the executive leadership team's mindset, your direct supervisor, and the people you'll work with closely—period!

Remember the saying, "People quit managers, not companies."[8] Originated by two researchers from the book *First, Break All the Rules: What The World's Greatest Managers Do Differently* by Marcus Buckingham and Curt Coffman. Ultimately, your department, team, and the individuals they report to have the most significant impact on your experience. Dig deep into the backgrounds of board members and the CEO. Investigate the person you will be working for and their background, character, and style. Rarely are two departments in a company the same, and many senior leaders are disconnected with what is really going on in middle management.

> *"People quit managers, not companies."*
> *—Marcus Buckingham and Curt Coffman*

Conduct extensive Google searches and explore their social media presence on platforms like Facebook, Instagram, Twitter, and LinkedIn. Evaluate their messages and posts and determine if their values align with yours. Look for diversity and a range of backgrounds and education among the leadership team. Leave no stone unturned, including checking platforms like Reddit, Glassdoor, and Fairygodboss. Don't fall into the trap of discrediting low ratings as a "disgruntled" employee; see the patterns in the comments. Also, be aware that they are likely examining you in a similar manner. Ask questions and follow your initial instincts.

Yes, it may require hours of research, but remember, you'll be investing your time and energy and building your future habits and programs in this environment. Remember the research and theory by Jim Rohn: "You are the average of the 5 people you spend the most time with!"

6. Many Corporations Will Limit Us for Their Own Profit

While companies claim to want creativity and innovation, an unconscious desire for control often prevails. In the short term, conformity looks attractive, providing easier management and quicker uniformity. But this craving for control can stifle creativity, limiting long-term growth and profits at the expense of people—you and me!

In the pursuit of immediate conformity and control, corporations or workplaces might trade away your true capability. They are designed to hit short-term shareholder numbers and will easily sacrifice you to do that. The default then becomes making sure you don't get in the way of that goal.

Many levels of the hierarchy are designed to hide and mask your true abilities, even if it impacts profits in the long run. Very few are designed for or employ leaders for the long game. This is because "long-game" leaders will have the bravery to challenge the status quo and are often seen as "misfits" that would be disruptive to short-term Wall Street gains.

7. The Truth Behind Most Alphabet Soup Degrees Is Conformity

Our educational systems are designed to support our corporate systems. They are not designed to support what we naturally thrive at. They accomplish their cog-making with the reward of memorizing information and spitting it out on an exam, a thesis, or a report and rewarding you with a degree. The system is not designed to bring out your individual capability or help you learn how to tap into your unique gifts as an individual. It's also nearly impossible to compare education with pace of change and hands-on experience.

We get programmed to immerse ourselves in the world of the "MBAs" and other alphabet-soup degrees, meticulously designed to satisfy the insatiable conformity appetite of the corporate behemoth. While our degrees are meant to set us apart, they actually blend us seamlessly into a sea of similarly educated individuals armed with outdated information, theory-based knowledge, and fancy paper. They also don't educate or prepare us for what is mentally and emotionally required to heal, become aware, and thrive.

The corporate system, seeking conformity, readily accepts us as obedient contributors. It requires us to follow set rules and maintain the current state of affairs. Our degrees act as proof that we've passed through the educational system and are prepared to join in.

Now, don't get me wrong. Education has its merits, and there is value in learning foundational principles. However, it's vital to acknowledge the limitations of an outdated education system that simply can't keep up. Especially in the new world of generative AI, skills such as awareness and vulnerability, which used to be called "soft skills," are now critical skills.

"The percentage of US adults ages 18 to 29 who view college education as 'very important' dropped from 74% to 41% in just 6 years."

In fact, the Burning Glass Institute reported that the percentage of jobs requiring a college degree fell from 51% in 2017 to 44% in 2021. And according to Gallup, the percentage of US adults ages 18 to 29 who view college education as "very important" dropped from 74% to 41% in just 6 years.[9]

If you see some organizations still making this a requirement, it should be a red flag that they are not up to speed with the future, and you may want to think about whether this is where you desire to invest your time.

We must supplement our formal education with practical, real-world experiences, failures, and learnings and continuously update our skills to stay relevant in today's rapidly changing landscape. If you lack a foundational ability to learn as you go, what you pile on top will not be relevant. Unfortunately, no school system teaches us this!

8. Organization's Priority Is Not to Create Your "Career Path"

In the harsh reality of the corporate world, it's crucial to recognize the fallacy that has been maintained—the notion that the company will guide and shape your career path. The truth is, organizations are not equipped nor inclined to prioritize your personal growth and fulfillment. HR departments, learning and organizational development (L&OD) initiatives, and even leaders themselves primarily focus on maintaining the status quo and safeguarding their own interests.

To serve their interests, some individuals in leadership roles may attempt to make you feel incomplete or insufficient. It's essential to recognize that this isn't a reflection of your abilities or interests. Strangely, it's not a personal matter; it's their pursuit of short-term gains and shareholder profits. Without this awareness, you might find yourself sacrificing your life, chasing an elusive goal, and trying to validate your worth and prove your adequacy.

Never assume that all leaders are looking at the future of their business in 5 to 10 years and considering how that affects the talent and skills they require. They are just making short-term decisions.

Waiting to be chosen and relying on the company to pave the way for your career is a recipe for disappointment, self-sabotage, and total denial.

9. The Myth of Salaries and Pay Ranges

It can be an endless loop and trap: keep us thinking we are not good enough, don't have the degree, don't have the experience, don't understand fancy acronyms. Naturally, we would not have the courage and conviction to negotiate more money.

Salaries and pay ranges are another messy construct of the matrix. Salary is not solely based on your qualifications. And let's not put all our hopes on pay transparency laws either. While they may seem like a glimmer of hope, they alone won't solve this very deep-rooted issue overnight. Even with transparency, some companies will find ways creative ways to change the job and role-slotting classifications that impact pay ranges.

It's entirely up to you. The power lies in your negotiation skills, your ability to showcase your value and tell a compelling story, your willingness to advocate for what you deserve, and believing in yourself so much that you are willing to walk away.

"The power lies in your negotiation skills, your ability to showcase your value and tell a compelling story, your willingness to advocate for what you deserve, and believing in yourself so much that you are willing to walk away."

I can't tell you how many times people tell me they take a job only to find out later they are being paid less than their less-qualified counterparts. I made this mistake once myself. It builds a loop of resentment if not confronted.

But here's the catch: the system is sometimes designed to make us settle for less. Behind the scenes, many internal or external recruiters are incentivized to get us on board for the lowest possible cost. They're not there to always fight for our best interests or ensure we receive fair compensation. No, their goal is to keep labor costs down, follow company policies, and maximize the company's profits. So while they may paint a rosy picture of opportunity and growth, their true agenda is to secure your talent at the lowest price tag they can manage. That is how many are measured.

Remember, the lie of pay ranges is just another cog in the corporate machinery, designed to keep you in check and ensure their bottom line remains intact. It's up to you to break free from this illusion and advocate for yourself. The key here is that you must believe you are worthy of something better otherwise the sheer energy of your subconscious limitations developed from your past will hold you back.

10. Human Resources Is Not Your Advocate

Let's venture further into the complex realm of Human Resources (HR). In many organizations, but not all, HR is just an administrative office. They follow the policy and procedures that are in the employee handbook, meticulously built around your country, state, and city employment laws. They are set up to protect the company, not you—period! The former Microsoft VP of HR gives advice that HR should be the last place you go. "HR is not your friend," he writes as he echoes where the priorities are.[10]

If you ever find yourself needing to engage with HR, approach it as if you're entering a courtroom—meticulously presenting your case with caution. Although this may sound unsettling, it reflects the unfortunate reality, as many employment attorneys will confirm.

This approach is crucial because HR's loyalty lies squarely with the company, not with you. They possess expertise in navigating legal waters and prioritize protecting the organization's interests above all else. Therefore, when you require HR's attention, gather your facts, familiarize yourself with the documented company policies such as the code of conduct and any relevant documented references, articulate your grievances, and maintain a composed demeanor. Do not expect empathy or automatic advocacy from them. Instead, approach them armed with details, facts, and proof.

Remember, in the realm of HR, the focus is not on justice or fairness; it revolves around safeguarding the company's reputation and avoiding legal complications. Don't hesitate to seek legal counsel and consider opening cases with organizations such as the Equal Employment Opportunity Commission (EEOC) for unresolvable extreme matters.

11. "Hard Work" Is a Fallacy

Let's debunk the prevailing myth that hard work alone guarantees recognition, promotion, and success. It's a common misconception that if you put in long hours and work tirelessly, you will automatically achieve your desired outcomes. This is another lie you are sold to keep you a part of the efficient cogwheel. If you think work is meant to be "hard," then that is what you will create and get.

The reality is that success in the workplace is not solely determined by your effort and dedication. Instead, it involves understanding the intricate dynamics at play, including the importance of building connections and aligning with leaders you are working under and those in positions of power.

Putting all your eggs in your boss's basket, assuming that they will notice your hard work and advocate for your recognition and advancement, is a risky approach. While your boss may appreciate your efforts, they might not always be aware of the full extent of your contributions or have the ability to advocate for you effectively.

> *"The most important decisions about your career are often being made when you're not in the room."*

I have sat in on hundreds of succession planning meetings and advised companies on plans, and I can confirm that the most important decisions about your career are often being made when you're not in the room, from loaded assumptions, biases, and people echoing a 5-minute conversation they had with you as fact.

Sometimes it's personal, and they think you could replace them and are intimidated. Sometimes they just don't have the capability or courage to advocate or use their voice for you, or they have no clue about how the inner politics or promotion system even works or how to tell a compelling story about you. Sometimes they are not well respected by their peers or senior management. Yet we somehow under a delusion make them the source of our progression without asking questions.

Contrary to popular belief, success is not solely measured by the number of hours worked, arbitrary metrics tracked by your manager, or your output volume. It's based on visible initiatives that higher leadership levels can see and who is advocating for you. If you don't have an advocate, you are flying solo—period.

The secret is not to work harder. The secret is to be smarter and more aware. If you put your head down and aimlessly grind just for the sake of "working hard," you are unlikely to stop and ask yourself if the work you're doing or the dynamics of the organization at large are truly in line with your values and with the future you want to create.

12. The Same Company in the Same Role for 10-Plus Years Is Not Always a Badge of Honor

The days of working for a company for 10, 15, or 20 years like a badge of honor are quickly fading. It's not always something to celebrate—doing the same role, in the same culture, and settling for a couple promotions as the golden path for everyone. Some of us desire vast, diverse experiences. Either way is not wrong, yet if you put your head down and think, *This is what I'm supposed to do*, you will miss out on creating the path you actually desire.

Job hopping, once stigmatized as "hobo syndrome" in the 1970s, has evolved. In today's job market, where company loyalty is waning, frequent role changes, or job hopping, especially among high-performance workers, are on the rise. The recent "Great Resignation" has further fueled job hopping, with a significant number of Gen X, millennial, and Gen Z workers planning to leave their current employers for long-term gains. This shift reflects a broader change in attitudes toward careers, emphasizing autonomy and personal control over traditional career ladders dictated by employers.[11]

Organizations will often make us feel like we are wrong for switching jobs, trying new things, or having résumé gaps. They will even question your loyalty. It's part of the conformity belief to limit us and take away our choices. If we do not become aware of this or of our values, goals, and where we desire to be, we will look up one day after working somewhere for 5 years and realize our ladder was on the wrong building working for the wrong leader.

> *"Organizations will often make us feel like we are wrong for switching jobs, trying new things, or having résumé gaps."*

We often hear the rallying cry of "never give up" as a mantra for success, encouraging us to push through challenges and overcome obstacles. Even worse is a comfortable, slow death to never reaching our true potential, capabilities, or aspirations. It's often harder to walk away from something that is OK, something we fail to realize should be freaking phenomenal.

Sometimes, we find ourselves invested in a particular career, project, or relationship, only to realize that it's not bringing us the sense of fulfillment or satisfaction we had hoped for. It takes immense courage and self-awareness to pause, reflect, and acknowledge when our efforts may be misplaced, and freaking pivot and change it. We are not victims; we have choice!

Buying into crazy limited beliefs that are programmed into us is what causes our misery. Things like the idea that "a résumé gap is career suicide" are sold to us as real but are outdated and not true or relevant.

Taking time off to travel, learn, explore, care for a child, or recover from burnout should be celebrated rather than stigmatized. It's crucial to question whether we want to work for companies that don't recognize the value of personal growth and life experiences.

13. Our Opportunity Cost Relationship with Work

For whatever reason, we buy into the misconception that we are the ones that constantly need to prove our value to the organization. They dangle the carrots of more money and a promotion while we chase it like good little rabbits.

Have you ever stopped to ask, *What value do they provide me? What is the opportunity cost here?* No, I'm not talking about your salary, bonus, time off, or access to a private jet.

Wherever we are working or spending our time is a cost because it's time we could be spending doing something else or learning something else. We need to place a currency or number on our time. This does not always mean literally billing someone but gauging the value. It's about becoming aware of the value an hour provides to us, and the value of that time we could spend learning or growing in something else

For example, in my case, my time is worth $1,000 per hour in time and energy. So, when I work, help someone, or do anything, it costs me that amount. This is time I could use elsewhere. How often are we in meetings or with people that don't add any value or are not receiving our value (aka, a radio silence interaction)? Using my rate of $1,000, it's a $2,000 loss for me—$1,000 spent and another $1,000 I could've gained or contributed to someone or something else.

Nothing is free. If you join a "free" class or training, it's actually costing you. When someone says "free" to me, in my head I ask, *Is this worth $1,000?*

For example, a manager I once worked for would schedule one-on-one weekly meetings with me once a week to talk about "air"—nothing of value. I decided it was costing me way too much and started asking for an agenda, and if there was no topic then I would ask her to cancel. She was stunned. Yet later she was inspired to do the same thing.

Value needs to be two-way. We are programmed to think we are the ones that need to prove or show our value. That is not true and is the biggest misconception. It is another way we give our power away.

14. Capitalization of Judgment, Comparison, and Competition to Keep Us Limited

The corporate world capitalizes on the societal program of judgment, comparison, and competition, which is now a hundred times easier to target, thanks to Instagram and LinkedIn, etc. It's easy to fall into the trap of constantly measuring and judging ourselves against others.

The pressure to outdo our peers and achieve more can be overwhelming. Comparison and competition have a way of consuming us in the corporate world, leading us to lose sight of our unique journey and place in the world. They are designed to keep us in a constant cycle of self-judgment, which keeps us from creating what is true for us.

The relentless pursuit of external validation and fitting in can ultimately burn us alive. When we constantly compare ourselves to others and strive to outshine our peers, we sacrifice our authenticity and true selves.

If we allow the fear of judgment and the need to fit in to dictate our decisions and actions, we risk undermining our own future. The desire for acceptance and the pressure to conform can be powerful forces that suppress your true self and smother your inner flame.

Engaging in constant judgment and striving to outperform others can be draining and demoralizing, especially when we find ourselves on a playing field that doesn't align with our values or passions. It's essential to take the time to evaluate our environment and consider if it truly resonates with our unique strengths, aspirations, and vision of success.

Don't lose sight of this: If you are in competition with sheep, you will become a better sheep. If you are in with lions, you can become a better lion. The challenge is that there are *many* sheep pretending to be lions in the workplace. It's critical to stay present and aware.

15. Insanity Behind Performance Reviews and Feedback Systems

I fell into the trap of never being good enough and always trying harder, big time. Doing more and staying late. Taking "feedback" seriously. Falling into the trap of endlessly being judged and projected at and obsessed with "beating the competition" or "improving weaknesses" instead of doubling down on my own unique strengths.

Let's delve into the world of feedback and performance reviews, shall we? In an ideal universe, feedback would serve as a catalyst for personal growth and improvement, nurturing our unique talents and unleashing our true potential. But alas, we live in a world far from ideal.

Instead, feedback often becomes a tool used to mold us into compliant cogs within the grand corporate machine. It's no longer about fostering our individuality; it's about fitting us snugly into predetermined molds and predefined roles. Anything that strays from the norm is swiftly deemed as not meeting the system's expectations.

Beware of this kind of feedback, for it seeks to sever the very qualities that make us extraordinary. Remember, the system's insatiable desire for conformity should never outweigh the importance of your authenticity. Keep your discerning eye sharp and differentiate between feedback that genuinely serves your growth, and that which is just another attempt to mold us into a cog.

In fact, a HuddleUp survey and research found that on average, 85% of employees quit after an unfair performance review, 95% of managers aren't happy with traditional performance management, and 80% of workers are dissatisfied with their performance reviews.[12]

Sometimes performance reviews masquerade as fair assessments, but their true purpose is to erode our individuality and reduce us to a series of checkboxes. They magnify our weaknesses while overshadowing our strengths. It's a twisted dance of "right and wrong" narrow perspectives that often lack any real meaning or relevance.

16. The Corporate Construct Feeds on Your Childhood Trauma

Within the intricate web of the corporate world, the workplace can act as a constant reminder of the limitations and traumas that linger from our childhood. It is a system that often perpetuates and reinforces these deeply ingrained beliefs and wounds, makes us think we are constantly wrong, and traps us in repetitive patterns from our childhood homes.

In the workplace's confines, our childhood limitations subtly resurface and are reinforced. The same fears and insecurities that once hindered us reemerge, manifesting as even deeper self-doubt, proving imposter syndrome and a nonstop unconscious need for validation.

The hierarchical structures, power dynamics, and competitive nature of the corporate environment magnify these limitations. They compel us to continually prove our worth, seek external validation, and buy into the lie that if we can "work" harder and do more we will "be enough." Take your childhood limitations and pile on the corporate programs, and before you know it, you are lost deep in the abyss.

"Take your childhood limitations and pile on
the corporate programs, and before you know it,
you are lost deep in the abyss."

We get stuck in a loop because as powerful creatures, we create our realities. What you subconsciously think about yourself is what you project and create. Unfortunately, the workplace often fails to provide an environment for healing, growth, and expansion. Instead, it becomes a breeding ground for unresolved childhood traumas. Past experiences of rejection, abandonment, and criticism echo through harsh feedback, micromanagement, and an unrelenting pursuit of perfection.

While people often make light of past job experiences and share anecdotes about their "jobs from hell," the truth is that emotional workplace trauma, often termed *CTSD* (corporate traumatic stress disorder) or business/career trauma, is a prevalent issue. This trauma stems from capitalizing on our pasts.

These triggers can be overwhelming, pulling us back into familiar patterns and restricting our ability to reach our full potential. Although the workplace may not actively foster healing, growth, or expansion, we can reclaim our power by cultivating self-awareness.

17. Immigrants Face Unique Challenges in the Workplace

If you left your country of origin, you are forever an anomaly.

Differences in culture, language barriers, and biased attitudes can combine to foster feelings of alienation, thus making one feel like an outsider. The emotional and physical toll of this is something I had not fully grasped before.

While the term "country" is used, this experience is not limited to international moves; even transitioning from a familiar small

31

town to an unfamiliar city can classify you as an "immigrant" in this context.

Contrary to common belief, hailing from another country and speaking multiple languages are assets rather than liabilities. For example, research supports the cognitive advantages of bilingualism. A study in the *Journal of Experimental Psychology* found that bilingual individuals were 20% more efficient in task-switching compared to their monolingual counterparts.

> *"The harsh reality is that the terms 'diversity' and 'inclusion' are often mere buzzwords utilized to satisfy legal and compliance obligations rather than to instigate genuine change."*

In the highly competitive and often unforgiving corporate landscape, both internal and external appearances hold significant weight. If we dare to deviate from societal norms—be it in speech, thought, or appearance—prepare yourself for judgmental glances and whispered conversations in hushed tones. This is not exclusive to racial or ethnic minorities; immigrants contributing diverse perspectives and experiences are subject to the same scrutiny.

The harsh reality is that the terms "diversity" and "inclusion" are often mere buzzwords utilized to satisfy legal and compliance obligations rather than to instigate genuine change. Companies may tout their commitment to these ideals, yet their actions frequently unveil a facade, carefully erected to maintain a politically correct image and sidestep legal consequences.

It is crucial that we acknowledge this reality without the distortion of rose-colored glasses. Understanding that being an immigrant adds another layer of strength is vital, but recognizing the unique attributes that come with it is equally important.

18. Toxic Leadership Is Rewarded More Than We Realize

This one really punched me in the face. I spent years being gaslighted and emotionally abused by a senior leader. Let me tell you, it took a toll on my self-worth like you wouldn't believe. I wasn't dealing with just any self-centered boss; I worked for a full-blown narcissistic sociopath. When you and your peers start Googling a leaders' behaviors, trust me—you have crossed over to potential abuse.

A study published in the *Journal of Applied Psychology* suggests that about 1% of the general population exhibits psychopathic traits, but this figure rises to approximately 3% to 4% among business leaders. Similarly, a survey from psychologist and author Robert Hare estimated that the prevalence of psychopathy among corporate professionals could be as high as 4%, compared to the general estimate of 1% in the broader population.

It's paramount to exercise caution and not be swayed solely by charismatic and persuasive leaders without conducting a thorough assessment of their character and behavioral patterns. While magnetism and rhetorical prowess can be captivating, they can also serve as veils that obscure underlying toxic traits, detrimental to both your well-being and career trajectory.

When evaluating or engaging with someone in a leadership role, it is essential to be vigilant in detecting warning signs of toxic behavior. Indicators commonly associated with narcissistic or sociopathic tendencies—such as pronounced self-importance, a lack of empathy, manipulative behavior, or a blatant disregard for others' emotional or practical needs—ought to serve as immediate red flags.

19. Women Do Not Support Women, and Men Are Also Wearing Masks

Let's shed light on the fallacy of "women support women" in the cutthroat landscape of the corporate world. While we may hope for a sisterhood of unwavering support and solidarity among women, the truth is far more complex. Gender alone cannot guarantee a cohesive support network when there are limited seats at the table and as self-interest and power dynamics transcend gender boundaries. Women, like men, can succumb to toxic behaviors and perpetuate a harmful power struggle, and in many organizations those actions are rewarded.

Within the workplace, phenomena like the "boss babe" and the "queen bee syndrome" can emerge, where women vie for power and recognition, sometimes at the expense of their peers. Men, too, face their own struggles under societal expectations of masculinity. In this environment, support and camaraderie often give way to competition, insecurity, and fear of being left behind.

As we consider the masks we are forced to wear to survive in corporate culture, we should pay special attention to men. 60% of men think it's weak to be vulnerable in the workplace.

Yet a Harvard research study shows that male children are actually more emotionally expressive than female children. The journey from emotional child to invulnerable employee is not always linear, but the impact of this suppression is disheartening. In the United States, over 6 million men are affected by depression, and 80% of suicides are committed by men. This is a major indication that our men are lacking support to be uniquely seen.

20. Flying "Under the Radar" Means Suppressing Your Abilities

The notion that remaining inconspicuous or always agreeable in professional settings is a safe path to success is not only flawed but also self-limiting. This belief—often a coping mechanism rooted in fear and control—constrains personal growth and stifles both creativity and innovation. The cost isn't just individual; it has collective repercussions.

When we opt to go unnoticed, we're essentially dimming our own light, withholding innovative ideas, and stifling our unique perspectives. In doing so, we inadvertently foster a workplace culture that undervalues individual contributions and suppresses diversity of thought. This self-imposed limitation doesn't just keep us from realizing our full potential; it impoverishes the intellectual and creative fabric of the organizations we are a part of.

The tragedy is twofold: not only are individual talents and capabilities left untapped, but the collective environment also misses out on the richness of diversity and innovation that could otherwise fuel progress. By choosing to suppress our brilliance and capabilities, we perpetuate a cycle of conformity and miss the opportunity to add unparalleled value to our work and lives.

In Short

There are so many more I could share with you that happen on a daily basis. This is why I strongly recommend you invest in a phenomenal coach, not a résumé writer or recruiter, but a coach who will point out the truths and lies and keep you aligned and centered with your values, goals, and who you are. In part two, I take you through the ones that impacted my journey and the research and tools I used to overcome them.

On average, humans access only 5% of our potential because we are on autopilot, unconscious, or in survival mode. It's important to recognize that raising awareness about the falsehoods we've embraced as real and true isn't about playing the victim or placing blame on corporations. It's about understanding the reality of what we often call normal, without rose-colored glasses and actively working toward personal change. Without awareness, nothing can be transformed.

The time is now for us to open our eyes, to not buy into the misconceptions and lies designed to limit us, and to take back the brilliance we gave away for free.

CHAPTER 2

The Time Is Now: Igniting the Human Revolution in the Age of Machines

"To be nobody-but-yourself—in a world which is doing its best, night and day, to make you everybody else—means to fight the hardest battle which any human being can fight; and never stop fighting."

—*E. E. Cummings*

The world and humanity are at a major inflection point. Our old methods and approaches that once maintained the status quo are no longer sufficient for our future. We are living in a time when past experiences, often rooted in the need to control or force things into existence, are proving counterproductive. It's crucial to ask ourselves: How can we adapt to the rapid advancement of generative AI, which is reshaping our connection with machines, without furthering our unhealthy relationship with them?

Reflect on this: In 1993, our journey of integrating human lives with machines began, granting us access to information. The World Wide Web transformed our world, even though early web browsers had their hiccups. In 2007, the iPhone revolutionized our interaction with machines. Additionally, in 2004, the advent of social media, exemplified by Facebook, introduced a complicated relationship where we presented idealized versions of our lives through machines.

Fast forward to 2022, and ChatGPT has facilitated two-way conversations with machines, attracting 100 million users within two months of its 2023 launch.

What we are avoiding looking at is that we are also functioning like machines, especially in modern workplaces. Just look at the way we talk to each other in workplaces—it's definitely not like humans.

> *"What we are avoiding looking at is that we are also functioning like machines, especially in modern workplaces. Just look at the way we talk to each other in workplaces—it's definitely not like humans."*

I got curious and asked ChatGPT, "Can you give me the standard canned response to sound intelligent that leaders unconsciously respond with when asked about their company's strategic plans?"

It was pretty accurate. Take a look:

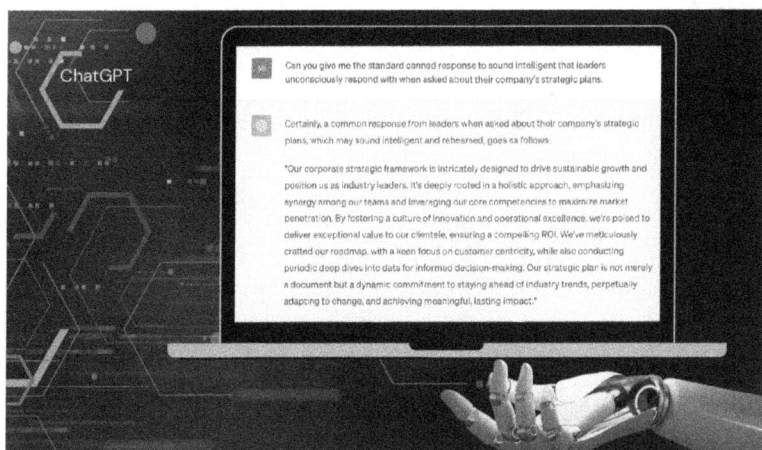

In this emerging world, our ever-deepening relationships with both humans and machines are rapidly evolving. However, we currently find ourselves in an unhealthy state, often unaware and masking our true selves. This state poses a substantial threat to our humanity.

If we fail to recognize and pivot, it could alter not only our future but also that of our children and the course of human evolution as we surrender to machines.

A senior global executive from a successful European company reached out to me for advice on how to address the challenges facing his team. The more he pushed them to do more with less, cut costs, work harder, and be creative, the more counterproductive it became. People, including his seasoned direct reports, were experiencing burnout and calling in sick. His team was disengaged, and even high-performing "go-getters" were resigning or taking sabbaticals. Our conversation took a confidential turn when he expressed his desire to resign as well.

He admitted that he could no longer maintain the mask and the facade. He was tired of the politics and weary of the games, and he had reached his limit with his peers. Now, he was tasked with figuring out generative AI and how it could propel the business forward. He exclaimed, "At this pace, they won't just replace us; they could potentially control us."

We've relinquished so much of our creativity, self-compassion, and authenticity in order to conform, and as a result, we find ourselves in a dire situation. This poses a significant threat—the prospect of even deeper, unhealthy relationships with machines.

Our minds and bodies are genuinely suffering. They are weary of concealing our true potential to fit in and tired of perpetuating what is no longer true. There's a fear of being labeled "negative" if we acknowledge the stark reality: as a society, we are grappling with the highest levels of stress, anxiety, burnout, addiction, depression, and suicide.

Research has consistently demonstrated that changing, hiding, and abandoning our authentic selves takes a toll on our minds, bodies, and souls, creating a state of dis-EASE., taking away our body's natural state of ease. Disease is a term derived from "dis-," denoting a lack or reversal, and "-ease," symbolizing comfort or well-being. It encapsulates a state of discomfort or illness in which well-being is conspicuously absent.

Psychologists report that hiding one's true self is one of the top contributors to depression. 7 out of 10 people report mental health issues.

We must reconnect with ourselves, get more vulnerable, step into more awareness, and give up unconscious behaviors that distract us from being us and creative. These autopilot behaviors are often disguised as:

- Shame
- Guilt

- Anger
- Hate
- Regret
- Fear

If we do not consider this, we could give into unhealthy relationships with machines, and all of our human connection and true power will be diminished.

In some workplace environments, the behaviors above are unconsciously taken advantage of through misconceptions and lies within narratives that include these:

- Negative performance reviews if we don't fit in
- Put our heads down and just work hard to get ahead
- Compete against our colleagues or other businesses in your industry
- Hide ourselves and be "perfect" so we can fit the mold

"81% of individuals conceal aspects of their identity in the workplace."

81% of individuals conceal aspects of their identity in the workplace, with 75% admitting to masking various facets to avoid exclusion from professional growth and promotions. In the US alone, this normalized practice results in an annual cost of $406 billion due to reduced engagement, diminished creativity, and lower productivity.

We get boxed into corporate metrics that manage everyone the same way and encourage us to look, think, and be the same. We are constantly judged, made wrong, or rejected until we fit into a monkey suit and try climbing the tree like everyone else. Then and only then do we get a nice, neat check that we "meet or exceed expectations."

"Employee disengagement costs the world $8.8 trillion in lost productivity, equal to 9% of global GDP."

Research from BambooHR found that job satisfaction has suffered a steady decline since 2020 and taken a sharp drop this year, saying, "Most simply accept that morale is getting worse." People are simply no longer happy. In fact, Gallup reports that employee disengagement costs the world $8.8 trillion in lost productivity, equal to 9% of global GDP.

What we are not connecting is this—it's not that generative AI and machines are going to replace us, but that we are leading *ourselves* to extinction. We already function as robots on an autopilot program.

We were born to embrace our true selves and connect and contribute to one another. Our purpose is not conformity, concealing, or normalizing the suppression of our identities as a coping mechanism just to navigate through each day.

We are our worst enemies—not social media, iPhones, or machines—and we can choose to become aware of and change this.

What Are We Doing to Ourselves and Our Children?

What are we doing? Why do we buy into this box of programs?

Glaring hashtags on social media aren't just for show; they're a collective shout, a wake-up call. From *#quietquitting* to *#greatresignation* and the oh-so-revealing *#greatbreakup*, we're all screaming for a shift.

And let's not even talk about the ridiculous glamorization of struggle with hashtags like *#grit* and *#hustle*. Come on, are we celebrating burnout as normal?

Look, burnout is real. It's not some fable or initiation rite into adulthood. It's a chronic, soul-sucking state that's swallowing individuals in all roles and sectors. And here's the kicker—this toxic culture doesn't stop at the office door; it's teaching our kids that this insanity is perfectly normal.

What are we telling the next generation? That it's OK to suppress their uniqueness, to grind away their best years in pursuit of what—more burnout? We're programming them to dim their own lights, to hustle in silence and call it *#grit*. By setting this example, we're unintentionally disempowering them, clipping their wings before they even have a chance to fly.

It's time to question these so-called norms, both for ourselves and the young minds we're shaping. The long-term cost of this "keep your head down and grind" mentality is way too high—it's not just robbing individuals of their brilliance; it's stealing the future's potential for innovation and human richness.

> *"Many people don't realize that this mindset, limitation, survival program, and autopilot only allow us to tap into 5% of our natural capabilities and potential."*

Many people don't realize that this mindset, limitation, survival program, and autopilot only allow us to tap into 5% of our natural capabilities and potential—5 freaking percent. If we think hard about this, it's a traumatizing way to live because it does not allow us to tap into the natural joy, creativity, and courage that we are born with and could thrive in.

Human Revolution Is Underway—the Deal Has Changed

What we really have is a fire brewing—the collective is becoming more conscious! Every single one of us around the world is becoming more and more aware of what is important. We are slowly beginning to realize that we are running under a program. This outdated program is being kept alive by corporations that are perpetuating and encouraging us to hide and be the same as each other. Especially in the workplace, we have finally realized we have an epidemic on our hands and have disconnected from being humane and compassionate.

In both Deloitte's and Gallup's human capital and engagement surveys, the key theme behind burnout and quiet quitting was that over 78% of employees desire to contribute to meaningful work that drives creativity and change. The Gallup 2023 report found only 23% of employees feel they are thriving in the workplace.[13]

We are all demanding more than a reactive and survival mindset.

The human deal has totally changed! The big debate about working from home, in-office, or hybrid is a microlevel debate of ants. What is actually happening is a demand for radical flexibility and inclusion. It's not that people don't want to come to the office. We want to feel autonomous. We desire to have deeper connections and feel understood and included. We yearn for personal growth and to feel valued.

> *"Only 23% of employees feel they are thriving in the workplace."*

What we are not understanding is that we cannot have creativity and innovation in the structure and hierarchy of command-and-control environments and leadership mindsets that exist in most organizations. We require a radical restructuring if we ever hope to achieve our full potential, as people or as organizations.

Pushing through Stress, Anxiety, and Burnout

The consequences of workplace burnout are far-reaching. Physically, individuals may experience fatigue, sleep disturbances, headaches, and a weakened immune system. Emotionally, burnout can manifest as feelings of cynicism, detachment, and irritability, leading to strained relationships with colleagues and loved ones. Mentally, it can contribute to a sense of diminished accomplishment, reduced productivity, and a loss of motivation and creativity.

The cost of all of this is astronomical in 2022. Burnout cost organizations in the United States alone over $400 billion annually in talent retention, engagement, and ability to drive productivity and innovation. Jack Flynn of Zippia reports that 89% of workers have experienced burnout within the past year in 2023.[14]

One significant contributor to this exhaustion is the constant hiding and masking we engage in, both professionally and personally. As researched and reported by Dr. Nicole LePera, known as "The Holistic Psychologist," the consequences of this self-imposed hiding and masking are far-reaching. It not only stifles our individuality but also hinders our ability to form deep and meaningful connections with others and is behind the epidemic of burnout.

Authentic human connection thrives when we can show up as our true selves, vulnerable and unfiltered. Yet the constant need to hide and conform inhibits this connection, leaving us feeling isolated and disconnected from those around us.[15]

We wait until we are exhausted and burned out, hit rock bottom, or are diagnosed with an illness. Some even wait until their deathbeds to realize, *Wait, I was living in a program. I wasn't living my truth. I was hiding this entire time.*

Is there a do-over button? No, there is no do-over button!

Hospice nurse Bronnie Ware cites the following as the top regrets expressed by people nearing death:

1. "I wish I had the courage to live a life true to myself, not the life others expected of me."
2. "I wish I hadn't worked so hard."
3. "I wish I had the courage to express my feelings."
4. "I wish I had stayed in touch with my friends."

These regrets scream, people, for God's sake, show yourself! How many of these are you already experiencing? Now is the time to un-hide and stop fitting in. Be true to yourself.

Losing Ourselves Behind Our Masks

Hiding and masking downplays parts of yourself that you feel might be stigmatized. It may be so instinctive or unconscious to you that you don't even realize you are doing it. Hiding can include sexual orientation or things we don't talk about, like your education, marital status, religion, or where you're from.

We are all so unique, but we are desperately trying to be the same and fit in, especially in the workplace. What we don't realize is that we are also hiding and masking what we were born with. Curiosity, courage, vulnerability, the ability to connect and learn. All these are cornerstones to creativity and innovation and creating a thriving future.

The creative mind is the most potent force on earth. No oil well or gold mind can compete with wealth-producing possibilities of just one creative idea. Yet we cannot have creative ideas if everyone is trying to be the same so that they are not rejected from the survival environments we have normalized.

What we are not getting is that in many organizations we put our heads down and spend our time and energy on repetitive, low-value commodity tasks or things that have zero alignment with our personal goals and values. We give up the time we could be spending consciously working on things we are in alignment with, yet most of us are so hard-core on the survival wheel that we barely know what that can even look like.

If we don't wake up and we keep doing this, we will soon realize when it's too late—on our deathbeds—that we never looked at what was true for us. We fell into an unconscious trap.

The time is now to wake up and say *no more* and take back what we were born with as a child: curiosity, uniqueness, creativity, and a lens of possibility, not of limitation.

A Machine Will Replace Us If We Don't Wake Up and Elevate!

We all just got a promotion! Instead of worrying about whether machines will take over our jobs, we need to focus on reigniting the skills we had as kids—curiosity, a hunger for learning, a willingness to experiment, and the courage to explore. Let the machines do the boring work!

Why do you think every company is losing its mind over generative artificial intelligence (e.g., ChatGPT, LLM, etc.)? Because brainless, controlled work is a thing of the past. Generative AI is causing chaos in a controlled, status quo environment. It's adding to people waking up to the realization that stupid tasks can now go away.

It's waking people up to the fact that we have been on a "controlled" hamster wheel, surviving but not elevating and thriving. We have been controlled into our choices; we have been controlled into keeping an image, being like everyone else.

Chaos, not order and control, is actually the secret behind creation. Look at Mother Nature and how planet Earth was created through chaos and then evolved. Chaos is what creates infinite possibilities, not rigid control.

Chaos is created when we all bring our unique abilities to the table.

Critical Skills We Need to Elevate Human Potential

To truly harness the power of combining human and AI intelligence to drive creativity (applied innovation), it's crucial to elevate the development of human skills in this collaboration. These critical human skills embody what makes us uniquely human compared to machines. Here are the results if we choose to embrace and prioritize them:

Human Skill	Description
Empathy and compassion	Connecting and caring for people's well-being
Effective communication	Clear communication for collaboration in "human speak," terms a 5th grader can understand and explain.
Critical thinking and ethical judgment	Objectively evaluating information
Adaptability and continuous learning	Staying open to asking questions and changing
Courage and resilience	Leaning into the discomfort and bouncing back from challenges

Human Skill	Description
Creativity and problem-solving	Connecting the dots and innovatively searching for better ways to do things
Teamwork and cultural sensitivity	Collaborating with respect for diverse cultures
Emotional intelligence	Understanding emotions and perspectives for better relationships

Here's the crux of the matter: accessing these skills, which are not merely soft skills but critical ones, requires us to become vulnerable, look in the mirror and reflect on ourselves, and undergo a process of healing. It also entails understanding and unraveling the autopilot programs, outdated beliefs, and misconceptions we've accepted as reality, both in the workplace and our personal lives.

These skills are often locked away within a vault concealed behind layers of conditioning that have built up over the years.

> *"Accessing these skills, which are not merely soft skills but critical ones, requires us to become vulnerable, look in the mirror and reflect on ourselves, and undergo a process of healing."*

To truly harness adaptability, resilience, curiosity, communication, and accountability and to address unconscious bias, we must embark on a journey of vulnerability, honesty, and self-reflection. Here are the imperative actions we must take, or else the crucial skills above will remain locked away:

Imperative Foundational Actions for Elevating Human Potential
1. Expose your childhood programs
2. Understand workplace misconceptions
3. Elevate and choose from awareness
4. Tap into the skills we need for the future
5. Get in touch with what is true for you and distinguish your genuine viewpoints from learned ones
6. Regain the gifts of your authentic self that you gave up to feel included, belong, and fit in
7. Reclaim your voice
8. Rediscover the leader within you

The journey of personal growth and self-awareness is intertwined with developing the critical skills required for the future, when humans and AI collaborate. By looking inward, healing past wounds, and shedding misconceptions, we empower ourselves to fully embrace these skills and navigate the evolving landscape with wisdom and purpose.

So now what?

Wait and see? Quit your job? Get a new one? Start a business?

No matter what you change about your work, nothing will change unless you choose to become more of you. It will actually fall apart because it's not true for you! Most of us are still unaware, unhealed children living a program of limitation in an adult body.

"Most of us are still unaware, unhealed children living a program of limitation in an adult body."

The life you have in all areas is a reflection of what you subconsciously, deep down, think and see about yourself. We then unconsciously pull in people and tolerate environments that reflect what we think of ourselves so we can be "right." I know . . . mind-blowing. Changing this requires courage. Courage to become aware, then to look at yourself and make different choices.

The goal of the rest of this book is to open your eyes and empower you to choose who you are beyond the survival mode programs in workplace environments and unleash your unique identity and capability.

My purpose is to ensure you never lose the most valuable resource on earth—YOU!

PART II

IT ALL STARTS WITH YOU

Chapter 3

Starts with You: Courage to Look in the Mirror and Become Aware

"True courage, bravery, and power is taking the mask off, unhiding, and having the willingness to see all of ourselves first before we can expect others to see us and definitely before we can truly see and include other people!"

—*Mehrnoosh Bazargan*

Now that we've explored the reasons people wear masks in order to more successfully survive corporate culture, let's consider the possible implications of this act. What most people don't realize is that when we put on masks to keep ourselves safe and fit in, what we are actually doing is hiding, judging, and rejecting ourselves.

I know—mindfuck!

People can't see or include us when we don't see or include ourselves and look at what is true for us. Read that again and again.

Dr. Joe Dispenza explains in his research from his book *Breaking the Habit of Being Yourself* that "95% of who we are, by the time we are 35 years old, is a memorized set of behaviors, emotional reactions, unconscious habits, hardwired attitudes, beliefs, and perceptions that function like a computer program"[16, 17]—meaning we do not know we are doing them. 95% of what we choose is on autopilot. We unconsciously scan the environment and then morph ourselves into what is "normal" to fit in.

This leaves us with just 5% of our conscious mind to think differently from the mold we have created for ourselves.[18, 19]

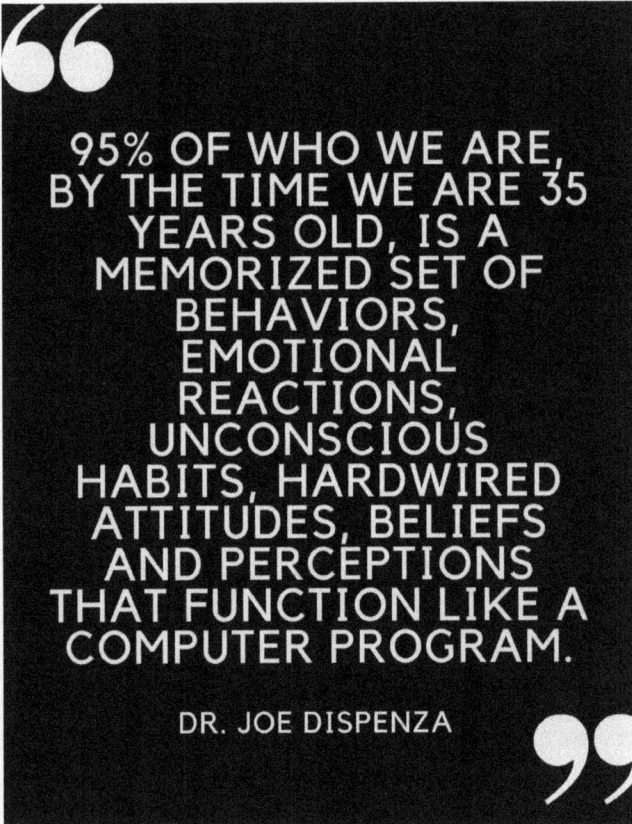

> **95% OF WHO WE ARE, BY THE TIME WE ARE 35 YEARS OLD, IS A MEMORIZED SET OF BEHAVIORS, EMOTIONAL REACTIONS, UNCONSCIOUS HABITS, HARDWIRED ATTITUDES, BELIEFS AND PERCEPTIONS THAT FUNCTION LIKE A COMPUTER PROGRAM.**
>
> DR. JOE DISPENZA

As much as we like to point the finger at the workplace and the environment, oftentimes we are unaware of what we are doing to contribute to the problem. We are part of the problem because we all hide aspects of our identity every day in our micro-behaviors in the workplace, and we have normalized everyone doing the same. We must get to know ourselves and then stop divorcing ourselves to fit into the lies and boxes. As believed to be originally said by Alexander Hamilton, "If you don't stand up for something, you will fall for anything."

> **"If you don't stand up for something,**
> **you will fall for anything."**

Without the courage to look in the mirror and do the hard work on yourself to build awareness of your blind spots, patterns, unconscious behaviors, and habits from all your life experiences, it is nearly impossible to grow and thrive. We end up creating a life that is for others, not what is real and true for you. A life that taps into only 10% of what we are capable of creating.

When we are hiding ourselves, over time this shows up as whispers and eventually shouts of pain. Pain often creeps up in the physical body in the form of fatigue, anxiety, aches, pains, sickness, cancer, autoimmune issues, and so much more.

Emotionally, it shows anxiety, depression, and even a reaction as extreme as suicide. It can also show up as a lack of purpose, drive, and contribution to the world. This is what all of us are witnessing in the workplace.

The only way we can truly un-hide and be a courageous leader in our lives and for others is to understand what is real and true for us, looking past what we believe we are supposed to be or do.

Autopilot Programs Learned as Children

For me, I was forced into feeling shame about where I was from. What did I do? Naturally, I had to fit in, so I learned to mask and hide aspects of my identity as tight as I possibly could. The name of the survival game was to be *unseen*. I learned that who I was would not be accepted, and I was convinced those parts of me were wrong and shameful, so I hid them and never spoke of them again.

Only several years ago did I realize that what you're made to believe is wrong about you is what's strong about you, and my journey and the things I had hid and thought were wrong about myself were what was actually strong about me: courage, grit, curiosity, tenacity, the lens of reinvention and believing truly anything is possible, which are traits of many immigrants from around the world.

How could it have taken this long for me to see this?

Subconscious programming! I know it's hard to fathom because we are made to believe that if our eyes are open, we are conscious, but we are all walking, talking, unconscious programs from our past experiences and environments.

We all desperately desire to be the same so that we are not judged, rejected, and alone. I know because I hid and locked the key away for half my life until one day I woke up and didn't recognize the person in the mirror and said, "Enough! I am not hiding me anymore." The scary part was I had no clue who I was even hiding anymore.

"What you're made to believe is wrong about you is what's strong about you."

As I became curious, I asked myself: What belief is mine? What point of view is mine? What have I bought as reality from parents, teachers, organizations I worked for, leaders, media, friends, partners?

I started seeing how not only was I hiding, but so was everyone else. I started seeing that not only was I in an adult body reenacting my childhood, but so was everyone else.

As I delved into research and observed patterns in interactions with various organizations and leaders, a stark contrast emerged between those embracing infinite and abundant "we" mindsets and those stuck in limited, finite "me" mindsets. It became apparent that many of us were unwittingly operating on survival scripts without questioning them. The root of numerous issues lies in our inability to effectively communicate our needs and desires, in exclusionary behavior, in overly personal or overly detached reactions, and in the struggle to navigate conflicts that could benefit everyone without resorting to fighting, people pleasing, or shutting down.

I got insanely curious as to why on earth human beings behave this way, and then I recognized the autopilot program that every single person is being taught at a young age. How awareness, being present, abundance, and looking at what is true for us is rarely taught in schools or valued in organizations. Sadly, what is valued and taught is lack, wrongness, rightness, and diminishing us to fit in and be liked.

Here's why: As babies, we land in this galaxy with literally nothing. A clean slate. We look around and think, *Whoa, how do they do it in this weird place called Earth?* Then we start collecting points of view and beliefs and start filling our luggage.

We think the adults are physically bigger than us, so they know what they are doing. So we start picking up points of view . . . from our mothers, fathers, or other caregivers. We learn from our communities and friends; we take on the religion passed down to us, like our names. We pack our Star Wars lunch boxes, head off to school, and hand our young, fresh minds to a system and to teachers who we also think have all the answers.

Then the madness and craziness happens. We get this "be the same" chip inserted into our minds that hits right at our basic human instinct for survival (thanks, cavemen and ancestors), the need to fit in with the tribe and not become a failure and end up alone.

So we quickly learn that if we study and memorize and vomit the answer, then we are right; we get an A; if we are wrong, we get an F. Seriously, who even came up with this outdated madness?

How These Programs Are Connected to Corporations and the Workplace

As adults, we unconsciously carry this program of right and wrong into the workplace. Just look at any industry and you will find a connection from educational systems to corporate profit constructs.

The Carnegie and Rockefeller families, driven by their immense wealth and influence, exerted significant control over the pharmaceutical industry as soon as breakthroughs in chemical synthesis and the understanding of medicinal compounds led to the production of standardized drugs. This control allowed them to shape the production, pricing, and distribution of drugs, potentially prioritizing profits over public welfare. Through their extensive financial resources, Carnegie and Rockefeller also had the means to heavily influence the education system.

Critics argue that their involvement in education allowed them to mold curricula to serve their interests and ensure a compliant workforce that maintained the status quo. It is suggested that these influential families strategically positioned themselves within the education system to promote their industrial interests.

> *"Critics argue that their [Carnegie and Rockefeller] involvement in education allowed them to mold curricula to serve their interests and ensure a compliant workforce that maintained the status quo."*

By educating doctors and medical professionals, they could influence the approach to health care and pharmaceutical practices, potentially leading to a medical system that heavily relied on pharmaceutical interventions and disregarded alternative or holistic approaches.

That is just one industry! You can find corporate compliance baked into the educational pipeline at all levels and across all industries.

The principle in neuroscience called Hebb's rule kicks into full gear—"nerve cells that fire together wire together." As you repeat the same patterns and habits through your life, they get unconsciously reinforced. This is why the need to be right repeats itself when we are adults, as it's enforced by corporate structures and systems, just like when we were in school. As Dr. Joe Dispenza's research shows, we become neurochemically attached to the thoughts, feelings, emotions, and conditions in our lives. In time we begin to "think in the box" unconsciously!

As he articulates, your brain now starts firing a finite set of circuits that then create a mental signature that most people call their personality. Imagine that! Our personalities are directly shaped by the industrial education system through which we were led since childhood.

The majority of education is an outdated program designed around the needs of industrial-era factory workers so they can prepare you to become a cog in the wheel in many corporations. Many businesses and leadership education are also taught command and authority (hence the boxes and titles), all to control the workers just like the assembly line.

Factory owners saw people rather like cogs: they didn't need the best cogs, they needed ones with minimal variance in the system. The point of all this programming was not to make us all unique thinkers and beings, but to make us all linear and the *same*.

We buy into this insane command-and-control system and leadership mindsets as normal, then we wonder why we are disengaged and cannot be creative. Chaos, not order and control, is the secret behind creation; that's why people struggle with change.

Being unique and in a constant flow of change feels foreign to all of us because it gets sucked out of us the minute we enter the school system and then the workplace and corporate constructs. What was once comfortable and fun becomes a limitation.

Rich Layers of Our Identity We Hide and Undervalue

We often conceal aspects of ourselves and our varied thoughts and experiences. This self-concealment can occur for various reasons, such as societal expectations, fear of judgment, or a desire for self-preservation.

We may hide our true feelings, beliefs, or identities to conform to societal norms or maintain acceptance. Additionally, past experiences, traumas, or insecurities can lead us to bury certain thoughts and emotions deep within us.

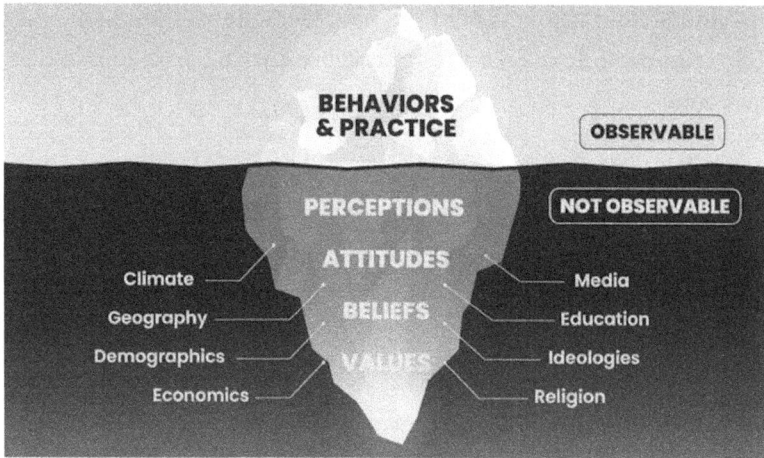

Cultural Behaviors[20]

By concealing these aspects, we create a facade that shields us from vulnerability and potential discomfort. However, embracing our diverse thoughts and experiences allows for personal growth, self-acceptance, and genuine connections with others.

Remember that we often hide the parts of ourselves that are different from the norm. This is particularly harmful to us and to our society at large because, as we discussed earlier, those exact differences that we are hiding actually generate quantifiable benefits within the communities or workplaces of which we are a part.

Even circumstances traditionally seen as disabilities, like autism, dyslexia, ADHD, or using a wheelchair, should be reframed as unique abilities.

We get conditioned that who we are outside of the workplace and the skills we have, like coaching our kids' soccer league, playing piano, or being a mother with multitasking abilities, are irrelevant skills that don't transfer into the workplace. In fact, these diverse traits are our unique superpowers—it's just that many leaders lack the understanding of managing dynamic uniqueness; they are often conditioned to follow linear approaches that tend to standardize everyone.

"Many leaders lack the understanding of managing dynamic uniqueness; they are often conditioned to follow linear approaches that tend to standardize everyone."

Think about the layers of identity we reveal to others and those we keep hidden, often without even realizing it. Many of these rich, unique layers of our true selves are concealed in the depths, beyond what can be readily observed.

Layers of Identity	Examples
Life experiences	Traveling, relationships, achievements
Trauma	Abuse, loss, accidents, violence
Cultural background	Ethnicity, nationality, traditions
Country of origin	Area or region born in
Language	Native language, dialects, fluency
Beliefs and values	Religious beliefs, political ideologies
Gender and sexuality	Male, female, transgender, gay, straight
Personality traits	Introverted, extroverted, compassionate
Interests and hobbies	Sports, arts, music, cooking

Layers of Identity	Examples
Education and knowledge	Academic degrees, areas of expertise
Socioeconomic status	Wealthy, middle class, disadvantaged
Physical appearance	Height, weight, facial features
Mental health	Anxiety, depression, bipolar disorder
Family background	Parental relationships, siblings
Transferable skills	Leadership, communication, problem-solving
Neurodiversity	Autism, ADHD, dyslexia, sensory processing differences

I get it, no one has given you permission to be you. So 99% of us literally have no clue how to even do that.

We are powerful creatures, so if we choose to hide, shrink, and disappear, we will. We will meet a leader or manager 3 or 4 times and they will barely remember us. We walk down the hall and people look right through us.

Life and the universe are a mirror. So if you choose to hide and become invisible and disappear that is exactly what will show up. This was a harsh reality I had to accept.

Yes, I had trauma and a million reasons to keep hiding. It was actually easier and within my comfort zone to hide, not to be vulnerable or fully seen. I never realized that by doing this I was comfortably rejecting myself while blaming others for rejecting me.

Here is a very rough truth to face: people will only include you to the degree that you are willing to include yourself.

"People will only include you to the degree that you are willing to include yourself."

So if you do not see yourself as a unique gift, a miracle, who has unbelievable capabilities that no one else has . . . how do you expect others to see that?

Here are some other ways we hide ourselves:

- We don't give our opinion because it's different from what other people are saying. Or we wait for someone else to go first so we are not judged or rejected.
- We avoid eye contact or we speak very softly and timidly.
- We slouch and hunch over in an effort to shrink ourselves down.
- In conversation we don't offer up anything about our lives, our feelings, our interests, our thoughts.
- We make assumptions and tell ourselves stories about people so we don't have to let them in.
- We just take what is handed to us and don't ask questions or push back.

When we hide and shrink ourselves down, we literally diminish our light. We literally become invisible and unseen. People look right through us, walk around us, and forget us because we made the choice to disappear, separate, and exclude ourselves.

The Cost of Image: Losing Touch with Our Authentic Selves

When we are unwilling to connect with our true identity and be seen, we create a safe and controllable image instead. We create an image purely based on what people see as our value at work and lose our true authentic selves. We become rabbits unconsciously chasing carrots in the form of salaries, titles, and bonuses as the promise to happiness.

An image refers to the way we present ourselves to others, often shaped by external factors such as societal expectations, cultural norms, and personal perceptions. It can be influenced by how we dress, behave, and communicate, and may not always reflect our true thoughts, feelings, and experiences.

On the other hand, our real identity is the authentic core of who we are, encompassing our genuine beliefs, values, emotions, and personal history. It goes beyond the surface-level image we project and represents our unique combination of traits, experiences, and perspectives that make us who we truly are.

While an image can be curated and manipulated, our real identity is an inherent part of us, shaped by our individuality and over time. Embracing and expressing our real identity allows us to live authentically and connect with others on a deeper level.

> *"Our society's fixation on maintaining a polished image has triggered an identity crisis."*

Our society's fixation on maintaining a polished image has triggered an identity crisis. By sidelining our unique backgrounds and identities, we've lost sight of our true selves. This obsession with image doesn't just manifest in our online personas; it deeply influences our behavior, especially at work.

Many people think this only has to do with people on Instagram, but that's not true. Even if you don't use social media, how often is your entire image of how you present yourself in the workplace your title and company logo?

Telltale signs of focusing on image at the workplace include these:

- Presenting purely professional facades, sidelining emotions
- Hiding personal challenges to appear competent
- Conforming to fit in, driven by a need for acceptance
- Silence in meetings due to fear of judgment
- Dimming our unique skills to blend in
- Suppressing our true selves due to stifling company cultures
- Setting aside personal passions if they don't tally with our roles
- Concealing stress to keep up appearances
- Valuing image over authenticity for career progression
- Abiding by workplace hierarchies that reward conformity

It's time we recognize and challenge these behaviors. Only then can we embrace authenticity and fully leverage our unique strengths.

Obsession with a certain image has profound consequences, including these:

- By hiding our greatness, we cap our potential
- Concealing creativity chokes innovation
- Not showcasing courage curbs our growth
- Suppressing our true self mutes genuine connections
- Masking genuine feelings and thoughts strips authenticity

- Muffling unique perspectives limits diverse ideas
- Undervaluing our skills and talents reduces our contribution
- Keeping our experiences in the shadows stunts learning
- Sidestepping our passions denies us fulfillment

Only if we are present and aware can we embrace and display our authentic selves and change this narrative.

What You Think Is Wrong about You Is Actually Strong about You

In the corporate world, or workplaces in general, it's common to believe that certain aspects of ourselves are flaws or weaknesses. That is why we create images or mask ourselves. We fear that being different will put us at a disadvantage, so we conform to fit in. However, it's important to realize that what we perceive as wrong about ourselves can be sources of strength.

Our unique qualities bring fresh perspectives and innovative solutions. Thinking differently and questioning norms demonstrates critical thinking and creativity. Being an immigrant or having a diverse background brings resilience, adaptability, and a broader perspective to the table.

Instead of hiding or suppressing these aspects, embrace them. Recognize their potential and value. By being true to ourselves, we can tap into our strengths and make a significant impact in our organizations.

Authenticity and self-acceptance lead to fulfillment. Embrace your uniqueness, leverage your strengths, and create positive change. Don't doubt yourself or think something is wrong with you.

When we choose to be ourselves, we are illuminated like a beacon in the night for the right people and experiences to come right at us. Let's play.

Pen to Paper Homeplay: Tools and Exercises

I call the following exercise home*play*—not home*work,* throughout the book. We should not think getting to know who we are is "work"; it's a playful exploration to the real, brilliant you! These are all the tools and exercises I went through to un-hide myself, and I still turn to these when I get disconnected.

Our modern society's preoccupation with image often conceals our genuine identities, and what is true for us, leaving us feeling disconnected and unauthentic.

To bridge this gap and live a fulfilling life, it's imperative to delve into a deeper understanding and appreciation of who we truly are. This reflection exercise offers a comprehensive exploration of your multi-faceted identity.

1. Layer-by-Layer Exploration

Use the chart below to explore each layer of your identity. Jot down your reflections, experiences, and insights for every dimension. These are all things that should be uncovered and celebrated, not hidden and concealed.

Openly talk about these and share stories with people. Those who are for you will be genuinely curious, and you will open a vulnerable space and possibly inspire them to be themselves too.

Layers of Identity	Insights/Actions
Life experiences	Recall the places you've been, milestones achieved, and transformative moments from the time you were born, to adolescence, and into vast life experiences. Ask close family or friends and look at pictures to ignite your memory
Trauma	Recognize and acknowledge challenges and adversities faced
Cultural background	Reconnect with your ethnic roots, traditions, and heritage. What does your name mean? Who were your ancestors across generations?
Country of origin	Consider how your birthplace has shaped your perspective
Language	Reflect on your native language, dialects, and languages learned
Beliefs and values	Identify core principles guiding your life decisions
Gender and sexuality	Delve into your gender identity and sexual orientation
Personality traits	Consider whether you are more introverted or extroverted, get bored easily and require a challenge, or prefer slower change, and other defining traits
Interests and hobbies	Celebrate your passions and pastimes

Layers of Identity	Insights/Actions
Education and knowledge	Acknowledge your academic pursuits, learning, and hands-on experiences. Even things like what you learned by being a waiter in college or working in a mail room in high school. Every little experience gives you a nugget of knowledge
Socio-economic status	Reflect on how your economic background has influenced your worldview. Whether you struggled for money or grew up wealthy
Mental or physical health	Identify mental or physical health challenges or experiences you've navigated
Family background	Think about your family dynamics, memories, and relationships
Transferable skills	Catalog skills you've cultivated that apply across various contexts. Being a soccer coach, mother, or community event planner
Neurodiversity	Celebrate and value your unique cognitive attributes such as ADHD, autism, OCD, dyslexia, PTSD

2. Reflections: What Is Strong about You

This one is about vulnerability and honesty with self. Make a list in one column of the top 10 things you think are wrong with you, you judge yourself for, or things others have told you are a weakness and have rejected you because of it.

Now take that list, do a 180, and flip the script. Next to that column write the antidote and ask this question for each one: What is actually strong about me? What is right about this? Acknowledge you, celebrate you, and see yourself.

Here are a few examples of mine:

Wrong (Reaction: let me hide and morph)	Strong (Choose: I'm unique and different)
I'm from a country that is in the media and known for terrorism. I will just say I'm American.	I come from a beautiful country that most have no idea has ancient history and beauty and is one of the oldest cultures in the world. Let me share, celebrate, and educate.
I won't speak up because I have an accent and people will say, "What did you say? I can't understand you."	Yup, I have an accent. It means I speak another language. It means I have courage because I left home in search of different possibilities.
I'm a troublemaker and a misfit. I can't seem to fit in and align and agree with what everyone sees.	I see the world from a lens of possibility and change. Because of my background, I see the forest through the trees naturally.
I get bored easily.	I'm extremely creative, so when a task becomes repetitive, I get curious and explore.
I'm stubborn and I don't let things go.	I don't easily give up and I have courage to see the vision and possibility in how things could be.

Unmasking your true self begins with recognizing the societal scripts and behaviors you've unconsciously accepted as normal. Self-awareness is your ally in this journey. Pause, reflect, and become conscious of the genuine you that's been overshadowed.

Ask yourself, "What is true for me that may not be like anyone else or true for anyone else?"

This is not a one-time event; it's a continuous exploration and life cycle. Embrace these transformative steps:

- **Dive into Your Values and Strengths:** Connect with your passions and what drives you.

- **Champion Genuine Expression:** Surround yourself with spaces and people that applaud your true self.

- **Live Your Values:** Don't bend to societal whims; let your actions resonate with your beliefs.

- **Establish Personal Boundaries:** Safeguard what is real and true for you.

- **Prioritize Open Communication:** Cultivate transparent, genuine interactions.

- **Celebrate Your Distinctiveness:** Harness and honor your unique strengths and outlooks.

Committing to this introspective path is a tribute to your authentic self. Recognize, value, and cherish every part of you. By embracing your truth, you rekindle the childlike wonder and creativity inherent in all of us.

CHAPTER 4

Trauma: The Silent Epidemic Shaping Workplace Behaviors

"With your level of CPTSD, I want you to know you are a walking, talking miracle! I'm surprised you are not either dead, hooked up to an IV in a mental hospital, or a severe drug addict and haven't committed suicide or been killed!"

—My EMDR therapist

If you search on Amazon for books on leadership, how to accomplish goals, how to perform at your peak, etc., you will get something like 50,000 results. I've read a lot of them.

Yet no one talks about the real foundation that will keep you in reaction and survival mode and stop you from truly thriving in the workplace, business, and life: trauma.

Tears flowed down my face as my EMDR therapist looked me dead in the eye and said, "On a scale of one to ten, your CPTSD is a 9.5. Terror of escaping a war, leaving everything you knew and your family behind, rejected when coming to America, beatings and physical and emotional abuse from a father that also had his own rage and unhealed severe trauma, growing up too fast and becoming a responsible adult taking care of your family by age 10, sexual abuse. The only thing that is missing from your background and experience is a family member that is incarcerated in jail."

I honestly thought those were normal hardships everyone goes through. I was conditioned by my environments to get up, not cry, work hard, and never play the victim. Until that point, I did not realize the impact my experiences had on me emotionally, psychologically, and even physically.

I have never cried for so many hours in someone's office. I felt sheer relief that what a lot of people—including myself—had judged, rejected, and made wrong about me was actually strong about me! I never imagined in a hundred years that this was all a miracle in disguise.

I was a deer in the headlights when she told me that the majority of people are walking around carrying this level of trauma from past experiences, and it's all relative. Especially "high performers" and those with the "image" of success. I was stunned and had a moment of clarity and compassion for behaviors of those I knew that were visibly successful and, just as much, for those that lash out in hate and anger.

> *"The majority of people are walking around carrying this level of trauma from past experiences, and it's all relative."*

Even as a little girl I was highly aware and empathic and could feel not only the fear of my mother but the terror of the others that boarded the bus with us leaving everything behind. This awareness made me physically sick to my stomach, and I threw up and had diarrhea along our journey. The bus had to keep pulling over, and my mother and I would get off so that she could change my pants. To this day I remember the chill in my body from the cold, the pitch blackness of the night, and the strange noises in the background that sounded like bears or wolves.

I remember vividly men with machine guns boarding the buses and checking passports when we made it across the border. They sent several families and young children back to a war right before our eyes. We were some of the lucky few who made it across the border.

I had zero clue that this experience would be locked in my body, right down to my cells, and that no matter how much I went to regular talk therapy or changed it to an "adversity story," it would still show up as a trigger of fear, shame, pleasing, fitting in, and hiding the real me—or the other extreme of fighting, proving, anger, because I was programmed so young that when you are *you*, you could die.

> **"I was programmed so young that when you are you, you could die."**

The sad truth is that it doesn't take an experience as dramatic as mine to learn the very same lesson. We all have varying degrees of these thoughts that we have experienced over time, so we quickly learn to mask up, shield up, and protect ourselves.

We think hiding and burying parts of ourselves shows strength and power. We convince men and women that "toughening up" and "not being emotional" especially in the workplace is the power.

Guess what? This is literally killing us.

You might believe you had a great childhood and lived a privileged life. Yet if you grew up on planet Earth, had parents, went to school, played sports, or worked for bosses or companies, you have experienced trauma.

A National Council for Mental Wellbeing study indicates that 70% of people globally have undergone some form of trauma that they either aren't aware of or choose not to confront. As insane as our world has become, we could argue that statistic is 100%.[21]

Trauma and CPTSD manifest primarily in our behaviors and responses to external factors, including personal relationships and work dynamics with bosses, colleagues, and even the organization itself.[22] Until we really look at our past and our trauma, it will own us, blind us, control us, hide our unique ability, and slowly not only kill our creativity and the gift we each uniquely bring to the world but physically make us sick.

Regardless of whether you are seen as an exceptional and flawless athletic performer or if you're in need of assistance and undergoing rehab, it's essentially the same situation —it's only society's view of "success" that makes it different.

Trauma is also often the leading cause of suicide. A nationwide study found longitudinal evidence that PTSD was associated with increased suicide rates. Take the likes of beloved performer "tWitch" Boss, Anthony Bourdain, Kate Spade, overachiever and Miss USA Cheslie Kryst, Bed Bath & Beyond CFO Arnal Gustavo, Reddit entrepreneur Aaron Swartz, and so many more.

Alice Miller's book *The Drama of the Gifted Child: The Search for the True Self* explores the impact of childhood trauma on personality development. Miller discusses how unacknowledged trauma can lead to patterns of self-sabotage, self-destructive behaviors, and a disconnection from one's true self.

The book emphasizes the importance of confronting past emotional wounds and uncovering repressed emotions as a vital step toward healing and personal growth. Miller's work underscores the significance of understanding the influence of childhood experiences on adult behavior and the journey to rediscovering one's authentic self.

> *"We often buy into motivational platitudes like 'the past is not my story' or 'be stoic,' forgetting that the past is indeed part of our narratives."*

We often buy into motivational platitudes like "the past is not my story" or "be stoic," forgetting that the past is indeed part of our narratives. This past is deeply embedded in our subconscious mind and body, influencing our adult behaviors, choices, and attractions. It's deeply embedded into everyone we interact with and yet judge.

What exacerbates this issue is the corporate world's intricate design which serves as a constant reminder of limitations and traumas lingering from our childhood. It's a system engineered to perpetuate these deeply ingrained beliefs and wounds. Within this work environment, our childhood limitations resurface and are magnified by hierarchical structures, power dynamics, and the inherent competitiveness of the corporate culture. These settings amplify self-doubt, imposter syndrome, and the incessant need for external validation.

The silver lining of the devastation caused by COVID-19 has been a societal willingness to speak openly about trauma. This openness has spotlighted trauma-informed care, offering us the chance to begin healing not only as individuals but also as a society—and to address the wounds we've inherited and labeled as "normal."

Trauma's Imprint: Where It Comes from and How It Shapes and Impacts Us

In Oprah Winfrey's book *What Happened to You?: Conversations on Trauma, Resilience, and Healing,* coauthored by Dr. Bruce Perry, she explores how childhood experiences shape our brains, personalities, behaviors, and life outcomes.[23] The book emphasizes the question, "What happened to you?" as a key to self-discovery and unlocking personal growth and shifts the focus from asking, "What's wrong with you?" This change in perspective leads to a seismic shift, allowing individuals to delve into past adversity, trauma, and dysregulation to find support, safety, new perspectives, resilience, and peace.

Dr. Perry differentiates between "capital-T" trauma (such as abuse and natural disasters) and "small-t" trauma (continuous experiences of feeling excluded or not belonging). Both types can have lifelong impacts, affecting an individual's emotional, physical, and social well-being.

The book highlights the fact that many people carry some degree of trauma, which manifests in various ways, such as difficulty being vulnerable, lacking curiosity, and struggling with self-understanding.

Brené Brown, in an interview with Dr. Perry, shares an "aha" moment she had regarding the power of trauma-informed care. After opening a girls' school in Africa, Brown discussed with Dr. Perry why some students were not responding positively to the opportunities given to break the cycle of poverty. Dr. Perry's response shifted the focus from, "What's wrong with these kids?" to "What happened to these kids?" This change in perspective helped Brown realize the importance of understanding the impact of past experiences.

Asking the question "What happened to you?" has a significant influence in fostering empathy, connection, and a deeper understanding of the effects of trauma.

Trauma has a lasting impact on who we are, including on our brains. Dr. Daniel Amen and Amen Clinics have used advanced brain scans to study the effects of trauma, and they have found visible changes in the brain as a result. These changes can affect our emotions, thoughts, and behaviors even long after the traumatic event has occurred.

Recognizing the profound influence of trauma on the brain is crucial to providing compassionate and effective support. This research emphasizes the importance of trauma-informed care and creating safe environments for healing and resilience.[24]

We Inherit Family Trauma, and It Unconsciously Shapes Who We Are

Most of us will experience at least one conscious trauma in our life-time that could lead to post-traumatic stress disorder (PTSD) or, in cases like mine, complex post-traumatic stress disorder (CPTSD). I say *conscious*, meaning you have some memory of it happening.

It could be anything from a car accident to sexual or physical assault, to combat, to witnessing death or injury. It can also come from the moment you are conceived or your early childhood experiences that you don't remember, which also become marked in your unconscious.

Additionally, trauma can be inherited and passed on from generations and passed from your ancestral lineage. If a traumatic event occurs in one generation and isn't resolved or processed, its effects can be inherited by the next generations, affecting their mental and emotional well-being.

The book *It Didn't Start with You* by Mark Wolynn delves into the research and profound concept that inherited and unresolved family trauma is passed down from one generation to the next. [25] Drawing from the field of epigenetics, the book presents research indicating that traumatic experiences can influence gene expression, through the DNA code itself.

One pivotal technique to unearth such hidden traumas is the core language approach, which underscores the importance of our frequently used words and phrases as potential indicators of ancestral pain.

For example, if you are of Iranian descent like me, the trauma you inherit might encompass layers beyond personal family experiences. The Persian Empire's long and storied history, the recent political changes, revolutions, and wars, all contribute to a collective trauma experienced by its people. Epigenetics studies show, regardless of your family's ancestral country of origin or your generation, we all have generational trauma passed to us in some capacity.

When personal trauma, like your mother's experiences, is layered onto this collective backdrop, the emotional inheritance can be complex. It can have profound effects on her behavior, emotions, and the ways she interacts with her environment. The stress, fear, and traumas associated with things like fleeing a war and personal abuse can influence her gene expression (as per epigenetics), which could theoretically influence her offspring. This trauma can manifest in various ways: anxiety, hypervigilance, distrust, nightmares, or even physical symptoms. This is why understanding your ancestorial history is a critical component to understanding yourself and healing.

In my case, the rich cultural backdrop of Iran, with its emphasis on family honor, tradition, and societal expectations, might mean that many traumas are kept silent or internalized, adding another layer of complexity to their expression and transmission.

The next layer of what we inherit is what we are absorbing at the time of conception; for example, whether we were conceived in love or conception was forced, like in arranged marriages or through rape or sexual abuse. These things are often inherited into our bodies and DNA.

From that comes the experience your mother is living while you are in her womb. Specifically, from the time you are in mama's belly until about 7 years old, you are absorbing and learning the energy of everything around you, and even if the experience is not directly yours, the energy is still being stored in your body.

In my case, my mother was in a constant state of fear of my father abusing her while I was in her belly. I never knew I was predisposed to a high state of anxiety because of this. Add in escaping a war and being rejected in my new home country, and it's a recipe for a constant state of hypervigilance.

The next cycle includes the subtle experiences you inherit. For example, if you had busy parents in survival mode working 24-7, you may have been unintentionally raised without having your core emotional needs met. These needs are foundational in the way we are developing.

When our core needs are not met by our caregivers, we develop unconscious behaviors such as people pleasing, avoidance, and defensive or highly reactionary responses—meaning we do not know we are doing them.

To heal and break the cycle, it is essential to recognize these layers of trauma, understand their origins both personally and within the larger cultural context, and work toward addressing and resolving them.

Yup—this is extremely hard work, yet it brings the keys to unlock total freedom.

In my case, it took reconciling with my identity as an Iranian growing up in America. I had to unpack the profound influences of Iran's storied history, intertwined with personal narratives, underscoring the complexity of the traumas many of us bear.

Truly healing and finding our place in such a rich cultural tapestry necessitates recognizing these multilayered traumas, understanding their roots, and embarking on a journey of both personal and collective reconciliation. But the exploration doesn't end there.

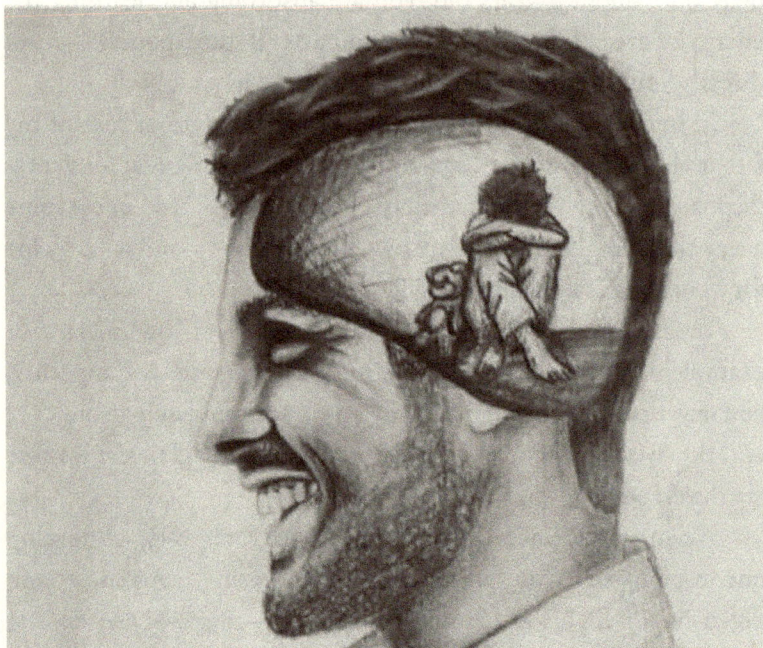

Unknown

From Cultural Legacies to Complex PTSD

Enter CPTSD. It's not solely a result of isolated traumatic incidents; often, it's the result of persistent, smaller stresses, especially during our formative years. It encompasses a range of behaviors and struggles that can have a profound impact on a person's well-being. Causes can include these:

- **Small Events Over Time:** Complex PTSD can arise from a cumulative effect of repeated small events, such as chaotic environments, financial insecurity, and witnessing dysfunctional or abusive relationships.

- **Harsh and Critical Punishments:** Experiencing harsh and critical punishments, whether physical or emotional, can erode self-esteem and create a constant sense of fear and inadequacy.

- **Witnessing Dysfunction and Violence:** Being exposed to dysfunctional or violent and abusive relationships, especially within the family, can cause chronic distress, fear, and trauma.

- **Parentification:** When a child is forced to take on adult responsibilities and become the caregiver for their parents or siblings, it disrupts normal development and overwhelms them with stress and responsibilities beyond their years.

- **Emotional Neglect:** The absence of emotional support, validation, and nurturing can leave deep emotional scars, leading to feelings of emptiness, isolation, and difficulties in forming healthy relationships.[26] Dr. Brené Brown is well known for deeply researching and writing about shame, empathy, and vulnerability, and she connects these three very closely:

"The difficult part about trauma is that it feeds feelings of shame. Shame is the concept of, 'I am bad,' 'I am unworthy,' and 'I am undeserving.' And yet, when we are able to dig deep within ourselves, allow ourselves to be vulnerable, and tap into our courage while being met with empathy and compassion, we are able to extinguish those feelings of shame and begin to heal."[27]

I spent a great deal of time understanding my CPTSD and how it was showing up. As I embarked on this journey, I started becoming aware and observing the behaviors in others and connecting just how many of us were carrying around CPTSD. You do not need to fight a war or escape one to have it.

It can show up in reactions to highly charged and stressful situations like the workplace, and it's critical for managers and leaders to build awareness and understanding around this condition.

From Shadows to Light: Unraveling Trauma's Impact in the Workplace

In our professional journey, personal traumas don't merely vanish when we clock in. In an age dominated by emotionally phobic workplaces and polished images on platforms like Instagram and LinkedIn, many silently carry burdens from their past. It's paramount that we comprehend these seldom-discussed challenges and their presence within professional settings.

Regrettably, it has become almost taboo to discuss past traumas, be it neglect, caregiver divorce, domestic violence, substance-abusing parents, or other challenges. These topics disrupt the facade of perfection we're encouraged to maintain.

There is also trauma instigated by the workplace, when employees undergo a one-time or ongoing distressing event at work, such as a workplace accident or continual stress like an overwhelming workload or an abusive supervisor. Oftentimes, abusive behavior is normalized in some toxic workplaces.

We fail to realize that not being vulnerable and portraying an image of perfection actually separates us from each other and eliminates our ability to connect. Vulnerability is the antidote.

"Portraying an image of perfection actually separates us from each other and eliminates our ability to connect. Vulnerability is the antidote."

The prevailing workplace culture, which often seems emotionally stifling, offers little room for openness or vulnerability. This isn't a call for the workplace to transform into a therapist's office but a plea to recognize that unspoken traumas can influence professional behaviors.

Most workplaces champion an idealized image, often to the detriment of emotional well-being. If unresolved trauma lingers, high-stress work situations can elicit strong emotional reactions. After all, the workplace is a common setting for stress. It's vital to understand triggers, which can prompt specific behaviors or reactions in individuals. These can stem from internal sources like memories or external cues such as sounds.

While negative trauma responses like anger or shutting down are evident, positive ones—such as excessive amiability or perfectionism—often go unnoticed. Recognizing both as trauma responses is crucial.

It is important to inspire everyone to ask their organizations, colleagues, and leaders about the topic and put practices in place to become trauma informed. There are very few detailed books published on this topic, so I hope this book will bring more awareness and drive change. *A Little Book About Trauma-Informed Workplaces* by Nathan Gerbrandt, Randy Grieser, and Vicki Enns and *Managing Trauma in the Workplace: Supporting Workers and Organisations* by Noreen Tehrani offer insights for creating trauma-informed workplaces.[28,29]

They emphasize understanding trauma's impact, fostering safe environments, and aligning policies while promoting well-being. These guides are invaluable for transforming workplaces with empathy and resilience and cover the following:

- Trauma-informed leadership and fostering resilience
- Aligning policies and procedures with trauma-informed principles

- Training and educating leaders and employees
- Establishing psychological safety for employees
- Promoting empathy and compassion
- Measuring progress and assessing trauma-informed practices

How Trauma Shows Up in Behaviors We Judge

Global researchers found that over 70% of the world's population has experienced some form of trauma; that is over 5 billion people. Awareness of these behaviors, whether in oneself or in colleagues, is essential. Here are ways trauma and triggers can manifest at work:

- Constant feelings of misplacement or self-doubt
- Shame, excessive self-critique, and feelings of being undeserving
- Overwhelming doubt, an urge to please, or a fear of decision-making
- Trust issues, leading to defensive barriers against others
- Disproportionate emotional reactions to workplace feedback
- Chronic physical symptoms like backaches or headaches indicating emotional suppression
- Either excessive defiance or a complete withdrawal from confrontations
- A tendency to equate self-worth solely with workplace achievements
- Overcompensating through amiability and a desire for recognition

- Pursuing perfection in every professional task
- High levels of hypervigilance and overly tuned to meeting other people's needs[30]

Reading this may bring up thoughts like *I do that.* This is not to judge yourself; it's to remember that what you become aware of can change. It's to identify these things, understand what triggers them, and apply tools to be able to see them happening.

Childhood traumas, especially if experienced during formative years, can be deeply ingrained and resurface during adulthood. The term "triggered" might be trending, but its implications are profound. These patterns infiltrate every relationship we hold—from self to friends, family to colleagues.

Unhealthy Empathy and Hypervigilance

Often when we experience trauma, we become overly empathic, aware, and highly sensitive. When we grow up on high alert, wondering when the next shoe will drop, we learn to tap into people's inner worlds in order to predict and protect ourselves from their next move.

The term "highly sensitive person" (HSP) was popularized by psychologist and author Dr. Elaine Aron. Dr. Aron conducted extensive research on individuals who have heightened sensitivity to various stimuli, including sensory, emotional, and environmental factors. She coined the term and wrote the book *The Highly Sensitive Person*, which has been instrumental in raising awareness and understanding of this personality trait.

When we are this in tune with our environment, it means 90% of the time we are picking up on other people's thoughts, feelings, and emotions and making them ours. We can literally "feel" when we disappoint someone when we say no. We "feel" when they've had a rough day and try to heal them. I experienced this to such a high degree it was paralyzing. It became my biggest curse and blessing in one.

Here's the crazy thing: oftentimes we make these thoughts, feelings, and emotions real and true for us personally. We take them on and give ourselves the job of healing and fixing people and things, all while giving up ourselves.

A tool I learned from Dr. Dain Heer and Gary Douglas is that before you make anything real and true for you, you should ask yourself—*Is this mine? Is this relevant to me? Is this my job?*

I use this tool every single moment as I need to make sure what I am perceiving and sensing is actually mine and not something I am picking up from someone else's head or body.

I also check in to make sure I am not repeating a past childhood belief that also was never mine but was projected at me. This tool has been a godsend for me, especially in the workplace, which for me is filled with hearing, sensing, and perceiving what is going on in others' worlds.

These traits can be falsely celebrated as positive behaviors when they are not, as people are quick to reinforce them as your identity. They make comments like, "You are so kind" or "You are so caring," when in reality we might be dealing with symptoms of trauma.

Often, we replay our childhood experiences in adult settings, especially at work, without realizing that we can choose to heal and alter these behaviors. Consider reflecting on the adult behaviors we exhibit at work (overly positive or negative) and tracing them back to past dysfunctional experiences. Recognizing these patterns is the first step toward positive change.

These behaviors can exist on a continuum of mild to extreme. Understanding this spectrum allows us to more easily recognize the behaviors in action. Here are two charts that give examples of the two extreme behaviors of people with CPTSD.

Examples of what we would traditionally label as "bad" behaviors in the workplace that could be the past repeating itself include these:

Workplace Behavior	How It May Appear to Others
Hyperarousal—overreacts or shuts down	Appears constantly on edge, easily startled, or jumpy; the other extreme uses silent treatment and is often dissociated
Flashbacks	May seem lost in thought or appear distressed
Avoidance	Avoids certain people, places, or activities
Emotional volatility	Exhibits intense and fluctuating emotions, including overly nice and sweet to anger and rage
Negative self-perception	Appears self-critical, has low self-esteem
Relationship difficulties	Struggles with trust, fear of abandonment, or emotional closeness
Hypervigilance	Seems overly alert or on guard, often scanning the environment
Memory issues	May have difficulty recalling certain events or details
Dissociation	Appears detached or spacey, may seem "out of it"
Physical symptoms	Displays physical discomfort, such as headaches or fatigue
Black-and-white thinking	Things or people are absolutes—"good" and "amazing" or "bad" and "awful"

Here are some additional workplace behaviors that are often labeled as "nice" or "good" or "high performance" and can also be present in individuals with complex PTSD:

Workplace Behavior	How It May Appear to Others
Lacks boundaries	For self and others with high expectations; inability to say no; struggles to assert personal boundaries and may be taken advantage of
People-pleasing	Constantly seeks validation and approval from others
Over-responsibility	Takes on excessive responsibility to avoid conflict or abandonment
Self-sacrificing	Puts others' needs before their own, often neglecting self-care
Avoiding confrontation	Tends to avoid conflict and difficult conversations
Excessive caretaking	Takes on a caretaker role for others, often neglecting own needs
Need for validation	Seeks reassurance and validation from others to feel worthy

Oftentimes we are just replaying our childhood experiences in adult bodies, especially in the workplace, and walking around completely unaware that we have the power to become aware and choose to change them.

As we become more aware of the ways in which our childhood selves inform our adult behaviors, we gain control over our actions, inside and outside of the workplace. This can be easier said than done though. It requires a deep inward journey to bring what is unconscious into the conscious realm.

I experienced this journey myself. Here are a few examples I went through and often observe in many others. Reflect on these, not only in you but to gain awareness in others as well.

Current Adult Behaviors at Work	Past Childhood Dysfunctional Experience
Overcommits and strives to maintain appearances at the cost of their relationships. Entire identity and happiness are tied to achievement and progress (athletics, workplace, business).	Perfection and achievement in school, sports. Proving to parents they are good enough and performing to gain validation of their worth and value.
Rose-colored-glasses syndrome and inability to see things as they are. Overly buying into the golden rule of do unto others as they do to you. Fantasizing about relationships with unavailable people or pursuing relationships that continue the pattern of self-abandonment. Positioning it as loyalty when it's one-sided or blind.	Isolating and dissociating alone in their room to cope with dysfunction of home or running away from home. Spending all time at friends' homes to avoid family home. Being the golden child or jumping from friendships to friendships or achievement to achievement.

Current Adult Behaviors at Work	Past Childhood Dysfunctional Experience
Responsible for fixing and taking care of everyone and everything. Overcompensates in relationships and hides their wants, needs, and safety in relationships.	Grows up fast and becomes the emotional caretaker to one or both of their parents. Becomes the compliant "good" child who doesn't want to add to stress or dysfunction in the home.
Hyper-independence, never asking for help. Self-protective habits like hiding behind career or avoiding close relationships (includes work) and getting "too attached." Hard time being vulnerable; hides behind image.	Parents were in extreme survival mode and overlooked needs. Avoiding getting close was modeled in the house by parents also being disconnected in the relationship (typically present in divorced parents). Affection was scarce or inconsistent.
High sense of fear of change, like changing companies or bosses even when they are limiting. Seeking comfort and safety in everything.	Unstable home with a lot of moving, fighting, and unknowns. Constant state of survival and abandonment to get basic needs met.
Everything is about power and control. Often seen as ego and entitlement. Used as a means to create the safety they never had.	Were highly controlled, bullied, criticized, or exposed to rage at home or at school.

It's imperative to recognize that these reactions are not sponta-neous occurrences. They are deeply rooted in our past, particularly in the environment we grew up in. In many ways, our relationship with the workplace acts as a mirror, reflecting the nuances of our childhood home.

Relationship with the Workplace: A Mirror of Our Childhood Home

Our childhood environment—the warmth, the tension, the conflicts, the moments of love—serves as a lens through which we perceive the world. This influence does not end at the doorstep of your family home.

It follows us, influencing how we perceive, react, and interact in the workplace. The correlation between childhood experiences and professional behaviors may seem abstract, but it's strikingly evident when observed closely.

Our first home becomes a blueprint. The values taught to us, the patterns witnessed, and the roles played shape our perceptions and reactions in the adult world.

Unless healed over time, these experiences can cause individu-als to develop protective mechanisms, which are often aggravated and escalated in many workplaces that are designed to make us feel like we don't fit in or are wrong.

This happened for me, unknowing the complex trauma I was carrying I unconsciously chose environments and people to work with that mirrored my very turbulent home. It was comfortably toxic. It was what was familiar to my childhood.

Drawing Parallels: Home Dysfunctions and Workplace Behaviors

Our childhood home plays a crucial role in shaping who we are as people. It's where we learn about values, beliefs, and behavior pat-terns that can carry over into our professional life. The dynamics, atmosphere, and experiences in our childhood home can influence how we approach work, handle challenges, and interact with others in the workplace.

For example, suppose you grew up in a supportive and encouraging environment, where your ideas and achievements were valued. In that case, you might develop confidence, a positive work ethic, and effective communication skills. These qualities can contribute to your success in the workplace, as you feel empowered to take on challenges and collaborate effectively with colleagues.

Conversely, if your childhood home was filled with conflict, negativity, or instability, it might impact your workplace interactions and performance. You might struggle with self-esteem issues, have difficulty trusting others, or find it challenging to handle stress and criticism.

Abuse, either emotional or physical, can also replay itself. In many cultures hitting a child is completely normal as a way to discipline, without understanding the long-term profound effects it has. I thought it was normal. My dad would have a rough day and be under pressure, and I would do something stupid like talk back to him, and he would rage beat me with his belt or anything he could get his hands on.

When a child cannot handle the trauma, they can go dark and split their personality, like my dad, and focus inward as protection for survival. This, for him, manifested in a high degree of narcissism.

Both of my parents were too busy in survival mode—trying to put food on the table, dealing with bullying and their own abuse in the workplace because of things like accents and mispronouncing words.

Abuse is not always clear-cut or linear, and trauma and dysfunction are not limited to early childhood. Each individual's experience varies, and a skilled trauma-informed therapist or physician who understands the neuroscience and mind-body connection is imperative.

Consider the following examples of a few parallels:

Childhood Home Dysfunction	Workplace Examples
Lack of communication or poor communication skills	Difficulty expressing thoughts and ideas clearly; avoiding conflicts or confrontation
Unpredictable or chaotic environment	Struggling with organization and time management; feeling overwhelmed or stressed easily
Emotional neglect or abuse	Difficulty forming and maintaining healthy relationships with colleagues; struggling with self-esteem and confidence
Lack of boundaries or invasive boundaries	Difficulty setting boundaries with coworkers or superiors; invading others' personal space or privacy
Unhealthy role models or lack of role models	Replicating unhealthy behaviors or toxic dynamics observed at home; struggling to find positive role models or mentors
Instability or inconsistent support	Difficulty handling change or adapting to new situations; seeking external validation due to a lack of consistent support

Childhood home dysfunction can have a profound impact on various aspects of our lives, including the workplace. Recognizing and understanding these patterns can help us break negative cycles and work toward creating a healthier and more fulfilling work environment for ourselves. The key is to not be under the illusion that any of this is normal.

Pen to Paper Homeplay: Tools and Exercises

1. **Get Curious and Shift the Question:** Instead of asking what's wrong with you or someone else, commit to start asking, "What happened to me or them?" Write this commitment down. This change in perspective opens up a space for understanding and compassion.

2. **It Starts with You:** Print out a picture of yourself when you were a child. How would you talk to that child? Can you still see the child in yourself and the ages you replay in the moments you are uncomfortable? For example, what happened to you at ages 6, 13, and 19? Do those personas show up when you are triggered? Can you see others through this lens when it happens in them?

3. **Observe Yourself:** Throughout your daily activities and build a habit to reflect in a journal. Ask yourself questions like these: How did I react (good or bad)? What came up for me in that moment? Where did I sense it in my body? What was my real "feeling" behind the "feeling"? Example: I lashed out in anger because I felt 10 years old again, when my needs never mattered. I felt a tightness in my chest like my heart was hurting again.

4. **List Ways You Can Learn:** Seek out information about your childhood and past. Ask parents, siblings, friends, or anyone

who has insight into the way you grew up. Look at old pictures and reflect from an adult lens of your experiences.

5. **Ask and Learn about Your Ancestors, Culture, and Lineage:** The science and research behind epigenetics show we carry genes in our DNA from our ancestors. If it's not in your DNA, you mimic and copy the behavior you observed to be true. This is why you could hear that someone in the family was an alcoholic, and it may have been passed to you. Find out about cultural norms and patterns that no longer apply.

   For example, in many Middle Eastern cultures, what the man says goes, and you are always wrong. Or hitting your kids is the way you discipline. This is not a blaming activity, but it is awareness and power for you to change history.

6. **Build a Support System:** Make a list of close friends or family that you can trust and be vulnerable with. See if there is space and a relationship to share with your bosses and colleagues. Some workplaces are very open and even have trauma-informed employee resource and support groups.

   Seek out a trauma-informed therapist who understands all of the points in this chapter across ancestral, cultural, mind, body, and soul connections. Be careful to avoid any who are eager to label you as a fixed diagnosis.

7. **Ask Your Employee Resource Group:** If there is an opportunity to champion and educate your organization on trauma-informed workplace options and create resources for employees and training.

Trauma creates ripple effects that can extend out and into every facet of one's future life especially in high-stress arenas that trigger us, like the workplace.

Anything we avoid, we may get away with for a while, but it will eventually show up through unhealthy behaviors, sickness, or illness in the mind or body.

Confronting, coming to terms with, and healing from that trauma is by no means an easy experience. It is more often a lifelong journey that involves equal parts deep, uncomfortable self-examination and patient, generous self-grace.

As you embark on your own journey toward healing, consider the resources available to you. When possible, consult with the right mental health professional or a trusted advisor. Equip yourself with a devoted support system and a toolbox full of self-care practices.

Remember that the majority of people have experienced some sort of trauma and that you are not alone.

Remember, too, how worthwhile a journey it will be. Just as trauma affects so many unforeseen avenues in one's life, so too does healing from trauma.

I would not take back any of the crazy complex trauma I have personally experienced as it has made me more aware, present, and an overall better person.

As you become a more whole, more authentic person, free or at least freer from the echoes of your traumatic experience, you will experience more success and fulfillment in every area of your life and take steps to uncover the real you.

CHAPTER 5

Childhood Shadows to Corporate Arenas: Breaking the Normalized Abuse Cycle in the Workplace

"Energy cannot be created or destroyed, it can only be changed from one form to another."

—Albert Einstein

"The executives know he's an abusive bully, but he's protected because he gets things done. You will get labeled as trouble-maker if you say something." These are the words someone said to me after I raised the issue that an executive was emotionally abusing people on a daily basis to the chief human resources officer.

I would find women crying in bathrooms and men with tears in their eyes saying they had a family to support and couldn't say anything. Little did I realize this was left to go on because he was the "deliver-at-all-costs guy."

In this toxic, cut-throat culture, leadership had made *emotional abuse* totally normal as the "cost" of doing business.

Years later, I found out that an HR VP who worked for him had transferred out to get away from the toxicity. Several other executives knew, but no one spoke up because it could mean getting fired and losing access to big bonuses and hefty retirement funds. This is what an "acceptance" and "lack" mindset looks like. Today, she has a "seat at the very top" and is in charge of many lives. I'm sure she generously contributes to numerous charities and avidly participates in "top women leaders" events—this is how the corporate-at-all-costs game works.

How have we developed tolerance for these things? Both those who turn a blind eye at the top and ignore these issues and those of us who, over time, consider environments like this to be normal. It's simple—childhood! Workplace dynamics and behaviors are often a reflection of our childhood home.

"Workplace dynamics and behaviors are often a reflection of our childhood home."

Our early family experiences echo in our adult interactions, notably in business, shaping how leaders manage pressure, teams, and relationships. Studies link executives' family backgrounds to their management styles, as they often mirror family dynamics in the workplace—known as transference. In essence, families form our first "enterprise," with parents and siblings constituting our initial "management team."[31]

Childhood trauma, especially when buried and left unaddressed, has a peculiar way of resurfacing. The corporate world, with its nuanced power dynamics, resembles the hierarchies and dynamics of a household in more ways than one might think.

Here, the bullying parent or the abusive elder might manifest as a manipulative boss or an oppressive colleague. The silent victim at a childhood home might reappear as the submissive employee, unable to voice against wrongdoings.

While the parallels between household dysfunctions and workplace behaviors offer insightful reflections, it is the confrontation with past shadows in the corporate halls that truly unravel the depth of their impact.

Professional environments replicate traumatic household dynamics, and this intensifies the cycle of abuse and has a severe impact on health, self-esteem, and long-term professional careers.

Dancing with Familiar Narcissism

Navigating the murky waters of corporate culture, I unearthed disturbing parallels to personal traumas of my past. It took me half my life to figure out my unconscious programming. To figure out what I was replaying from my childhood in the workplace. Not only was I attracting narcissistic and sociopathic abusive relationships but bosses as well. I was unconsciously the cocreator of this—it was normal to me.

The term "narcissism" has been diluted with casual usage, often misrepresenting its profound implications. It's not just about excessive self-love or vanity; it is an intricate web of behaviors that stem from deep-rooted insecurities of shame, self-hatred, and a distorted self-image. Narcissism is sometimes displayed as charismatic behaviors rooted in insecurities that can manifest as misleading leadership qualities that potentially harm organizational culture. This is why, even though research has shown that humble leaders with empathy make better leaders, we often confuse charismatic behaviors as leadership.[32]

In the workplace, these behaviors often mask themselves as leadership qualities. Aggression is mistaken for assertiveness; manipulation is seen as persuasion; and intimidation is misinterpreted as influence. Extensive research published in the National Library of Medicine by University of Berkley professors shows that these behaviors, left unchecked, not only harm the individuals at the receiving end but also poison the organizational culture.[33] Berkeley Haas Professors Jennifer Chatman and colleagues highlight in a new paper the significant negative influence of narcissistic leaders on organizational culture, revealing enduring detrimental effects on collaboration and integrity.[34] Through experiments and CEO studies, they demonstrated how narcissistic behaviors erode collaboration, ethics, and overall organizational effectiveness, emphasizing the critical importance of integrity for an organization's sustainability.[35]

> *"Narcissism is sometimes displayed as charismatic behaviors rooted in insecurities that can manifest as misleading leadership qualities, potentially harming organizational culture."*

I'm not talking about basic narcissism; or the healthy trait of putting yourself first; or the term used by someone who doesn't get along with someone else; or people who look in the mirror all the time and take selfies. I'm talking about the real deal—the abusive kind, the ones who emotionally abuse and gaslight us into thinking we are less than in order to take power from you. This is called *narcissistic personality disorder.*

Dr. Ramani Durvasula is the leading expert on the topic. She often emphasizes the distinction between narcissism as a personality trait and narcissistic personality disorder (NPD) as a clinical diagnosis.

Narcissism, as a trait, refers to a range of self-centered and self-focused behaviors that many individuals may exhibit to some degree. It involves an excessive preoccupation with oneself, a sense of entitlement, and a desire for admiration and attention. While narcissistic traits can be problematic, they do not necessarily meet the criteria for a clinical diagnosis.

On the other hand, NPD is a personality disorder characterized by a pervasive pattern of grandiosity, a constant need for admiration, and a lack of empathy for others. Individuals with NPD often display a sense of superiority, exploit others for personal gain, and have difficulty maintaining healthy relationships. Understanding this difference is crucial in recognizing and addressing the impact of narcissism on individuals and their relationships.

Unfortunately, the workplace only places focus on the physical abuse they can see. This is viewed as hostile behavior. Emotional and psychological abuse, bullying, and gaslighting are rarely found in an employee handbook, code of conduct, or checkbox compliance video training everyone is made to watch. Sadly, studies show many people in top leadership positions have narcissistic and sociopath traits and tendencies.

Actually, the entire corporate form, structure, and mindset is set up to be command-and-control and a form of abuse. Yes, abuse! If we bend and staple someone, put them in a box with their name on it, and call them wrong each time they try to break away or think for themselves, I'm pretty sure that is a form of abuse. This is how abusive leadership behaviors that we see as "normal" help keep this system intact. Controversial view, I know.

I finally discovered that my child program was being replayed in the workplace unconsciously. Who would pick an abusive boss willingly? I was replaying my mother who dealt with a father that I now know had narcissistic personality disorder as a result of a ton of generational and ancestral trauma. To cope, she would shrink, try to please him and make him happy, keep us perfect to keep the peace in the house. If that didn't happen, he would rage, usually triggered from a stressful day at work, and verbally abuse her or beat and come after me. I now know I often took it unconsciously as a way to protect her and my younger sister, as if in some twisted way I knew he had to get it out, and I thought at the time that I was the strong one.

Most people ask me if I hate my father, which is not my point of view. I believe he did the best he could with the level of deep trauma, awareness, consciousness, and tools he had at the time. Do I condone or excuse what he did? No way. Yet I made a choice a long time ago to have compassion for his childhood and forgive that part of him.

What mattered to me was this: now that I was aware, I needed to stop focusing on being a victim and, instead, shift my focus towards changing my subconscious patterns to prevent replaying my childhood dynamics in the workplace.

Through this healing process, I've discovered newfound strength and power beyond what I ever imagined.

I'm now profoundly grateful for my father and choose to focus on the invaluable lessons I learned from him, such as having unwavering faith, persistence, and courage. His most significant teaching was to never accept "no" for an answer and to persist until you find someone who says "yes."

Unconsciously Replaying and Allowing the Abuse

I was not only attracting these toxic situations and people energetically, but I was also turning into a scared, helpless little girl in an adult body when it would happen. Except, I had no idea at the time what was going on. I would know I was "frozen" but not why or how to undo it. Today, I understand that our bodies can transport us back in time, as if the same trauma is occurring again. In my case, it was like going back to being that frightened little girl who feared the belt.

There were 2 narcissistic and sociopathic bosses I worked for; one fully displayed who he was with abuse, anger, and rage, and the other was "nice," pretended he didn't know, and used the first to do his dirty work. I refused to see that they were the same.

What is sadder is that I bought into the rose-colored idea that, "We are friends and have each other's backs." I failed to recognize that no one can have your back unless you first have your own, and if you are unaware of what that looks like, you will fall for anything; yet I see people do this all the time.

"No one can have your back unless you first have your own."

With the help of a local therapist, I was able to uncover what I was dealing with. To make matters worse, this therapist said that although she could never reveal names, she could tell me that most of her clients were from my company, and they were telling the same story.

Around the time that I was going through this, I had the honor of giving a TED Talk. I know, don't ask me how I pulled it together with all this in the background. To this day when I watch the replay, I can see the turmoil in my eyes. What the pictures and videos do not tell you is that at the time I was feeling lack of confidence and belonging. It took me a while to figure out that the root cause was that I chose (it's always a choice) to work in a toxic environment.

I had surrounded myself with these same leaders above and a culture that thought instilling fear, bullying, gaslighting, and making thousands of people scared to voice the truth was the "power" strategy to get ahead.

When you look closer, these leadership behaviors stem from a place of deep childhood trauma, fear, insecurity, and lack. You would not choose to lead that way if you truly had a lens of abundance, security, and strength. Now I am fully aware that these leaders have significant unhealed pasts.

Toxicity is usually not a trait that is listed in the marketing brochures or best company rankings, but it is the ugly truth of some (not all) corporate cultures. It's crazy that these leaders and executives are hired or promoted to look out for the company's biggest asset—its people—and are rarely selected for their bravery or courageous skills. Most are not equipped to address tough, uncomfortable issues or recognize trauma within themselves or others.

This lack turns into power struggle behaviors that create toxic cultures, bullying, gaslighting, and let's call it what it actually is: abuse. Leaders are often chosen because of similarity, comfort, and unconscious bias, as most people subconsciously want to be around people who are like them. This is why we see leaders bring in or promote their "own" from within or from other companies.

Why? Because as humans we are wired for comfort and the easy-breezy road. Hence the comfort of the "Boy's Club"! Oh, and let's not forget the "Women's Club" either, and *yes*, that club exists as well, and women are just as guilty. With limited seats at the table, women also give in to their traumas and fears. The minute there is a risk of your outshining them, they will pull us down fast for fear of replacing them, instead of seeing the possibility of learning and growing together, which requires courage and confidence.

Although I already did not fit in, I *chose* to lean into the fear, muster the courage to speak up, and expose the abusive and toxic culture that was impacting thousands of lives.

I did this with the help of a therapist, one gem of an HR leader, 2 executives, and a lawyer friend who anonymously guided and coached me through the witness, documentation, and investigation process. The only way this would change was to go to the top.

At the time, I didn't think about why other leaders more senior to me who knew the abuse was happening didn't step up and do something; I just knew I needed to. (The research behind the "why" people remain quiet in the workplace is a topic for another book)

I sat with this for a while and asked myself, *If I choose this, what will my life be like in 5 years?*

Looking that far ahead gives us greater clarity on our fears, life, and choices. It helped me see that regardless of the outcome, I was not only building my courage muscle but also creating a higher standard for myself and opening a possibility for change for others, which to me was a win-win.

After many sleepless nights, I decided no amount of money was worth selling my soul. I chose to take a big step and meet with the newly appointed CEO with hard facts, tons of documentation, and a list of people to interview.

Was it hard? Extremely! Did I have fear? For sure! But for me, the pain of doing nothing was greater.

Did it change anything? Yes! Finally, everyone rallied to do the right thing, and both abusive leaders were fired.

I was asked to lay low until the dust settled, and since I'm not a "laying low" person, I decided to resign. Deep down, I knew that time would be better spent healing, uncovering myself, and moving on.

If you believe you might be dealing with a narcissist in your workplace, consider the following traits. How many align with your experience?

I urge you to take this seriously and not allow yourself, others, or especially HR to brush it off as "normal" or downplay what is happening. We can spin it how we choose, yet in the end our silence is acceptance—period!

Walk away! The impact to you will take years to uncover and heal.

Behaviors	Narcissistic Personality Disorder and Sociopathic Bosses
Lack of empathy	Shows little concern for others' feelings or needs, lacks empathy, and disregards well-being
Grandiosity	Has an inflated sense of self-importance, views themselves as superior and entitled
Manipulation	Uses manipulation tactics to control and exploit others, manipulates for personal gain without remorse
Exploitation	Exploits and takes advantage of subordinates for personal gain, uses people without regard for consequences
Lack of accountability	Avoids taking responsibility for mistakes or failures, shifts blame onto others
Lack of remorse	Shows little remorse for their actions or harm caused, lacks guilt for unethical behavior
Gaslighting	Manipulates others' perceptions, distorts reality to make victims question their sanity or judgment
Emotional abuse	Engages in harmful behaviors that cause emotional distress, belittles and humiliates others
Bullying	Engages in aggressive and intimidating behavior, targets and harasses individuals

Behaviors	Narcissistic Personality Disorder and Sociopathic Bosses
Anger range	Displays a wide range of anger responses, which can include explosive outbursts, passive-aggressive behavior, cold and calculating demeanor, or chronic irritability
Nice and charming	Can exhibit a pleasant and charismatic demeanor, often charming others with their words and behavior

Breaking the Chain

Awareness is the first step to healing and change. Recognizing these behaviors, tracing their origins, and understanding their implications are crucial. It is essential not only for victims but also for organizations to acknowledge the existence of these shadows.

Policies need to be in place, which not only focus on overt issues like physical abuse but also delve into the realms of emotional and psychological abuse.

For individuals, the journey involves acknowledging past traumas, understanding their impact on current behaviors, and seeking support to break free. It's about reclaiming control over one's life and ensuring that the traumas of the past don't dictate the narrative of the future.

As we reflect on the ways we may unknowingly recreate familiar patterns of abuse or get entangled in the web of narcissistic dynamics, it's essential to also examine the mechanisms we employ to cope.

Some of us numb through drugs and alcohol, and some of us might seek solace in routines and habits perceived as constructive or healthy. Yet, as we'll explore, even these can mask profound emotional scars. Behind every seemingly positive habit or achievement, there might be a hidden narrative, a story of trauma and evasion.

Behind the Badge of Honor: When Healthy Habits Conceal Trauma

There are both healthy and unhealthy forms of addiction. Healthy addictions are those that enhance our lives and well-being, while unhealthy addictions are those that harm us physically, emotionally, and socially.

Dr. Gabor Maté deeply researches addiction in his books *The Myth of Normal* and *When the Body Says No*. He emphasizes that we have normalized as a society addictive behaviors that are often destructive. He says, "An addiction is any behavior, substance related or not, that an individual pursues because they find pleasure, relief, or they crave it temporarily, so they pursue the pleasure and relief despite negative consequences. And they don't give it up, in the face of negative consequences. I said any behavior. So that could be sex, gambling, eating, shopping, work, relationships, or substances."

Healthy addictions might include activities like exercise, reading, creative pursuits, and socializing with friends and family. These activities provide a sense of pleasure, purpose, and fulfillment without causing harm or negative consequences. Unhealthy addictions, on the other hand, might include behaviors such as substance abuse, gambling, compulsive shopping, or overeating. These behaviors may initially provide pleasure or relief from stress, but they can quickly become harmful and lead to negative consequences.

Perceived healthy addictions can turn into unhealthy behaviors when they start to interfere with our daily lives and responsibilities or become a way to avoid and escape from emotional pain or discomfort hidden deep inside.

For me, my addiction to sports, fitness, and exercise became my perceived "healthy" habits that were even celebrated and admired.

I mean, come on, look at the exterior image and accolades: I ran a marathon on the Great Wall of China, the Chicago Marathon, and over 25 other marathons and half-marathons. I completed over 30 Century Rides on a fancy bicycle (100 miles is a Century for the non-riders). I've done over 15 triathlons . . . and the list, medals, and awards go on and on.

I was running and riding from unmasking all my pain, struggle, and trauma. I hid behind the badge of an accomplished athlete.

Don't get me wrong—I'm profoundly grateful for all my experiences. As my therapist pointed out, I could have easily lost my life, and it was athletics that kept me going. However, when we reach a point where we're ready to stop numbing our pain and summon the courage to confront the darker aspects of ourselves, we open the door to a world of profound growth, joy, and happiness.

What healthy and admired badge are you hiding behind? Signs of a healthy addiction turning into unhealthy behavior include:

- **Interference with Daily Life:** When an activity starts to disrupt work, school, or relationships, it may indicate an unhealthy addiction. For instance, if exercise overrides important commitments, it could be a sign of an unhealthy addiction.

- **Emotional Dependence:** Using an activity to escape emotional pain or discomfort suggests an unhealthy addiction. For example, relying on socializing to avoid loneliness or anxiety may indicate an unhealthy addiction.

- **Negative Consequences:** When an activity leads to physical or mental health issues, financial problems, or legal troubles, it can signal an unhealthy addiction. For instance, using alcohol as a coping mechanism but experiencing negative consequences indicates an unhealthy addiction.

For me this showed up as needing a hip replacement at 40 years old. In others, it shows up as knee replacements, back pain, and shoulder pain. For some, it may show up as autoimmune disorders, body aches, cancer, and more.

The body is always trying to tell us when something is off and wrong. If we stop and listen. Yet it is so common to get the joint replacement, get the cancer cut out, take the medication, and move on.

Reflecting on my habits, I started to see a pattern. What appeared as "healthy" behaviors on the surface were, in reality, mechanisms of avoidance and numbing. I was using the thrill of physical achievements to drown out the whispers of my body, ignoring the signs it was desperately trying to communicate.

This realization made me understand that trauma is not merely a mental or emotional concept. It leaves a physical imprint on us, as our bodies keep a faithful record of the pain we've experienced and the trauma we've been trying to avoid or numb.

Our bodies don't forget, even when our minds try to.

The Body Truly Keeps Score: Talk Therapy Tackles Only 2% of the Trauma Puzzle

The reason so many people have a hard time changing addictions through conventional talk therapy and mainstream books and training is that these are all focused on the mind. They cut out the body and the connections to neuroscience and quantum physics.

It is not enough to just gain "insights" about your past, as insights that the mind processes are only 2% of the puzzle.

In addition, even though the majority of people have been through some sort of trauma, most talk therapy is not trauma informed. Trauma is an entirely different ball game. It's like trying to heal a brain tumor with Tylenol or sleep.

Modern society often champions the development of emotional intelligence (EI) as a key to success and interpersonal relations. This matters, but many are discovering that conventional EI training can miss deeper-rooted issues, especially if one has experienced trauma, like we all have to a degree.

At the same time, the term "ego" frequently gets thrown around. While some perceive ego as a barrier to genuine understanding, it's essential to recognize the ego's protective role.

The ego often surfaces as a defense mechanism against deep-seated beliefs or traumas, trying to project an image contrary to an individual's innermost fears or insecurities. It might manifest in someone overly asserting their point of view, not because they're genuinely confident in their beliefs, but to mask their inner vulnerability.

"We strive to prove the opposite of what we believe is true about ourselves."

Ever meet someone who is trying to prove they are confident or knowledgeable or strong? Look at them through the lens of their childhood; they would not be doing that if they actually believed it to be true. We strive to prove the opposite of what we believe deep down is true about ourselves.

I went through 2 therapists and a business coach, and nothing worked. This is because the majority of people are not properly educated and trained in a holistic fashion; they are trained to surface-level "diagnose."

The reason is that the complex nature of trauma and its effects on the brain, cells, and nervous system cannot be changed simply by talking or using positive affirmations and memes that have become so mainstream. Trauma is locked in your body from the moment it happened. I really wish someone had told me this before I had wasted so much time and money on ineffective coaches and therapists who created vast amounts of suffering.

Memories Are Stored in the Body Down to Your Tissues

Despite the rise in awareness about mental health, mainstream therapy and pop psychology often stay on the surface. They might recognize trauma or "daddy issues" but struggle to address the profound physical and chemical imprints these experiences leave on our bodies.

It wasn't just my mind that I had to confront, but my body had its own revelations. When you're told to "listen to your body," it's not merely about physical signs like aches or fatigues, but more about the hidden emotional stories our muscles, bones, and cells might be preserving.

Through my journey of searching, asking questions, and healing, I came across a transformative resource. *The Body Keeps the Score* by Bessel van der Kolk sheds light on how trauma isn't just retained in memories, but it lingers in our very fibers and tissues. The book explores the complex nature of trauma and its profound impact on the brain, mind, and body, and delves into the neurobiology of trauma, explaining how it affects memory, emotions, and stress responses.

The book highlights the physical manifestations of trauma and its connection to psychological well-being. It explores various therapeutic approaches for healing, emphasizing the importance of addressing both the mind and body through many techniques I

tried and will recommend later in this section. The author emphasizes the significance of self-regulation skills and the healing power
of secure relationships in the recovery process.

The chronic pain in my back, the tension in my hips, the unex-
plainable weight gain even with my excessive athleticism were all
my body's desperate signals, alarms I'd been dismissing.

As I researched and talked to holistic and energy physicians and
practitioners, I was shocked to understand the bent bone that pro-
truded in my back was not from a motorcycle accident and which
I casually dismissed, but was a result of years of shrinking energetically, emotionally, and physically so I would not scare or intimidate
anyone.

*"Trauma isn't just retained in memories, but it lingers in
our very fibers and tissues."*
—The Body Keeps the Score *by Bessel van der Kolk*

I never fully grasped that things are locked into our bodies
down to our cells and tissues from the moment of trauma, and the
memory gets unlocked when the body senses any threat; this is
why we get "triggered." Threats bring up something from the past,
not the present. That is why certain words, people, locations, and
touches often do not match our responses; we go back in our bodies
to when we were 5, 10, 15, 21 years old.

A friend of mine was raped, and if anyone even lightly touched
her neck in the same place of the assault, she would be ready to go
into an all-out fight. In my case, if anyone raised their voice or yelled
or screamed, I would be set off into either complete shut-down and
freeze or anger and defense, as this would trigger my childhood
with my abusive father. In both cases, our bodies would physically
respond to external stimuli in ways that were beyond our control.

In other words, our trauma was repeating itself within the physical confines of our bodies.

Traditional talk therapy often falls short when it comes to addressing trauma. In cases of trauma, individuals can disconnect from their bodies as a survival mechanism. In similar situations, such as those encountered in the workplace, this disconnection can recur, even when it involves something as minor as receiving mild feedback.

Not until I read and researched this concept did I fully understand how I was replaying my past in my mind, body, and soul and how to heal from it.

Energy Imprints: Body, Mind, and Soul Connections

As quantum physics and holistic energy physicians and practitioners, like Dr. Bruce Lipton, have researched and taught, it is also critical to understand how energy can become trapped in the body and show up as chronic ailments. It can show up as emotional, psychological, or physical pain.[36]

Anytime you have chronic pain or aliment, ask what in your life could be contributing to it. Remember, we spend the majority of our time in the workplace, and it is nearly impossible for things that are occurring in the workplace such as stress, toxic cultures, and fear to not manifest in our bodies.

I had chronic pain in my back and hips. As a hard-core empath I was also picking up on thoughts, feelings, and emotions of everyone at my toxic place of work. I later learned that the hips are connected to the energy center that governs creativity.

The spiritual meaning of hip pain can be tied to old memories, traumas, and uncomfortable emotions like shame. The back is tied to feeling unsupported, a lack of belonging, and the inability to be in your power. It signifies that we are holding all of our potential power and potency behind us and are unable to share it with the world.

Embracing energetic wisdom, a holistic approach that focuses on creating harmony in one's mind, body, and spirit, allowed me to better understand the pain that I was experiencing and, eventually, to move beyond it. As with everything else in this chapter, that process involved contending with both the trauma I had experienced in my life and the trauma I was absorbing through other people in my life.

Energetic wisdom often views emotions and physical symptoms as manifestations of imbalances or blockages in the body's energy system. For example, chakras are believed to be energy centers within the human body that correspond to specific nerve bundles and major organs. These energy centers are thought to play a role in both physical and spiritual well-being, often discussed in the context of holistic health, yoga, and alternative medicine.[37]

Here are some examples of how energetic wisdom might interpret emotions and physical symptoms:

Emotion or Physical Symptom	Spiritual Interpretation	Energetic Interpretation
Anger	A call to assert boundaries and overcome obstacles	Imbalances in the solar plexus chakra
Anxiety	A call to surrender control and trust in a higher power	Imbalances in the root chakra

Emotion or Physical Symptom	Spiritual Interpretation	Energetic Interpretation
Sadness	An opportunity for introspection and reflection, leading to growth	Blockages in the heart chakra
Shame	A call to embrace imperfections and recognize inherent worth	Imbalances in the sacral chakra
Physical symptoms	Manifestations of energy blockages or imbalances	Sign of blockages in various chakras or energy pathways

Humans are complex creatures, and it takes an understanding of not only psychology but also neuroscience, quantum physics, and mechanics to understand how the body processes energy in relation to others and the universe.

Discovering What Truly Works: Body and Mind Combined

Think of humans as intricate puzzles, each piece representing a different aspect of who we are—our emotions, our body, and even our connection to the universe. Sometimes, those pieces get jumbled, and we need strategies to put them back in the right place.

When we feel any kind of pain in our bodies, it could be emotional, or it could be a physical manifestation like back pain or even autoimmune diseases or cancer. All of this comes from the resistance we have created to survive our insane reality.

Pain is often a bodily manifestation of whatever we are resisting in our lives. It's important to remember that often what we are resisting is **ourselves**—and what is true for us. That's why our society suffers from so much disease.

As a society we have to regain our power and pause! We must ask questions and choose with awareness, refusing to be robots. We must heal and connect the puzzle of how the reality around us is impacting our minds, bodies, and souls.

Over the past few years, I've explored various techniques, testing different solutions to solve that puzzle. I've found a combination of practices that don't just fit my pieces together but that can also help others in their own unique puzzle of life.

For the past two years, I've researched and incorporated various modalities into my routine, one of which is Generator Athlete Lab in Austin, TX. The lab offers the science-backed Generator Protocol, a holistic recovery approach that includes infrared sauna, alternating hot and cold plunge pools, Normatec compression therapy, red light therapy, and vibration plate treatment.

This method is known for reducing all-cause mortality and heart and brain disease deaths and improving mental health, sleep, and overall well-being by boosting dopamine levels associated with motivation. Low dopamine levels are connected to conditions such as Parkinson's disease, depression, and ADHD.

The results are astonishing, and I highly recommend it. Those I coach have also integrated this and have seen profound results in their overall work and life when it comes to managing stress, focus, writing, being calm and present, speaking, and so much more.

The other critical connection point is somatic breathwork, which helps you connect to your body and release what is stored in the body or work through a reaction or trigger. I highly recommend reading or listening to *Breath: The New Science of a Lost Art* by James

Nestor. It provides practical insights and exercises to help readers improve their breathing habits and, in turn, enhance their overall health and vitality. Also, look up breathing exercises such as the Wim Hof Method, straw breathing, 4-7-8 breathing, or box breathing.

It takes time, commitment, and patience to determine the best mix of what will unlock your limitations mentally, spiritually, and physically. There are so many modalities out there, and nowadays everyone is an "expert," especially on social media. It's important to do your research to find the right expert.

Here are a few things I tried that were extremely effective for me:

1. Cold water exposure, preferably cold to hot contrast intervals where you are in cold water for 3 to 4 minutes, then in hot water for one to 2 minutes. Swap for 3 to 4 rotations.

2. Infrared sauna heat exposure 2 to 3 times per week for 20 to 30 minutes.

3. Cognitive behavioral therapy (CBT), eye movement desensitization and reprocessing (EMDR), Internal Family Systems (IFS), and Somatic Experiencing or other types of modalities to go deeper than talk therapy, which may not help you recall everything.

4. Walk outside in nature to ground yourself. As an avid athlete this used to sound insane to me because there was no adrenaline of throwing weights around or racing a bicycle. Wait, no runner's high? Exactly. It's meant to slow down and become present and connect with something bigger that you—planet Earth.

5. Yoga, preferably hot yoga which supports your ability to get out of your head and be comfortable in the heat while doing flow movements.

6. Plant-based medicines monitored by physicians and therapists. These can span from ketamine, psilocybin mushrooms, and ayahuasca to many more. This has hit the mainstream and there are many "experts" out there, so it's important to do your research and homework.

7. Energy body work through Reiki masters or certified body practitioners. I leveraged both Access Consciousness, Reiki, and other modalities.

8. Meditate, meditate, meditate: a fifteen-minute minimum every morning like your life depends on it. I set an intention and a little prayer.

9. Schedule conscious check-ins: put alarms in your phone to check in with your body and breath or incorporate it into your meditation practice. It has a tremendous impact.

10. Journal! Get your thoughts out in front of you. Ask what triggered you today. How did you respond? If you reacted cool, how can you catch it next time? Remember, a trigger can be positive or negative (saying yes and people pleasing, or freaking out and getting angry, or shutting down and saying nothing).

Even when we think we're outrunning our traumas through distractions, our body has its own way of reminding and revealing what we've been trying to bury. Trauma isn't just a mental or emotional issue, but one that can physically manifest. We are complex, connected creatures, and it's crucial to connect modalities that work for you, not to just use what is conventional or what worked for someone else. Ask questions, try things, connect your own dots.

Raw Truths I Wish I Knew Sooner

With my newfound enlightenment came the raw truths, the hard-hitting revelations that I wished I had been armed with from the beginning. So as you embark on this journey of self-discovery, let me lay down some unfiltered insights and painful lessons from my experience:

1. **Everything You Avoid or Defend Will Eventually Punch You in the Face 100 Times Over.** When you are choosing distraction and are unwilling to become present you only hide you from you. Don't wait to hit rock bottom. Don't wait for an illness, burnout, or breakdown to look at these things.

2. **Let Go of Self-Judgment and Feeling That There Is Something Fucked Up or Wrong with You Once You Start Becoming Aware of These Traumas, Triggers, or Behaviors.** You made it this far and there is something very powerful about you that you were able to carry on this far and this long. Getting addicted to the "self-help" world and "fixing" yourself can have diminishing returns.

3. **Not Everyone Will Be Kind, Be Compassionate, or Understand, and That's OK.** Let them go and don't worry about the people or things that you may have lost. Most people don't have the courage it takes to look at their own traumas, and they will instead judge yours. Those that are aware will not be judging you; they are too focused on healing themselves. Focus on the road ahead.

4. **Exercise Patience, Allowance, and Kindness with Yourself.** This does not go away overnight; you have been carrying this your entire life. Make a self-care plan and commit to it. You will take 10 steps forward and 2 steps back,

but keep at it. Keep in mind that the majority of people never become aware of this and never have a chance to change it.

5. **Real Leadership Is Removing Your Mask.** Your story, your lessons, your mess-ups—they're all stepping stones. Use them. Don't just limp through life; own it. And for the love of all things good, remember: real leadership is doing the tough work on yourself. It's gritty, it's raw, but damn, it's worth it. Remember, no title required.

It's hard work, it will have its ups and downs, yet it is the only route to unmasking you, being more of you, and unlocking your courage, creativity, vulnerability, and true connection. Not just with others but with yourself.

Tools for Courageous Introspection and Unmasking You

True leadership in your personal life and the workplace is rooted in self-awareness, compassion, and the courage to change and grow personally. By leading consciously and being attuned to our traumas, we not only benefit ourselves but leave a lasting positive legacy in our lives, workplaces, and communities.

This requires staying present in each moment, seeing how and where the past is showing up, and choosing a different response to thrive.

How Are These Things Showing Up?

Remember that annoying thing . . . 95% of your choices, thoughts, and behaviors are unconscious. The other complexity to this is that you might be aware cognitively of what you desire to create, yet what actually shows up is different. For example, no matter how hard you try, you seem to have a lack of money or gain it and lose it and end up in debt.

This is because the trauma, beliefs, points of view hidden deep within us create how life shows up. This was a harsh reality I had to face as I was unconsciously picking bosses and environments that forced me to prove my worth, or leaders that would lose their mind if they were not able to control me. I would pick teams where I would work my ass off to hopefully be seen as worthy and validated.

Even more insane was this: there were three key ages I was mimicking in my behaviors in personal and professional life:

- 7-year-old Michelle who felt she never belonged, had to prove herself, had to hide and mask, and was shy and introverted

- 16-year-old Michelle who wanted to fight everything and everyone because she was carrying trauma and CPTSD

- 22-year-old Michelle who wanted to see the world with rose-colored glasses, had blind loyalty, and thought, *If I have their back, they will have mine*

- Adult present and aware Michelle—who trusted her knowing, observed people's behaviors and energy, not what was said or the promises made, and knew when things felt heavy and off

If you became present, what ages are you replaying? Heck, what ages are people all around you in adult bodies replaying?

Now go deeper. Think about the beliefs and behaviors you are picking up from your husband, wife, partner, friends, a boss you worked for at 22, a teacher or professor who pushed a point of view on you at 18.

Pen to Paper Homeplay: Tools and Exercises

- List all the areas in your life that are not showing up the way you desire. Money, leaders and bosses, colleagues, opportunities. Heck, might as well list out friends, partners, travel, adventure, and whatever else you desire. Now ask these questions for each area:

- Who am I being?
- Where am I being my mother?
- Where am I being my father?
- Where am I rebelling so I don't become my mother or father?
- Where am I defending them so I can validate their choices?
- Where did I pick up this belief or behavior? Am I mimicking my husband or wife or close group of friends?

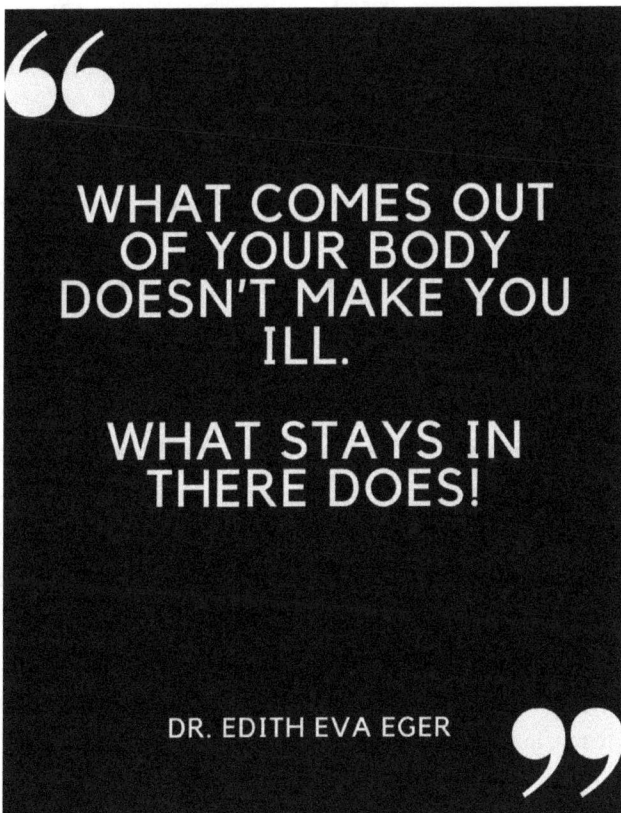

> ## WHAT COMES OUT OF YOUR BODY DOESN'T MAKE YOU ILL.
>
> ## WHAT STAYS IN THERE DOES!
>
> DR. EDITH EVA EGER

As we went through earlier, your body is more than just flesh and bones; it's a messenger, constantly relaying important signals. Those unexpected aches or sudden tensions aren't merely physical reactions. They're your body's way of signaling that something might be off-balance, not just physically, but emotionally or spiritually.

- Jot down your thoughts to the following questions. They might help you tune into what your body is trying to convey:
  - Where am I currently headed in life?
  - Does this direction align with my true desires?
  - In what areas do I feel emotionally or spiritually stuck?
  - If there were no limitations, where would I want my life to go?
  - Do I genuinely feel supported by those around me?
  - Am I truly expressing my full potential or holding back?

By understanding your body's signals and interpreting them, you can gain insights into your deeper emotions and desires. So the next time you feel an unusual ache or strain, consider it an invitation to reflect. Before seeking a temporary fix, take a moment to really tune in and listen to what your body might be telling you.

It's easier for most to pick up a book like *Atomic Habits*—but habit practices are 20% of the equation, and you cannot change your habits if you do not face the challenging inner work. Diving into the depths of your psyche, confronting past demons, and transforming them into pillars of strength? That's not just growth, that's leadership on steroids. And remember, it takes guts to embark on this journey. It's about evolving, not just for you, but for everyone after you.

This is the epitome of growth and leadership. It's a brave venture, one that promises evolution not just for yourself, but for generations to come.

From our childhood imprints to corporate dynamics, trauma's ripple effects are undeniable. But with the courage to confront these shadows and arm ourselves with introspective tools, we can transform our work environments and, most importantly, ourselves.

CHAPTER 6

Our Identity Crossroads: Embracing the Immigrant in All of Us

"Ewwww, that is gross. Why do you bring such strange food to school for lunch?"

"Why do you have a unibrow?"

"Why do you have a funny name? Mehrnoosh sounds like 'manure.' Your name means poop."

"I can't understand what you are saying with your accent. Where are you from, Mars?"

These are the kinds of questions I would get as a kid growing up in America. Aren't kids super fun? I wonder where they learn these behaviors . . . hmmm.

Funny how these behaviors and beliefs then get replayed as adults in the workplace with things like, "I can't understand you with that accent," or "Is there a shorter version of your name?," or "I can't pronounce that," or "Why can't you spell?," or "Why is your grammar off?"

No one teaches you that many people, regardless of the country they are in, never leave the street, town, or area they inhabit. And if they do venture out, it's often on a cruise ship just to post on Facebook that they are traveling. This doesn't necessarily mean they are curious or interested in learning about other countries, languages, and cultures.

No one teaches you that the reason you may feel like you don't belong has more to do with others' lack of knowledge, empathy, and awareness, rather than something inherently wrong with you.

"The big lesson often left unspoken is that your 'hard-to-pronounce' beautiful name, your accent, and those times when you mispronounce words are actually a demonstration of your courage, resiliency, and brilliance and your desire to create something greater."

The big lesson often left unspoken is that your "hard-to-pronounce" beautiful name, your accent, and those times when you mispronounce words are actually a demonstration of your **courage, resiliency, brilliance,** and your desire to create something greater. Yes, it's a significant strength, not a weakness!

Immigrants and the Workplace

Growing up with a "weird" name, accents, and eating "different" foods, you'd think I was from another planet by the way some kids reacted. Fast-forward to adult life, and it seems not much has evolved—especially in corporate corridors.

Sure, there are enlightened CEOs, like Hamdi Ulukaya of Chobani, who understand that diversity isn't just a buzzword or a box that gets checked off by hiring someone, but actually executes it; but let's face it, many are still operating with outdated notions.

In the midst of major talent and knowledge shortages, immigrants have become an important source of talent as well as a flash point for conflict in many countries. Many face identity and status changes when they move to a new country, along with the ongoing insecurity they feel as they work and live in a foreign land.

Here's the complex landscape: on one side, there are folks grumbling that immigrants have it too easy landing jobs. Flip that coin, and many immigrants find themselves marginalized, perhaps even subjected to mistreatment. If you deviate from the cookie-cutter norm, be prepared for judgmental glances and hushed, exclusionary talks.

In the unforgiving landscape of the corporate world, appearances carry weight. You might get hired for tokensim, yet *hired* versus *actually included in daily interactions* are 2 separate things.

Chances are, if you dare to appear different, speak differently, or deviate from expected norms, be prepared to face judgmental gazes and hushed conversations behind closed doors. This holds true not only for racial and ethnic minorities but also for immigrants who bring diverse perspectives and experiences to the table.

In response to remarks like, "I can't understand you," or "What?," or "Could you provide a shorter version of your name?"—stand tall. Refrain from diminishing yourself. Do not undermine your worth. Always remember—you are bold, courageous, and exceptionally brilliant. They are just clueless.

"How many of your brilliant gifts have you given up to be included and not rejected?"

One of the biggest behaviors that creates exclusion and marginalization is the reaction to accents, word mispronunciations, name scrutiny, and the ways these can make someone feel less than, and change themselves. How many of your brilliant gifts have you given up to be included and not rejected? Immigrants also face unique challenges once in the workplace. Cultural differences, language barriers, and discriminatory attitudes can all contribute to a sense of hiding or feeling like an outsider. I only recently began to understand the impact this can have emotionally and even physically.

If you find yourself standing out as an immigrant or a person from a diverse background, daring to be different, brace yourself for the scrutiny that awaits. Do not shrink or compromise your authenticity to fit into the narrow mold of acceptability.

Remember, authentic diversity and inclusion cannot be achieved through superficial policies and token gestures. They demand a fundamental shift in mindset, a genuine willingness to challenge deep-seated biases, and a commitment to fostering an environment where everyone, including immigrants, can thrive, regardless of their differences.

To safeguard your rights and authenticity, it's vital to be aware of marginalized behaviors and advocate for yourself. Such as comments like "we can't understand you," or "your people," or even being ignored in meetings or passed over for opportunities. These are not small things— they are big things. Don't be misled by superficial diversity and inclusion; seek spaces where your uniqueness is genuinely celebrated, your voice valued, and where you can be yourself.

The essential first step is to build awareness about the magnitude of these challenges, both in our lives and in the workplace and for yourself if you are an immigrant, as well as for your family, friends, and colleagues from different countries. The next step is to create space to talk about these experiences and feelings openly.

Also, it's crucial to develop strategies to overcome these challenges, such as seeking mentors or allies, building a supportive community, and enhancing cultural intelligence.

And here's an interesting perspective to round things out: we're *all* immigrants, in one way or another, navigating through unknown territories at various points in our lives.

We all navigate transitions—be it a new job, city, or life phase—that thrust us into unfamiliar scenarios. Essentially, we're all strangers navigating through unknown lands at various points in our lives.

> *"We're all immigrants navigating through unknown territories at various points in our lives."*

While the term "immigrant" is typically used to describe those who cross national borders, we can recognize the underlying theme of change, adaptation, and exploration that resonates with the immigrant experience in various aspects of all of our lives.

Even if we go back far enough in our collective history, we'll find ancestors who were bona fide immigrants, crossing continents and breaking new ground. So when you think about it, the immigrant experience resonates with each of us on some level. This makes the conversation not just about them, but about us—it's a collective endeavor to enrich our workplaces and communities by embracing the kaleidoscope of human experience.

The stories, lessons, advice, and tools in this chapter may resonate with you regardless of whether you immigrated to another country. They may resonate to those that always felt different and out of place or always had a sense of not belonging in the state, city, or town they were in.

There are many books that offer diverse perspectives on the immigrant experience, shedding light on the triumphs and trials faced by individuals and families as they navigate new cultures and environments. They often explore themes of identity, belonging, and the pursuit of a dream and new possibilities in the face of adversity.

"The highest form of knowledge is empathy—it's the ability to be authentically curious about another's world."

The highest form of knowledge is empathy—it's the ability to be authentically curious about another's world. One of the few people who was curious and fascinated about where I was from was my friend Steve Leveen. He inspired me to start stepping out of my shell and share my story, experience, and wisdom with the world. He encouraged me to stop hiding everything about myself and celebrate my uniqueness.

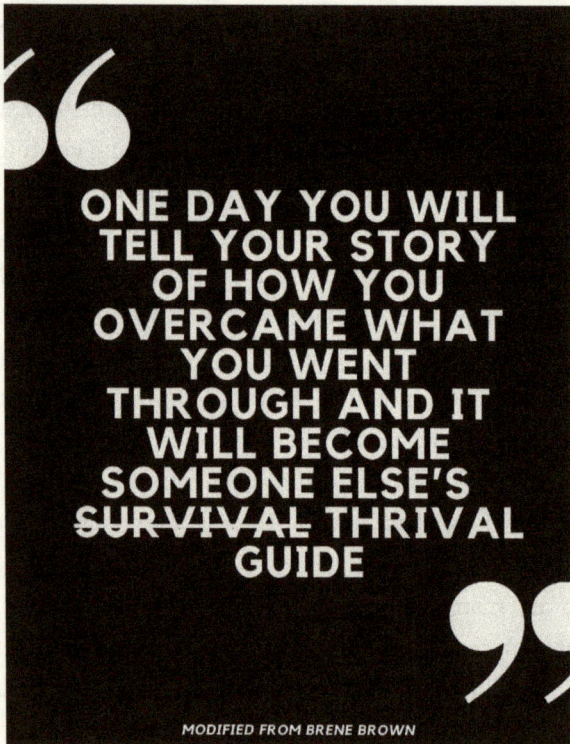

> ## ONE DAY YOU WILL TELL YOUR STORY OF HOW YOU OVERCAME WHAT YOU WENT THROUGH AND IT WILL BECOME SOMEONE ELSE'S ~~SURVIVAL~~ THRIVAL GUIDE
>
> *MODIFIED FROM BRENE BROWN*

Steve Leveen is the founder of the America the Bilingual Project, which delves into the surprising changes in bilingualism now taking place in the United States. He hosts a podcast with the project. Steve and his wife Lori Leveen cofounded Levenger in 1987 with a vision to provide Tools for Serious Readers.

Steve is also the author of *America's Bilingual Century: How Americans Are Giving the Gift of Bilingualism to Themselves, Their Loved Ones, and Their Country.*

I invite you to explore some of my favorite books that also went into the research for this book. These books offer vivid snapshots of immigrant experiences.

The Namesake by Jhumpa Lahiri delves into the challenges of a Bengali immigrant family as they navigate their cultural heritage and the demands of a new country.[38] In *The Book of Unknown Americans*, various Latin American immigrants residing in a single US apartment complex share stories of love, sacrifice, and resilience.[39] *Behold the Dreamers* by Imbolo Mbue sheds light on the disparities and struggles of 2 immigrant families in New York City during the financial crisis—one from Cameroon and the other from Wall Street.[40] *Exit West* by Mohsin Hamid weaves elements of magical realism into a tale of a couple escaping war-torn regions through mysterious doors, exploring themes of migration, identity, and belonging.[41]

All of these books have had a deep impact on the way I understand others and the way I understand myself. I suspect they will have a similar effect on you if you choose to engage with them.

Why Many Immigrants Hide Where They Are From

At what age did you look around and know you were totally weird, unusual, or different?

For me, it was when I came to America sporting a unibrow, frizz-ball hair, and not speaking English other than "hello." I remember sitting in class and wondering why everyone looked, walked, and talked the same. Why was my hair not blonde? Why were the desks perfectly organized in a straight line? Why on earth did I have a weirdo name that no one could pronounce?

This became worse as I entered the workplace and corporate environment. Yup, because adults are just kids in bigger bodies and able to filter their words slightly better.

Mehrnoosh what? Kids called me everything from "manure" to "my douche." There was no Google back then, so I would run home asking my mom, "What is a douche?" She would pull out the English to Farsi (Persian) dictionary and say, "Eyyy babbbba. Vaaa!" Translation: "What the fuck?" (Close enough translation at least ... that is how I took it.)

At ten I asked, "Can I pretty please pluck my eyebrows? The kids are making fun of my unibrow. And shave my legs?" *No* was usually the answer. They called me "Bert" (those old enough know it was Bert from Sesame Street) and "Amazon" I grew up fast in all ways. I was tall, already with boobs and hairy legs at 10 years old.

I felt totally odd and strange.

Like all that wasn't enough—every day my mom would pack my *Flintstones* lunch box with Persian food. I would open the container and the smell of rice and green sabzi stew took over the lunchroom. Followed by: "Gross!" and "What is that weird Amazon douche girl eating?!" I would run out of the lunchroom and eat in the corner by myself. Watch the movie *My Big Fat Greek Wedding* if you want the full visual of my experience.

I begged my mom, "Can I *please* just have a normal peanut butter and jelly sandwich like the rest of the kids?" Her response: "No, we don't eat that garbage." (P.S.—today most people beg me to have my mom cook Persian food, and I hate peanut butter sandwiches.)

My parents were super protective because they did not understand the relaxed American culture.

"Mom, can I sleep over at Amy's house?"

Accent and all, she would respond: "Vvvvwhatttt? Where we are from, we sleep in our own beds."

"Can I go over to Amy's house then?"

My dad would scream from the back, "NAAAAAHHH! Not until I meet both parents, have tea with them, and know who they are, what they do, where they are from . . ."

OMG, Dad, never mind. Alone it was!

If you curiously ask most immigrants, you will probably hear similar stories to mine. We struggle between 2 cultures while never fitting into either to determine what our identity is, all while confused about which set of norms to adapt to while in the home and out in society. We learn very quickly that unless you change and adjust, you won't fit in and will be ridiculed and rejected from both.

As adults in the workplace, there is often very little cultural awareness. The behaviors of children turned adults don't really change—we just get better at filtering what we say; yet ever so subtly, through small, unconscious micro-behaviors, we exclude people by doing these:

1. Not allowing someone to speak up because they think, speak, or look different than us.

2. Hiring "diverse" people but giving projects and opportunities to those we are more comfortable with.

3. Speaking over someone and rephrasing what they just said.

4. Saying statements like, "Let me paraphrase what you just said so they can understand you."

5. Saying, "Sorry, I can't pronounce your name," and moving along like it's no big deal.

These are a couple of examples of our unconscious behaviors that most people don't even think twice about or build awareness around. This also demonstrates that nothing has changed from childhood, other than we are big bodies pretending to be slightly more professional.

Hiding Identities Makes Immigrant Trauma Deeper

As mentioned earlier, everyone who is born on the planet Earth experiences trauma, just in varying degrees. The act of concealing or splitting one's identity adds another layer of emotional burden to the already-complex traumas facing first- and second-generation immigrants. For first-generation immigrants, hiding elements of their true selves may feel like a necessary survival tactic amid language barriers and potential discrimination. Yet this veiling of identity can deepen feelings of isolation and emotional dislocation.

Second-generation immigrants often find themselves in a cultural tug of war, trying to align with the expectations of their native-born peers while honoring their family's heritage. This often leads to suppressing parts of their identity in an effort to "fit in," which can exacerbate stress and inner conflict.

> *"Second-generation immigrants often find themselves in a cultural tug of war, trying to align with their native-born peers while honoring their family's heritage."*

In both scenarios, the act of concealing one's true self becomes a source of chronic stress, compounding preexisting traumas. This protective mechanism—while understandable—ultimately perpetuates a cycle of shame, self-judgment, and emotional struggle, making it more challenging to form authentic connections and thrive in a new environment.

The pathway to healing involves not just acknowledging these specific kinds of trauma, but also dismantling the walls we put up around our true selves. Supportive communities and professional help can pave the way for individuals to embrace their full identities, thereby reducing stress and enhancing well-being.

The thing with subtly adjusting yourself to fit in is it's an endless loop that has detrimental effects. I learned this the hard way. I changed my name, lost my accent, changed the way I looked, lost weight, got the makeover, the perfect body, the beautified image to fit into what I saw as "seen" and accepted in schools and the community. Then I landed in corporate America and guess what happened . . . the very things that I changed about myself so I would not be judged and rejected in school were now rejected by adults. I was labeled as:

- Too pretty
- Too fit
- Too intimidating
- Too vocal
- Too intelligent

I was called into my boss's office, a senior executive of a multibillion-dollar company, and told: "If you want to be promoted, I need you to wear a turtleneck and a suit every day, and please put your hair up." Later I heard: "You are too tall, and your fit arms are too distracting, you are intimidating and you are not seen as leadership material with that image."

I was too young and stupid to argue and thought this was normal, opting to stay quiet instead of saying, *Fuck you!* Regardless of your gender, if you are ever told this, make sure you reply: *"I am not intimidating. They are intimidated! There is a huge difference in that!"*

> **"You are not intimidating. They are intimidated!
> There is a huge difference in that!"**

Yet this is what we all unconsciously do. We look at people who are different and ask them to change. We think this is normal. What is worse is we abuse ourselves and actually change ourselves subtly over time until *we don't even know who we are anymore.*

The thing we miss is this: it is never enough and is a total endless pursuit because when we judge ourselves and change ourselves, we pull in more people who will judge us and reject us.

This is how we put ourselves in jail, stepping out of awareness and the choices we have because we have to automatically and unconsciously defend and reject anything that doesn't fit the "image" we have created.

That is how powerful we are. The universe listens to us and shows us more of what we think is true!

Perpetuating the Feeling of Never Belonging

When you are taught to change yourself and not see yourself anymore in order to fit in, you end up creating this constant deep feeling like you don't belong anywhere. The pursuit of belonging can often feel like a double-edged sword, particularly within the context of the workplace. It's a pervasive narrative that we've all been indoctrinated with: "Fit in, conform, and you will find your tribe."

But the irony is, the more we try to conform, the deeper we dig the pit of the unsettling feeling that we don't truly belong anywhere. This is compounded by a perpetuating falsehood that finds its way into corporate culture: we must find a workplace where we feel like we belong.

This misleading narrative often gets cloaked in well-intentioned corporate jargon, but the groundbreaking reality challenges this deeply embedded societal and professional dogma.

The truth is simple: *if we are in a constant state of growth, we may never "belong." And that's perfectly OK.*

"If we are in a constant state of growth, we may never 'belong.' And that's perfectly OK."

It's an uncomfortable truth, but one that bears profound implications. Growth is inherently unsettling. It's a dynamic process that requires us to try, fail, pivot, and transform. As we evolve, our environment and community may not always evolve at the same pace, and that's not a deficiency—it's an indicator of our own personal and professional progression.

This discordance doesn't signify failure. Rather, it serves as a litmus test that you are pushing boundaries, expanding your horizons, and defying the stasis that often blankets corporate environments. When you're growing, you're in essence outgrowing the very concept of static belonging.

Even after time passes, most people who have left the country and culture they were born into are often left with this deep feeling like they don't belong. It's definitely worse in the early stages, yet the sensation never really goes away.

I left Iran at an age when I had a solid understanding of my family, culture, and language. Despite growing up in America and embracing its culture, a persistent void lingered in my heart. It felt strange, like I didn't truly belong anywhere—neither in Iran nor in America.

It was as though my sense of home had vanished, leaving me in a state of homelessness. I could perceive what seemed like madness in both cultures. American culture, to me, appeared disconnected, fast-paced, superficial, and transactional. Meanwhile, Persian culture exuded warmth, sociability, and connection, yet it was also marred by judgment rooted in professional success, status, and image.

Growing up, we didn't talk much about where we were from, even with people who were also from other countries. Most people who came to America did their best to change, fit in, and morph themselves to belong. All while not actually belonging. I learned to carry all of this into the workplace. I also learned that the workplace was designed to perpetuate this in everyone.

Immigrants often feel disconnected and out of place in the workplace, especially in corporate environments where conforming is expected. The challenges include cultural differences, language barriers, discrimination, and the fear of rejection. It's essential for immigrants to acknowledge these challenges, embrace their uniqueness, and educate others about their experiences. Leaders must create an inclusive environment and educate themselves and their teams to become culturally curious and aware.

Here are some main reasons why immigrants may feel the need to hide their true selves:

Immigrants often mask and hide themselves in order to avoid judgment, rejection, or discrimination in their new environment. They may need to conform and assimilate to fit into the predominant culture, which can suppress their unique identities, gifts, abilities, and creativity. This self-censorship and limitation can stem from a fear of standing out or not being accepted. By concealing their true selves, immigrants may miss out on opportunities to contribute their diverse perspectives and talents, and this could ultimately hinder innovation and creativity in the workplace and society at large.

It's essential for both individuals and leaders to recognize this and cultivate an inclusive and welcoming environment where immigrants can openly express themselves. These qualities should be seen as strengths, not weaknesses, and it's important to understand that "belonging" can be an overused and sometimes deceptive concept. Embrace the idea that making space for conversations and raising awareness of unspoken topics may not always be comfortable, but it often signifies true leadership and inspires growth.

> *"Embrace the idea that making space for conversations and raising awareness of unspoken topics may not always be comfortable, but it often signifies true leadership and inspires growth."*

Here are a select few of the challenges immigrants may experience within and outside the workplace:

1. **Lost in Cultural Differences and Norms:** That feeling that everything you do is off, weird, or different, or you simply don't understand norms and traditions. Even when you try pretend to understand, it is awkward. For me, I never understood the work culture of people separating from each other and acting so cold.

Immigrants may feel a sense of cultural dissonance in the workplace due to differences in communication styles, work expectations, and attitudes toward authority. This can create feelings of isolation and contribute to a sense of hiding or not feeling like they belong.

Immigrants may also feel pressure to conform to mainstream cultural norms and downplay their cultural identity in order to fit in, which can lead to a loss of authenticity and a sense of disconnection from one's cultural heritage.

2. **Shame in Language and Accent Barriers:** Whether you speak the language of a new country fluently or not, you feel isolated and disconnected from those around you. You mispronounce things, says things out of context. Often you translate what you are going to say in your head and the words don't translate properly.

Language barriers can also present a significant challenge for immigrants, as communication is critical in the workplace. Limited English proficiency can lead to miscommunication, misunderstandings, and a lack of confidence in expressing oneself.

My mother often carried her Farsi-to-English dictionary back and forth to work. I would sometimes find her crying because as hard as she tried, people would make fun of her accent. As a young girl witnessing this at school, I somewhat understood why kids behaved this way. But adults? I never could wrap my head around that.

3. **Nostalgia for Home:** Many immigrants feel homesick and miss their families, friends, and cultural traditions from their home country, which can lead to a sense of disconnection and loneliness more than others may experience.

4. **Straight-Up Fear of Discrimination:** Fear of being excluded and discriminated against for your race, ethnicity, or national origin. That is why we change names and go to linguistics classes like I did. Discrimination and bias against immigrants can create a hostile work environment and increase the likelihood of hiding or feeling like an outsider. This can manifest as microaggressions, exclusion from social activities, or more overt acts of discrimination.

5. **Constant Fear and Survival:** For many Iranians who left Iran, survival became a pressing concern, as the media often portrayed all Iranians as terrorists. Simultaneously, during the war and revolution, Americans in Iran were taken hostage in the US Embassy. You could literally be brutally attacked walking the streets of Los Angeles. Could you imagine school and work? My father was attacked at work, called names, and given more work than others because his boss was prejudiced and told him he needed to work harder and prove himself because he was from another country.

6. **Identity Conflict:** Immigrants often also struggle to reconcile their cultural identity and values with those of their new country. It's very confusing and causes disorientation. Oftentimes you end up creating 3 or 4 identities or images to cope.

Helping immigrants un-hide in the workplace may include seeking out mentors or allies who can provide guidance and support, building a community of fellow immigrants or cultural affinity groups, and developing cultural intelligence to better understand and navigate cultural differences.

The key here is to build the muscle of just being different and true to who we are even if it feels uncomfortable. We must also take accountability for having the courage to step into who we are and realize hiding is cowardly, not noble, and only perpetuates the problem.

Having the Courage to Celebrate Where We Are From

What if every single immigrant had the courage to celebrate where they are from and help educate others?

I see way too many people, especially in leadership positions, hiding where they are from and not realizing they are casting a shadow to show others to do the same. When we do this, we don't realize we are disempowering ourselves and the people around us, and it's not a sign of leadership. We have a duty to educate each other by unmasking and showing ourselves and being open to being rejected or judged.

Most people know countries and cultures only from the television or social media, and their perceptions are usually one-sided. We can either help change their perspective and lens or help them realize their stupidity and closed mindset. To me that is a win-win. Doing nothing and hiding yourself keeps the world and everyone the same and does not contribute to evolution of mankind.

When I finally decided to un-hide and share the rich history of Iran and the warm culture and pictures, most people were shocked and taken aback. Iran was once the heartland of the mighty Persian Empire. An ancient, thriving society. Few were aware of these facts.

I once was invited to a meeting to share what was transpiring for the people in Iran during protests and burning of headscarves. I started full-on crying in a Zoom call with over 100 people. The old me would have used all of my power and might to shove down my emotions and not show "weakness"—yet in that moment I chose to be unapologetically me.

When I started sharing with thousands of people my hardship, what I was hiding, and my journey in keynotes and professional settings, I accepted the risk of judgment and rejection.

Instead, what I got threw me for a spin: admiration, honor, vulnerability, connection, gratitude, and kindness. Countless emails, LinkedIn messages, text messages thanking me for giving them the space and permission to have the courage to do what I hope you will do: step into the inner bold leader in you and un-hide, unmask, and fully embrace who you are!

In a corporate landscape teeming with buzzwords like "authenticity," "transparency," and "innovation," it's somewhat paradoxical that many individuals still feel the need to don a professional mask. But consider this—perhaps the most revolutionary step we can take is not to conform but to courageously unmask and reveal our full, authentic selves.

Un-Hide the Strength and Traits of Anomalies

If we flip the script 180 degrees on judgment, shame, and fear—which are not who we are—and look instead at the uniqueness to the "strange immigrant" story, we will find that people from other countries are anomalies in the US and bring with them their own cultural backgrounds, languages, beliefs, and customs that can enrich the cultural landscape of their new home country. They often have a unique perspective on life and can offer ideas and ways of thinking that can benefit their new communities.

The root of the word "immigrant" comes from the Latin *migrare* ("to move from one place to another"). Although the original meaning may mean to come from another country, it can also mean state or city; in either instance, you left the familiar and the comfort behind.

These are some core foundational strengths each and every immigrant has, which, most likely if you chose to read this book, applies to you as well. Read them, celebrate them, and if something applies to you, put it all over your résumé and share it with everyone you meet. Let's normalize not caring about people's titles or the companies they have worked for, and instead start caring about these skills and traits:

1. **Courageous:** Ability to face fear or uncertainty with bravery! Willingness to take on challenges, risks, and difficult situations, even when it requires stepping outside of one's comfort zone or facing adversity because you are breaking the status quo. Courage often involves standing up for what is right, even in the face of opposition or disapproval. It can also involve admitting to one's mistakes, taking responsibility for one's actions, and working to make amends. Courage is a valuable trait that can help individuals overcome obstacles, achieve their goals, and make positive changes in their lives and in the world around them.

2. **Highly Ambitious and Motivated:** Individuals who have taken a risk to leave their home countries (or cities) and start anew are not exactly lazy. To do this requires a great deal of courage, resilience, and adaptability. Many immigrants possess a strong work ethic and a determination to succeed that can make them valuable contributors to their new communities.

3. **Adaptability and Resilience:** Immigrants often have to adapt to new environments, cultures, and languages, which can require flexibility and resilience. They face unique challenges such as language barriers, cultural differences, and unfamiliar systems, which can make them more resilient

and resourceful. As Plato said, "Scarcity is the mother of invention."

4. **Creativity and Resourcefulness:** Immigrants may have had to overcome significant challenges and barriers to succeed, which can develop resourcefulness, problem-solving skills, and perseverance. They are able to come up with new ideas and solutions to problems, even in difficult situations. They have the willingness to embrace new ideas, perspectives, and experiences, which can facilitate innovation and creativity.

5. **Multilingualism and Cultural Awareness:** Many immigrants are bilingual or multilingual, which can be a valuable asset in today's global economy. They have often been exposed to different cultures and ways of life, which can foster an appreciation for diversity and an ability to navigate different cultural norms and expectations.

6. **Empathy and Compassion:** Immigrants may have a deep understanding of the challenges and struggles faced by others who are adapting to new environments, which can foster empathy and compassion.

Often these are called "soft skills"—but in the age of technology and automation, these are "critical skills" that are required to elevate, disrupt, and transform.

Overall, the experiences of an immigrant (again, anyone who either feels strange and different or has left the known behind) can foster the development of a range of core skills and traits that can be valuable assets in personal and professional life. The uniqueness in their diversity, experiences, and perspectives can bring a wealth of knowledge, skills, and cultural richness to their workplaces.

The key principle here is to not forget where you come from and the unique experiences that make you different.

Embrace Your Weirdness and Differences and Fuse Them Together

Every single one of us has an inner anomaly or "inner immigrant" that is unique. We all possess our own unique inner self that is undefined and holds expansive creativity. It can be a bit intimidating because it's unfamiliar, so many of us tend to stick with what's known and comfortable, even if it limits our true potential.

Being different, though, comes with both blessings and challenges. It requires a great deal of grit, courage, and resilience! Embracing this uniqueness means being willing to take risks and challenge the status quo, even if it invites criticism, judgment, or rejection from others.

However, when embraced and nurtured, it becomes the secret ingredient to creativity and differentiation. It's messy, it's not easily defined. That's why many organizations struggle to figure out what to do with it, as it doesn't neatly fit into a predefined box that can be easily managed and checked off.

In the context of immigrants, their diverse backgrounds and perspectives bring forth an even richer set of anomalies. By creating an inclusive and supportive environment, companies can tap into immigrants' immense creativity and potential. It's about recognizing and celebrating the unique contributions and perspectives that immigrants bring to the table, rather than trying to fit them into existing molds. When companies embrace and harness this diversity, they can unlock innovation and thrive in an ever-changing world.

Wholeheartedly embracing everything that makes you different is a powerful way to unlock your full potential. Here are a few points to remember when deciding to share what is unique and different about you:

1. **Get Uncomfortable and Stay Uncomfortable!** Don't be afraid to step outside of your comfort zone and challenge yourself. Growth happens when we push ourselves beyond what feels familiar and safe. Embrace new experiences, take risks, and be willing to learn and adapt along the way. Remember, the magic lies just beyond the boundaries of comfort!

2. **Celebrate Your Differences and Your Unique Experiences.** Put them in your bios and résumés, tell them in meetings and to everyone you meet. Your differences and unique experiences are what make you stand out from the crowd. Instead of hiding them, celebrate them proudly. Let your authentic self shine through. Share your stories and perspectives in meetings and conversations. By doing so, you not only contribute to a more diverse and inclusive environment but also inspire others to do the same.

3. **Vulnerability Is Created through Our Personal Stories, Lessons, and Experiences.** Lowering your walls and barriers and sharing your personal stories, lessons, and experiences is a powerful way to connect with others on a deeper level. It creates a sense of authenticity and fosters empathy. Vulnerability is not sharing what you are "comfortable" with; it's about sharing what you think you will be judged for. When you open up and share your own vulnerabilities, you give others permission to do the same. This opens the door for meaningful connections and allows for individual and collective growth.

So remember to embrace discomfort, celebrate your uniqueness, and be open and vulnerable in sharing your stories. It's through these actions that you can truly unleash your full potential and create a positive impact in your personal and professional life.

Acknowledge the Critical Skills Immigrants and "Anomalies" Bring

In today's fast-paced and dynamic world, the traits of an immigrant extend beyond their personal lives and have become increasingly vital in the workplace. These traits encompass a wide range of characteristics that not only shape individual success but also contribute to the overall productivity and growth of organizations.

Recognizing the importance of these critical skills is key to harnessing the full potential of immigrant talent and creating innovative and inclusive workplaces.

Trait	Definition
Adaptability	Natural adaptability by quickly adjusting to new lifestyles, climates, cultures, and communities in their host country
Self-discipline	Ability to control one's impulses, focus on long-term goals, and take consistent action toward them
Resilience	Ability to bounce back from setbacks and challenges, and to persist in the face of adversity
Perseverance and grit	Willingness to keep going and not give up, even when faced with obstacles or failure
Flexibility	Frequently exhibit flexibility and a willingness to embrace change; able to adjust to changing circumstances and situations
Curiosity	A desire to learn and explore new things, and to ask questions to gain knowledge

Trait	Definition
Open-mindedness	Being receptive to new ideas, different perspectives, and alternative ways of thinking
Responsibility	Taking ownership of one's actions, being accountable for one's decisions, and fulfilling one's obligations and commitments
Gratitude	Feeling and expressing appreciation for the people, things, and experiences in one's life
Optimism	A positive outlook and belief in the possibility of positive outcomes
Courage	The ability to face fear, uncertainty, and adversity with bravery and resolve

The traits discussed in this chart highlight the multifaceted nature of immigrant success, both in life and in the workplace. These qualities are not only individual strengths but are also essential for building cohesive teams and thriving organizations.

Pen to Paper Homeplay: Tools and Exercises

1. Reflect on your unique experiences and qualities—what have you gone through in your life that makes you different from others? Think about various ages—6, 10, 17, 25, etc.—and all the stories.

2. What was the core foundational trait in you? Did it appear in different ages and stages in your life and shape your unique journey? (Use the list above for a reminder.)

3. Highlight these aspects and traits in your personal life and professional life; these are critical skills needed in the

workplace to build the future and drive creativity, inclusion, and innovation.

4. Instead of trying to fit in with the crowd, embrace and celebrate your unique qualities. Update your bio, résumé, and LinkedIn, and share your different qualities everywhere—in meetings, with colleagues and friends, on social media.

5. Schedule coffee, lunch, or a Zoom call with someone you normally would not connect with.

6. Put a sticky note on your monitor or workspace to remind yourself of these traits in yourself and in others.

7. Share with people where you are from, your roots, no matter how exotic or simple; share to educate and inspire them.

To combat the challenges faced by immigrants in the workplace, it's crucial to raise awareness, educate others, and create a supportive environment. Being different is hard because it does not have a definition; it's advantageous because it has no limits.

Being an anomaly can be lonely sometimes, so it's essential to surround yourself with people who support and encourage you. Seek out like-minded individuals who share your interests and values. (You are not for everyone, and that's cool—it means you are being you.)

By sharing our journeys, experiences, and backgrounds, we help bridge the knowledge gap and promote inclusivity. Encourage open dialogue, advocate for policy changes, promote cultural exchange, and offer resources and support to other immigrants. Each of us having the vulnerability to be ourselves inspires others to do the same.

CHAPTER 7

Shattering the Myth: Toxic Masculinity and Femininity in the Workplace

"When a man is both masculine, driven, visionary, powerful and also soft, loving, kind, and accepting, and at peace, that man is powerful! That man is unstoppable!"

—Danny Morel

"Boss babe," "queen bee syndrome," and "masks men wear" represent real challenges that can hinder the development of strong, supportive workplace relationships. Moreover, toxic masculinity and femininity are pervasive in the workplace, which gives rise to an "emotion-phobic," robotic culture, preventing genuine connections, vulnerability, and the full expression of each individual's unique power.

The good news is that we can work together to overcome these issues and create a healthier workplace for everyone. In this chapter, we'll explore how we can move beyond these programs and lies that we have bought into and work together to build stronger workplace relationships.

The present moment provides us with the opportunity and the canvas to embrace our true selves and reclaim what may have been taken from us. It's a chance to shed all the obsolete beliefs and programs that hold us back from thriving.

Misconstruing the Strength of Masculinity and Softness of Femininity

We are all born with a mix of masculine and feminine energies, regardless of our gender. For context, when we talk about the feminine energy, we can think of it as embodying the essence of Mother Nature and the creative force that brought forth our planet. It's the nurturing and life-giving energy, much like the womb from which we all originated. The feminine energy is associated with qualities like intuition, empathy, compassion, and the ability to foster growth and connection.

On the other hand, masculine energy represents the creative and active force of creation. It's the energy that drives innovation, problem-solving, and taking action to manifest ideas into reality. Masculine energy is characterized by traits such as assertiveness, logic, ambition, and the ability to provide structure and direction.

In acknowledging these energies, it's crucial to recognize that we are not strictly confined by the labels of "masculine" or "feminine." These are only constructs that serve the discourse within our reality.

At our core, we are all infinite beings, pure energy encapsulated for the moment in gender-defined bodies. In the grander scope of existence, energy doesn't subscribe to masculine or feminine; it simply is. However, for the purposes of our discussion and understanding in this lifetime and reality, we utilize these terms to dissect complex dynamics.

Both masculine and feminine energies are essential catalysts for growth, offering unique strengths that can inspire us to step into our hidden courage and inner leadership. In doing so, we un-hide, unmask, and fully embrace all aspects of ourselves, fostering an environment where we can thrive as complete beings.

Together, the feminine and masculine energies complement each other, just like the yin and yang. They are both essential for a harmonious existence. It's not about placing one above the other or devaluing any specific energy. Instead, it's about recognizing and appreciating the inherent power and beauty in life's nurturing and creative aspects.

These energies can manifest in various ways. For example, masculine energy is often associated with assertiveness, competition, and being task oriented, while feminine energy can be seen as kind, openhearted, and relationship focused. These energies complement each other and create a balanced approach to life.

In relationships, whether it's at home or in the workplace, yin and yang symbolize a partnership where we support and complement each other. There are times when nurturing, empathy, and understanding are crucial, and there are also moments when we need to be strategic, driven, and analytical. It's not about one partner overpowering the other and the other taking orders, as many personal and working relationships are unconsciously set up.

True complementarity is not about one person being submissive and the other dominant. That's a major misconception that limits our potential. In reality, complementarity means embracing each individual's diverse strengths and qualities at *each moment*, regardless of gender. A man can be kind and caring in a moment when it is required and dominate, strategize, and take action the next. Just like a woman can be direct and assertive when required and have empathy and compassion in another moment. These behaviors are gender-neutral or nonbinary and are actually an energy we all can choose to set in and out of like a song in harmony.

So it's not about being solely masculine or feminine, which have manifested separately in the workplace. It's about embracing the diversity of traits and qualities within ourselves and others and understanding that we can all contribute to a successful partnership by combining the nurturing and strategic aspects when needed. It's a dynamic balance that allows us to have each other's backs and create fulfilling relationships at home and work.

How We Have Twisted This in the Workplace

But here's the thing: in the corporate world, it seems like everyone has turned to their masculine energy in order to compete and succeed. It's like we've built this culture where vulnerability and embracing our "feminine" traits are seen as weaknesses. It's as if we're all wearing masks and hiding our true selves just to achieve what society deems as success. We're constantly putting up armor and shields, which can be exhausting and even traumatic.

The modern workplace often prioritizes masculine energy, which is defined by competition and goal orientation and thus leads to low creativity. This focus sidelines the softer, more nurturing feminine energies, which are essential for emotional well-being and authentic relationships (i.e., the cornerstones for being creative). By neglecting this balance, we're left in a state of perpetual "doing," causing mental and physical exhaustion. Integrating both masculine and feminine energies in the workplace is not just a nice thing to do; it is a must for creating a sustainable, fulfilling professional life.

We keep saying things like, *Why can't we be creative, productive, and innovative?* Duhhh—we are masking and hiding everything nature created and what we're born with as unique gifts to share with the world. It's not possible, and it's literally going to kill us.

As women, we are so concerned with not being seen as quiet or submissive, not leaning into our feminine energy, that we have taken it to the extreme and are living in our masculine energies at work. The phenomenon known as queen bee syndrome describes how women in leadership roles may undermine or mistreat other women in the workplace in order to gain or preserve power.

Queen bee syndrome has its roots in research conducted as early as the 1970s. This phenomenon includes a range of behaviors, from women belittling traits typically associated with femininity (such as saying, "Women are so emotional") to accentuating their own "masculine" characteristics (like claiming, "I think more like a guy"). It can also involve dismissing claims of gender discrimination as unfounded.[42]

On the flip slide, the mask of masculinity is a phenomenon observed in men, where they hide or downplay what are traditionally considered feminine traits. This behavior stems from societal expectations and the pressure for men to conform to traditional gender roles. Men may feel compelled to suppress their emotions, avoid vulnerability, and prioritize assertiveness and dominance in order to fit the mold of a successful male leader.

We will get into both behaviors, how to recognize them in yourself and others, and how to begin to shift this madness slowly killing us mentally, physically, emotionally, and spiritually.

It's about time we address this issue and create a more inclusive and accepting work environment. Embracing our authentic selves, regardless of gender, is crucial for our individual well-being and the overall success and productivity of organizations. It's time to let go of these outdated norms and allow everyone to bring their unique blend of masculine and feminine energies in harmony to the table.

My Big Punch in the Face of Corporate Gender Reality

I started in the field of technology when I was about ten years old. My parents didn't have money for a babysitter, so I would go to computer engineering classes with my dad at the University of Miami, quietly listening and absorbing. We used to laugh that I got a free computer engineering degree.

I was the only girl in the room, yet this never fazed me. I never noticed it, as my dad's college classmates didn't treat me differently. I coded with them and went on to build computer systems and run networks with my dad and his team of engineers at his startup. It was the best experience. I did sales, marketing, accounting, and even shipping. (I know how to pack better than the UPS dudes.)

I genuinely saw no gender in my young eyes. Sure, I noticed that people would look at me funny when I knew a lot of detailed, technical technology information, but I didn't realize it was because their perception was that a girl wasn't supposed to know those things. I was oblivious.

Only once I entered the corporate environment did I have my *holy shit* moment. My *holy shit* moment was also part of the biggest lie we have bought into: that women stick together.

Consider as evidence this feedback I received from 2 executives following my first-ever presentation at an organization:

- **From a Man:** "That was rock star status. You are a natural storyteller and presenter. I think you had a major impact on the final decision."

- **From a Woman:** "Just so you know, we have a pantyhose policy, and if you wore a jacket, they could hear what you're saying and not look at your chest."

When I went on to work at other organizations, it hit me like a freight train. Oh crap, there is this weird "boys club" and "girls club" thing that I was sheltered from. I had assumed that since women were underrepresented in business and technology, we would be on the same team and have each other's backs. Biggest punch in the face.

They absolutely did not have my back and not only stabbed me in the back more times than I could count, but some stabbed me in the forehead.

> THERE IS A SPECIAL PLACE IN HELL FOR WOMEN WHO DON'T HELP EACH OTHER.
>
> MADELEINE ALBRIGHT

I grew up as a tomboy, so I was more comfortable hanging out with the guys, which worked against me even more. In the women's eyes, there was no way I could be attractive, into sports and fitness, and kind and smart. I was perceived as a threat because I was different. At its core, feeling threatened or jealous of someone versus being inspired or admiring them taps into deeper self-esteem wounds. Genuine inner confidence is when you are inspired by someone unthreatened by differences. In my 25-plus-year career, I have had more allyship and support from men than from women. To this day, I can count 2 women who genuinely have supported my growth and progress.

> **"Genuine inner confidence is when you are inspired by someone unthreatened by differences."**

Don't get me wrong—I have encountered my share of sociopathic, raging, abusive assholes of men in the workplace, so I'm not saying all men are saints. Yet women are eager to set up big women's events, exclude men, and make them the enemy. This is called **separation**.

It's a major myth that the women-only "kumbaya" meetings we all have been invited to or attended—which we think are a movement and a step into inclusion—are not helpful! We have amazing men walking on eggshells unsure of what to say and how to support us because we set up "diversity and inclusion" meetings and then *exclude* the very humans that can support us.

This isn't to say that women's experiences and challenges in the workplace aren't unique and important; they are. But if we're truly aiming for an inclusive culture, we must encourage dialogue that includes all genders. This means tackling issues holistically, not in isolated bubbles. Exclusion, even when well-intentioned, can't be the path to true inclusion.

Therefore, while women-only events might offer temporary relief and a sense of community, they can paradoxically become barriers to the broader goal of full workplace equality and inclusion. We should focus on cultivating spaces where everyone—regardless of gender—feels seen, heard, and equally invited to participate.

I have several amazing women in my life today that have my back and are 100% supportive, yet this is only because I have chosen to unapologetically step into more of me. Those that never had any genuine interest in rising and growing with me rarely show up anymore in my personal or work life; and if they do, I'm so aware that I'm able to get rid of them at lightning speeds. When you become more conscious and more authentically you, it's amazing how the aligned people show up and the rest disappear.

Author Richard Bach wisely conveys, "Like attracts like. Be your authentic self, composed, lucid, and radiant. Continuously ask yourself, "Is this what I truly want to do?" and take action only when the answer is "yes." This process repels those who have nothing to gain from your presence and draws in those from whom you can learn and who can learn from you in return.

Unraveling Toxic Femininity and Queen Bee Syndrome

During a speech at a women's conference, US Secretary of State Madeleine Albright famously quipped, "There is a special place in hell for women who don't help other women."

Albright's intention behind the statement was to highlight the significance of women standing together and advocating for one another. She wanted to emphasize the idea that women should uplift and assist each other in order to overcome societal challenges and gender inequalities.

She probably also said it because, unfortunately, the total opposite is true. Many women have shared countless experiences of not only the lack of support for women by women, but of sabotage, defamation, stealing each other's work, and ensuring other women don't reach the top. I think some women behave this way because of a lack of awareness, unhealed trauma, unconscious wounds from their relationships with their mothers or fathers, or retribution for having to suffer themselves in their career.

The queen bee syndrome exists in many companies, and women in positions of power tend to exhibit behavior similar to their male counterparts. This phenomenon arises as women try to assimilate into male-dominated environments, often adopting traits and characteristics traditionally associated with masculinity. The pressure to conform to these masculine norms can lead women to distance themselves from their femininity and adopt an image of being tough "like a man."

Queen bees are women in positions of authority who can be overly critical of their female subordinates. Often, these women, consciously or unconsciously, become part of the problem, per-petuating the stereotype about women at the top need to "act like men" to get ahead in the workplace. They may do this due to a scar-city mentality regarding available opportunities or because of unre-solved personal traumas.

What's more, they frequently lack the awareness or the cour-age to speak up, address problematic behaviors, and support other women, especially those they perceive as competition. Sponsoring "women's events" is easier than using your voice.

I see way too many women kicking the can down the road because they experienced this, so they perpetuate the cycle instead of standing up and becoming a cycle breaker. This issue is visible in unequal promotions, hiring, opportunities, and pay, as well as in the application of stereotypical labels to women, and it's often more pronounced among women than men.

Let's break it down. On one hand, there's been a growing awareness about the lack of gender diversity and appreciation for successful women who have risen to the top despite facing adversity. Nonetheless, this appreciation has at times evolved into an exaggerated glorification, resulting in the commercialization of models such as events, awards, and lists exclusively for women. While some of these recognitions may be authentic, a significant number can be acquired through financial means, creating an artificial sense of distinction.

Research has shed light on various factors contributing to these dynamics. One concept called the "power dead-even rule," proposed by Pat Heim, suggests that for a healthy relationship between women, their self-esteem and power should be perceived as equally significant.[43] However, this balance is disrupted when one woman is seen as more successful than the other, leading to a subconscious lack of support. Competition for limited opportunities and a mindset of "I figured it out, so you should too" also come into play, along with the notorious queen bee syndrome.

It's not uncommon for women to feel the pressure to conform to masculine norms and behaviors to succeed in male-dominated environments. They battle against stereotypes that label them weak, emotional, or not tough enough. And even when they manage to break into these circles, they face constant scrutiny and the burden of justifying their presence. With all these challenges, it becomes difficult for women to focus on helping and uplifting other women.

The assumption that women should always support other women regardless of circumstances contributes to the queen bee stereotype. Senior women in organizations are often expected to take on extra responsibilities in championing diversity, which can lead to resentment, while their male counterparts are not held to the same expectations. If a woman chooses not to take on these roles, she may be labeled a queen bee, while men who don't engage in diversity efforts are not similarly judged.

The behavior of women not advocating for other women in their organizations can be attributed to "value threat," which arises from negative stereotypes in male-dominated workplaces. Women who have succeeded face constant battles against these stereotypes and may be hesitant to support other women if their qualifications are questioned, which could reinforce the negative stereotypes.

The limited opportunities available to women, often in the form of implicit quotas or the phenomenon of "tokenism" (appointing 2 women but not more to leadership roles), can create competition among highly qualified women for a small number of positions. This competition can lead to women not supporting each other as they vie for these limited opportunities.

Instead of solely fixating on changing women's behavior, the focus should shift toward improving organizations and creating an inclusive and supportive environment for everyone.

Take a look at some of the different unconscious patterns, behaviors, and antidotes related to the queen bee phenomenon and the unconscious pattern and how this behavior shows up. We cannot change anything we are not aware of, so this list is to empower us to do the following:

- Recognize these patterns as not normal or acceptable in yourself or others
- Call these actions out and remember that silence is acceptance
- Recognize the antidote and the possibility that is actually available to every single one of us

Often, we lose sight of how big and abundant the world is and forget there is plenty to go around. The movie *Auntie Mame* (highly recommend) said it best: "Life is a banquet, and most poor suckers are starving to death."

"Life is a banquet, and most poor suckers are starving to death." —Auntie Mame

Below are some examples of the unconscious patterns and behaviors we have all either observed or fallen into the trap of:

Unconscious Pattern	Behavior	Antidote
Unresolved and unhealed trauma	Perpetuating childhood wounds and mistreatment toward others	Courageous mindset: acknowledge and heal personal wounds
Lack mindset	Viewing other women as threats	Abundance mindset: think bigger; embrace collaboration and support
Survival lens	Lack of confidence and jealousy	Seek inspiration: learn from and uplift other women
Suppression of masculine and feminine energies	Discouraging or dismissing feminine qualities	Embrace gender diversity: celebrate and value both masculine and feminine strengths

Unconscious Pattern	Behavior	Antidote
Withholding support and opportunities	Blocking advancement of other women	Advocate for inclusivity: support and empower other women
Undermining and criticizing	Diminishing the achievements of other women	Promote unity and encouragement: celebrate each other's success
Gatekeeping	Excluding other women from opportunities	Foster inclusivity: open doors and create equal chances
Thinking, "Well, I suffered, so you should too"	Resisting support or empathy for others' struggles	Cultivate compassion: recognize and empathize with others' experiences
Falling into false competition trap	Engaging in unnecessary rivalry and sabotage	Collaboration over competition: build strong networks and support each other's growth
Marginalization in corporate setting	Facing limited opportunities and implicit quotas	Drive inclusivity: advocate for equal representation and dismantle systemic barriers

Remember, it's important to actively address these behaviors and patterns. If you witness someone engaging in queen bee behavior or perpetuating unhealthy dynamics, you can choose to speak up publicly and use your voice to raise awareness and encourage change. If you prefer a more private approach, you can offer coaching and support to individuals involved, guiding them toward a more inclusive and supportive mindset.

By understanding patterns and implementing the suggested antidotes, we can contribute to a healthier and more empowering work environment for everyone.

Toxic Masks of Masculinity, Un-Hiding, and Including Men

The workplace in general has been traditionally emotion-phobic until now. We have been taught to mask and hide aspects of ourselves for fear of not fitting in or excelling.

Especially men!

As kids, little boys are taught various things that shape their understanding of the world. They are often encouraged to be strong, adventurous, and independent. They are taught to explore, take risks, play sports, and engage in physical activities. They might be told to "be a man" or to "toughen up" when faced with challenges or emotions.

As Lewis Howes, ex–professional athlete writes in his book *The Mask of Masculinity*, "I don't think men are fundamentally flawed or broken, they are just trapped. I know that's how I felt for 30 years of my life." He delves into the prevalence of the false mask of "stoicism" instead of leaning into real strength that comes from being able to be vulnerable and communicate.

> BECAUSE EVERY MAN MUST BE INVULNERABLE AND TOUGH, EMOTIONS ARE CAREFULLY MANAGED AND SUPPRESSED. THERE CAN BE NO CRYING, NO PAIN, NO FEELING. SO HE PUTS UP A WALL BETWEEN HIM AND THE WORLD TO PROTECT HIMSELF, TO PRETEND HE DOESN'T FEEL THE THINGS HE DOES.
>
> WHILE WEARING A *STOIC MASK*, HE VIEWS WEAKNESS IS AN INVITATION TO SCRUTINY, AND JUDGMENT AND REJECTION.
>
> ONLY THROUGH ITS REMOVAL CAN HE FEEL EMOTIONAL FREEDOM, EXPERIENCE DEEPER RELATIONSHIPS, AND MOVE TOWARDS INNER HEALING.
>
> LEWIS HOWES

Society often places expectations on boys to conform to traditional gender roles, such as being assertive, competitive, and less expressive with their feelings. They may receive messages about what toys, games, and activities are considered suitable for boys.

Overall, boys are influenced by a combination of family, friends, media, and societal norms, which can shape their perspectives and behaviors as they grow up. The message they get is clear: showing emotions will get you beat up! Being vulnerable is for girls and losers!

This is having a significant impact on aspects of mental health that are often not talked about, such as men have higher suicide rates than women and often suppressing their emotions for fear of appearing week.

MEN ACCOUNT FOR 75% to 80% OF DEATHS BY SUICIDE

- Canada: In Canada, men account for 3 out of every 4 suicides.
- UK: In the UK, where nearly 12 men lose their lives to suicide every day, men die by suicide at rate 3 times more often women.
- USA: In the United States, the suicide rate among males is 4 times higher than among females

SUICIDE IS A LEADING CAUSE OF DEATH FOR MEN UNDER AGE 50

- Canada: Suicide is the second leading cause of death
- UK: Suicide is the single largest cause of death
- USA: Suicide is the second most common cause of death for men under the age of 45[44]

"In fact, 60% of men think it's weak to be vulnerable in the workplace."

The reasons why men hide or conceal certain aspects of themselves are influenced by various factors. Society often imposes expectations and stereotypes on men, defining what is considered masculine or acceptable behavior. This societal pressure can lead men to hide certain traits or emotions that are perceived as vulnerable or that do not conform to traditional masculine norms.

One reason men may hide is from the fear of being judged or ridiculed. They might worry about being seen as weak or less masculine if they express their true thoughts, feelings, or struggles. Society often places a premium on stoicism and emotional toughness for men, which can create a culture in which vulnerability is discouraged.

Additionally, men might hide aspects of their identity to fit into certain social or professional environments. They may feel the need to conform to specific expectations in order to be accepted or respected. This can involve suppressing certain interests, downplaying emotions, or conforming to traditional gender roles.

Another factor that contributes to men hiding is the fear of losing power or control. Masculinity is often associated with authority, dominance, and independence. When men feel that their masculinity is being threatened, they may resort to hiding or engaging in harmful behaviors to reassert their sense of control and power.

Recognizing that these societal expectations and pressures can have negative consequences is important. Men may suffer in silence, experiencing mental health issues or struggling with self-acceptance. This can also show up for them physically in back pain, joint pain, sleep issues, anxiety, heart issues, cancer, and even death.

Research has also shown that when men feel that their gender identity is being questioned or threatened, they are more likely than women to respond with aggressive and toxic behaviors. Masculinity is found to be a fragile identity, and even minor threats can lead men to engage in harmful actions to prove their masculinity.

The studies conducted with working adults revealed that when men perceive threats to their masculinity at work, they tend to exhibit behaviors such as anger, rage, bullying, ignoring, yelling, cutting people down, withholding help, mistreating coworkers, stealing, and lying for personal gain. These can escalate to the full-blown narcissistic behaviors we previously discussed.

In order to create a more inclusive society and workplace, it's crucial that we expand our understanding of masculinity. Instead of valuing sole characteristics like aggression and physical strength, let's celebrate the idea of being a "good man" rather than a "real man."

This means recognizing that manhood can encompass qualities such as civility, fairness, gentleness, and a nurturing and collaborative nature. Particularly in male-dominated teams, where men often feel pressure to conform to certain masculine ideals, it's essential for male leaders to actively role model this positive form of masculinity. By doing so, they can inspire others and promote a healthier approach to manhood.

Additionally, HR teams should promote these leaders and increase their visibility within the organization, highlighting their positive influence as something to aspire to. Together, we can challenge outdated stereotypes and create a more inclusive and respectful environment for everyone.

Managers and leaders can dismantle toxic structures that threaten men's masculinity. Organizations should promote a positive version of masculinity, including traits like civility, fairness, and collaboration. In male-dominated teams, male leaders should model this healthier masculinity, and HR teams should promote and highlight their positive approach. By rethinking reward systems that prioritize competition and by giving employees more autonomy, workplaces can reduce the need for men to prove their manhood through harmful behaviors.

It's important to focus on specific problematic behaviors instead of using loaded terms like "toxic masculinity" and to create an equitable culture that validates everyone's gender identity.

This benefits men, reduces destructive behavior, and creates a more inclusive workplace. Encouraging open conversations, breaking down stereotypes, and creating environments where individuals can be authentic and accepted for who they are can help address these challenges and promote healthier expressions of masculinity.

It's interesting how society often portrays fitting in as being strong and powerful, when in reality, it is actually a sign of weakness. People may feel the need to conform to certain expectations and maintain a facade of strength because they fear being judged or rejected if they show vulnerability or embrace their true selves. But the truth is, true strength lies in being authentic and comfortable with who you are, rather than constantly trying to fit into a predetermined mold.

It takes courage to embrace vulnerability and show your true emotions, and that's where real strength can be found. So instead of trying to fit into a narrow definition of strength and power, focusing on being true to ourselves and embracing our individuality is important.

To all the amazing and vulnerable men I have had the honor to cross paths with, your courage contributed to me being me and unhiding. Thank you! I see you!

The following are summaries and examples of frequently observed unconscious patterns, behaviors, and possible remedies. It's essential to approach these with empathy, whether you notice them in your own behavior or in others. However, considering them as normal is similar to endorsing toxic feminine behaviors. It's crucial to raise awareness, acknowledge these behaviors, address them, and initiate change.

Unconscious Pattern	Behavior	Antidote
Mask of masculinity	Putting on a tough and unemotional front to appear strong	Embracing vulnerability and expressing emotions authentically
Toxic masculinity	Engaging in aggressive and domineering behaviors	Promoting healthy communication and respectful behavior
Attack on identity	Feeling the need to conform to societal expectations	Embracing individuality and being true to oneself
Childhood wounds	Carrying unresolved trauma from interactions with parents	Seeking therapy or support to heal and grow
Personal trauma	Experiencing traumatic events that impact self-perception	Seeking professional help and engaging in self-care practices
Unhealthy definitions of masculinity	Associating man-hood with traits like aggression and dominance	Broadening definitions to include qualities like empathy, compassion, and collaboration

Unconscious Pattern	Behavior	Antidote
Need for acceptance	Seeking validation from others based on traditional masculine standards	Cultivating self-acceptance and finding value in personal growth
Fear of weakness	Trying to fit in as strong and powerful despite internal vulnerabilities	Embracing authenticity and recognizing strength in vulnerability

Choose to Get to Know What Is True for You

The ultimate goal here is becoming present and aware of unconscious toxic behaviors that limit all of us and hide our abilities and gifts. Of the lies and programs we have bought into since childhood that separate us. Of our ability to lean into healing and become fluid between the energies that are required regardless of our external body suit, gender identity, or expression.

This includes embracing and acknowledging the diverse range of identities such as transgender, nonbinary, and other identities within the realm of gender diversity. The goal is to create an inclusive space where individuals can authentically explore and express their unique selves without judgment or limitations based on traditional gender norms.

Below are a few examples of masculine and feminine energies. Remember, these are nature's given energies. These energies are not inherently tied to gender, and individuals can express a mix of both masculine and feminine energy, regardless of their gender identity or expression. These traits can also be influenced by cultural and societal factors and may vary across different workplaces and industries. So think through your background and environment as well.

Masculine Energy	Feminine Energy
Assertive	Nurturing
Logical	Intuitive
Analytical	Empathetic
Competitive	Collaborative
Goal oriented	Process oriented
Direct	Indirect
Dominant	Submissive
Independent	Interdependent
Aggressive	Passive
Task oriented	Relationship oriented
Problem-solving	Creativity
Decisive	Flexible
Confident	Supportive
Results driven	People focused
Ambitious	Empowering

Pen to Paper Homeplay: Tools and Exercises

1. **Reflect on Your Experiences with Toxic Masculinity and Femininity.**

   - List out the times you have felt the consequences of behaviors in the sections above from a woman or man and made it about you, when in reality it was about them.
     - How did they behave?
     - How did it make you feel?
     - What do you think was the core unconscious mindset you saw displayed?

   - Now reflect on the times you behaved this way toward someone else and answer the same questions above.

   - What can you commit to do differently to combat this and make the unconscious conscious in yourself and others?

   - Instead of avoiding, defending, or ignoring, how can you commit to have the courage to use your voice or to change your own unconscious behaviors?

2. **What Is Uniquely True for You?**

   - Get vulnerable with yourself and list out what energies are true for you and your true essence as a human, and in what situations, regardless of gender.

   - List and consider ways to enhance your presence and disengage from autopilot mode. Take the opportunity, in each moment, to consciously select the energy above that aligns with your true self.

- List ways you plan to blend the energies to become more balanced and a way you could hold yourself accountable. Maybe it's an accountability partner at work or in your personal life.

If we choose to evolve and have the courage to lean in, be both energies without shame or fear of judgment and rejection, and create environments where people feel safe to be themselves in this era, we can un-hide the emotions that are foundational to leadership and innovation:

1. Compassion
2. Vulnerability
3. Connection
4. Creativity
5. Inclusion

Together we can question the way it's always been done and pave a more humanized workplace where we are all seen. If we choose courage over comfort, we have a chance to create a better future for ourselves and our children. One that robots, machines and AI will never replace.

PART III

UNLEASHING THE BOLD, CONSCIOUS LEADER

CHAPTER 8

Reclaim Your Power: Realignment with Values and True Desires

"When I look up in the universe, I know I'm small, but I'm also big. I'm big because I'm connected to the universe, and the universe is connected to me."

—Neil deGrasse Tyson

"You know what's wrong with you, Michelle, and will hold you back in the corporate world? You are way too intimidating, ask too many questions, and think way too big. And you are too attractive . . . if you could tone it down and fit in you would probably get promoted."

This was exact feedback from an executive vice president of a billion-dollar company who I once called a mentor, a brother, and a friend because of his "image" of success.

This is what I bought into as true. I was young and stupid and thought if I followed him I would grow. I "toned it down" in the way I talked, walked, dressed—basically everything about me—to fit into the box so I could get promoted. Guess what, it worked. I got the title in the same box.

At what cost? The cost of losing *all* of me.

Yet we all do this all the time, and we have been programmed to think it is completely normal and to even ask other people to do the same, and we call this "coaching." We are taught crap like "never give up" and "quitting is for losers" so much so that we think we're totally wrong, even when it is costing us our lives. Steven Bartlett said it the best "They trap you in the toxic narrative that quitting is a weakness, an easy way out or, worse yet, that quitting is failure. I assure you—quitting is for winners and quitting is a skill."

> **"They trap you in the toxic narrative that quitting is a weakness, an easy way out or, worse yet, that quitting is failure. I assure you—quitting is for winners and quitting is a skill."**

We have bought into the myth that success means hiding who we truly are, cutting off our uniqueness, and losing ourselves in the pursuit of conformity.

Who needs personal expression and authenticity when we can all be cookie-cutter versions of each other? It's absolutely amazing how we willingly sacrifice our individuality to squeeze into those tiny boxes, all in the name of fitting into the corporate world.

The harsh reality of all of this? We tolerate all of this; we create it. I tolerated it, I created it, and I watched it happen all the time without saying anything.

I was not crystal clear on my values, my boundaries, and my deal-breakers. Most people are not. Until I burned out and hit a wall and got tired of the abuse and madness.

Every single one of us does it, at least at some point in our lives. We lose precious time because we forget to pause. We forget to ask ourselves any questions. We make choices when we're in survival mode. We forget one simple, obvious, and crucial truth: that companies should align with our values and career aspirations. That they should provide an environment that supports our personal and professional growth and is also aligned with our overall well-being.

It is not your job to figure out what parts of you to cut off, hide, or morph so that you fit your company's values, culture, and goals. We must get courageous enough to look at what is true for us and choose from an empowered space so that we may thrive.

Ways We Give Away Our Power through Unconscious Micro-Choices

Often, as we unveil our true selves and peel back the layers of what companies and leaders prescribe, we'll discover a significant misalignment. This misalignment can lead to feelings of unhappiness, burnout, or even a massive skill gap that seems insurmountable.

Many individuals claim to have values, but frequently these values are vague and unconsciously acquired from sources like family, their workplace, or past leaders—values that don't genuinely belong to them. We disconnect from our own awareness and adopt what's handed to us, silently enduring the consequences.

Is this what success, empowerment, or thriving should look like?

How does this surrender of power occur? We suppress our awareness, relinquish our autonomy, and yield to external control.

In the workplace, a pattern emerges where we find ourselves trapped in survival mode. This limits our true potential and compels us to incessantly pursue success while fearing failure. The underlying message is that we're not "good enough" unless we conform to the established norms. It's as though our fear of falling short of expectations has been ingrained in us from our school days within an outdated system that taught us irrelevant life skills.

Now, imagine a world where we are fully aware, and because of that awareness, we are taught to choose values for ourselves and find our purpose instead of blindly buying into the idea that what is real for others is real for us. Imagine if instead of fearing getting an F or a bad performance review, we were taught a belief system and views that say we don't have to fit in—we can be ourselves.

Imagine if we were encouraged to seek and ask questions instead of being forced to have the answer for fear of failing. If we asked questions, we would be a little hard to control, right?

Understanding how our beliefs and perspectives shape our experiences is crucial. Getting to what is real versus what is a lie can either empower us to thrive and express our creativity or hold us back from being our authentic selves. If only someone had told us this earlier!

When we give away our power by becoming overly attached to things like our job, partner, home, car, or money, we allow them to have control over us. Our emotional well-being and sense of control then depend on these external factors. It's important to maintain a healthy balance and remember that true power comes from within ourselves.

For example, if we derive our entire identity and happiness from our job, we become vulnerable to its fluctuations. If we lose that job or face challenges in the workplace, we may feel a significant loss of control and confidence. The same applies to relationships— if we rely solely on our partner for our happiness, their actions or absence can greatly affect us.

Similarly, if we tie our self-worth and security solely to material possessions like our home, car, or money, we become susceptible to their loss. Suppose our financial situation changes or we encounter unexpected circumstances that force us to let go of these possessions. In that case, we might feel a loss of control and struggle to cope.

By understanding that our power and happiness come from within, we can develop a healthy detachment and regain control over our lives. This means valuing ourselves and nurturing our own strengths and passions, rather than relying solely on external factors for validation and fulfillment. By doing so, we become less vulnerable to the control of these external elements and gain the ability to shape our own lives according to our own terms.

> **THE ART OF LIVING DELIBERATELY IS THE ART OF EXAMINING THIS VAST STOREHOUSE OF BELIEFS, DROPPING THE OUTMODED ONES, CONSCIOUSLY CHOOSING THOSE THAT SERVE YOUR GOALS, AND CAREFULLY CRAFTING NEW ONES IN GREATEST ALIGNMENT WITH YOUR DESIRES.**
>
> SIR RICHARD BISHOP

It's never too late to break free from the school system programs and corporate illusions and to teach our children to do the same. In the corporate world, we can easily become consumed by titles, salaries, and the status quo, losing sight of our true values and purpose. We wake up one day and think, *How did I get here?* or *This is it.*

Please, avoid misunderstanding this as a call for reactive resistance, fighting, or avoidance, as those actions often exacerbate the situation. It's the other extreme. One extreme involves conforming and agreeing with the prevailing "this is the way it is" mindset. The opposite extreme, which can lead to burnout, is characterized by fighting and resistance. I urge you not to experience the suffering that I endured.

Instead choose to shatter this illusion, rediscover what truly matters, and uncover the importance of being clear on your values and purpose. By becoming aware, defining these core aspects of our lives, and having the courage to align every day in every moment, we can escape the corporate trap and embrace a fulfilling existence that aligns with our deepest beliefs.

Loss of Childhood Inquisitiveness and Questioning

One of the luxuries most immigrant families that are in survival mode don't get is time to pause and think about what they desire, their vision, who they are, and what they value. 99% of my family's time was spent learning a new language, new culture, and new slang like "get your ducks in a row." I remember the first time I heard that phrase was in school, and I thought, *We have to find a lake with ducks before I can take an exam?*

At the dinner table, our top-priority discussion was visas and citizenships and how to not get kicked out of the US and be forced to return to a war-torn country. We really didn't have the space to talk about anyone's dreams, desires, or values. I never ever in my wildest dreams realized this had nothing to do with being from another country; everyone was living this way.

In many Middle Eastern cultures, your education and career options are usually doctor, lawyer, engineer, or any PhD will do. I asked my dad, "Why?" His answer, with a thick accent, was, "Because otherwise you will be an idiot." I miserably went with it and agreed to be a doctor. I even interned with a surgeon and almost passed out at the sight of blood every time. I convinced my parents to let me change to computer engineering and business. Even that bored me to tears. I could barely follow along.

I called my mom and asked, "Why do I need to read about how something is done when I could just do it?" I convinced my parents to let me start working at the family technology business at the ripe age of 16. I never had the college experience. I would work all day and go to school at night.

By the time I graduated college I had learned how to build computer systems, run networks, program, run the warehouse, sales, marketing, accounting, finance, customer service, public relations, event management, and everything else it takes to run a business. I even remember that sometimes I would read things in books at night and think, *How on earth would someone understand this unless they were doing what I was doing during the day* (aka, our outdated school systems, which are really a business entity that feed the matrix)?

When I entered Corporate America, I had no idea that my "asking why" curse (blessing) was not a childhood thing that I would grow out of. I questioned everything. I didn't realize that because of my experience in running everything at a very young age, my mind did not understand silos, bureaucracy, politics, and corporate structures.

Once again, I was confused. That feeling of *I'm from Mars, and where is Scotty to beam me up?* came back. There was so much to go around, and we all worked for the same company; why so much lack and behaviors like it's the apocalypse and the world is ending? I guess it's because of the same people who buy 100 rolls of toilet paper when there is a hurricane or a pandemic.

I realized we are programmed stop asking questions, cut off all of our awareness, and believe that success is just doing what we are told. Luckily for us, it doesn't have to be this way.

Courage to Question Absolutely Everything

Contrary to our program and subconscious, questions—not answers—create empowering possibilities. Answers are actually disempowering because they tap into our old points of view that are based on judgment and conclusion and the need to be right. These all create limitations and are based on the past. Remember, that annoying 95% subconscious programming.

The lie we have been sold is that we must have the answers to be in control. This program is taught everywhere in school and corporations. In actuality, chaos and being out of control is what creates the future. The only way to create this chaos is through asking open-ended questions of yourself and others with zero judgment, conclusion, or point of view. I know it's hard, yet it's the only way to create an unprogrammed future.

Bringing back your childhood inquisitiveness and questioning everything can be a powerful antidote to the stifling corporate boxes we often find ourselves in. Remember those days when you constantly asked "why" and explored the world with curiosity and wonder? Well, it's time to channel that inner child and unleash your curiosity once again.

To this day, I ask "why" a lot, and usually if you ask enough ways and enough times to multiple people you will end up receiving the truth: "That is the way we have always done it."

Start questioning the norms, the status quo, and the limitations imposed by the corporate world. Ask yourself why things are done a certain way and if there's a better, more innovative approach. Embrace a mindset of curiosity, always seeking to understand and learn. Don't be afraid to challenge the rules and assumptions around you.

By bringing back your childhood inquisitiveness, you'll open up new possibilities, spark creativity, and inspire others to do the same. So let your inner child roam free and let the questions fly. Who knows, you might just uncover amazing insights and pave the way for positive change.

Pen to Paper Homeplay: Tools and Exercises

I sound like a broken record, but we cannot change what we don't become aware of. Here are the actionable steps to serve as a tool for self-reflection and growth:

1. **Self-Awareness:**
   - How am I showing up in my thoughts, beliefs, and actions?
   - Am I practicing mindfulness and being present in the moment?
   - How can I enhance my awareness and emotional intelligence to navigate situations authentically?

2. **Question Assumptions:**
   - Am I cultivating curiosity and challenging the status quo?

 - Do I actively seek different viewpoints and reflect on the consequences?

 - How can I explore alternative approaches and embrace continuous improvement?

3. **Embrace Uncomfortable Questions:**
 - Am I courageously exploring difficult questions?

 - How can I foster a learning environment and embrace diversity?

 - Do I encourage open dialogue and create safety for others? Or do I judge them?

4. **Getting Comfortable with Confrontation:**
 - What fears or beliefs hold me back from expressing myself assertively?

 - How can I overcome these fears and beliefs?

 - What communication or conflict resolution skills can I develop?

 - How have past experiences influenced my hesitation to assert boundaries, and how can I heal and grow from them?

By using these questions as a tool for self-reflection, you can gain deeper insights, challenge your own perspectives, and foster personal growth in navigating the corporate world with authenticity and continuous improvement.

The Externally Focused Program behind Loss of Power and Burnout

The belief that the external things we put on a list and check off—like cars, homes, wife, husband, kids, jobs, or titles—lead to happiness, purpose, and fulfillment is the biggest program and lie we have bought into. We use this lie to judge ourselves if we don't acquire or do acquire things, and then we figure out it never led to the promised land.

Society, school, the workplace, and organizations often reinforce the idea that unless we have these things that can be checked off, we will be judged and rejected because clearly there is something wrong with us.

While external things can provide temporary pleasure or a sense of accomplishment, true and lasting happiness usually stem from within ourselves. It's about finding meaning, fulfillment, and inner peace. Below are some reasons why relying solely on external factors for happiness may not be sustainable and often leads to negative outcomes that we see all the time, like these:

- Burnout and exhaustion
- Stress and anxiety
- Depression
- Detachment
- Unfulfillment
- Exclusion
- Lack of Belonging

The 2 main reasons this happens are these:

- **"The Next Thing" Dopamine Chase:** Humans have a remarkable ability to adapt to new circumstances. Once we acquire a desired possession or reach a specific goal, the initial excitement or joy often diminishes over time. Our desires tend to evolve, and we may start seeking something new to maintain that fleeting happiness. This perpetual chase can lead to a never-ending cycle of dissatisfaction.

- **Hedonic Treadmill of Validation:** The hedonic treadmill is a psychological phenomenon where we constantly strive for more, thinking it will make us happier. However, as we acquire more material possessions or external achievements, our expectations rise along with them. This can create a never-ending pursuit of external validation, always seeking the next best thing but never finding lasting satisfaction.

In life, we often give away our power and let external forces control us. But reclaiming our power is essential for personal growth and fulfillment. Here are some common ways we lose our power and accompanying antidotes:

- **External Validation:** Seeking validation from others. **Antidote:** Cultivate self-acceptance, self-acknowledgment, and gratitude for yourself. Ask, *What can I appreciate about me today?*

- **Attachment to Outcomes:** Becoming overly attached to specific results. **Antidote:** Focus on the process and what you are going to or did learn. Ask, *What awareness did I gain from this regardless of the outcome?*

- **Comparison and Competition:** Constantly comparing ourselves to others or competing with them. **Antidote:** Practice self-compassion, celebrate your unique journey, and ask yourself, *Am I like them? Is everything as it appears in the image?*

- **Fear of Failure:** Allowing fear of failure to hold us back. **Antidote:** Embrace failure as an opportunity for growth and develop a growth mindset. Flip the thought to learning and ask, *What will I learn? What will I become aware of?*

- **External Circumstances:** Letting external events control our emotions and well-being.
  Antidote: Cultivate inner resilience and the ability to respond rather than react. Pause to get into your body and literally put your hand on your belly, then take 3 deep breaths and visualize expanding out to the size of planet Earth. Then ask, *Is this relevant to me and where I am going?*

- **Negative Self-Talk:** Engaging in self-limiting beliefs and negative self-talk.
  Antidote: Cultivate self-awareness, challenge negative thoughts, and replace them with positive questions. Ask, *Is this really true? When did I buy this as true? Is this a program I bought as mine?*

- **Giving Energy, Time, and Focus to Others:** Depleting ourselves by excessively giving our energy, time, and focus to others.
  Antidote: Practice healthy boundaries, self-care, and prioritizing your own needs. Ask, *Is this a contribution to me and what I desire to create?*

Remember, these are common ways we may give away our power; the key is to become aware of these patterns and actively work on reclaiming your power. When it comes to giving away our power and feeling controlled, other people and our relationships can play a significant role and often the biggest role.

Genuine happiness often comes from nurturing a relationship not with others, but with yourself first, pursuing meaningful experiences, and aligning our actions with our values. No matter how hard it is and what you will lose, there is so much to be gained. These internal aspects of happiness are more sustainable and not dependent on external circumstances.

That being said, external factors can contribute to our overall well-being to some extent. For instance, having a stable job can provide financial security, which can positively impact our mental and emotional state. Similarly, a comfortable home can create a sense of safety and belonging.

However, it's crucial not to rely solely on these external factors for our happiness and well-being, as they will lead you down an empty road. What we are actually seeking when we do so is the *feeling* we think those things will give us—not the actual "checkbox" we are chasing such as a title or money.

Here's a list of internal experiences we often think external pursuits will create:

- Joy and excitement
- Freedom to choose
- Belonging and being part of something
- Happiness and laughter
- Fulfillment and purpose
- Love and caring
- Acknowledgment of our capabilities
- Embracing our uniqueness
- Authenticity and being seen
- Feeling good enough
- Gratitude and appreciation

Remember, these internal experiences are not solely dependent on external circumstances. They are influenced by our mindset, self-acceptance, and inner growth. Focus on cultivating these qualities within yourself to truly experience the fulfillment and happiness you seek. By shifting our focus to internal factors and nurturing our inner selves, we can build a more resilient and authentic happiness that is less dependent on the ever-changing external world.

Pen to Paper Homeplay: Tools and Exercises

One tool you can use to explore the external things you desire and uncover what you truly seek internally is a simple exercise called "Desire Mapping," a concept developed by Danielle LaPorte.[45] Her work focuses on helping individuals align their goals and aspirations with their innermost desires and feelings, creating a more fulfilling and authentic life. Here's how you can do it:

1. Create 2 columns: one for external things and one for internal desires.

2. Begin by listing out the external things you believe will fulfill your desires. For example, you might write down material possessions, achievements, relationships, or experiences that you think will bring you joy, freedom, belonging, happiness, or any other desired feelings.

3. Once you have listed the external things, take a moment to reflect on each one. Ask yourself, *What is the underlying internal desire or feeling that I associate with this external thing?* For example, if you wrote down a luxury car, the underlying desire might be a sense of status or validation.

4. In the second column, write down the internal desires or feelings that correspond to each external thing. This could include qualities like love, self-acceptance, purpose, connection, or personal growth.

5. After completing the exercise, review your list of internal desires. Take note of any patterns or recurring themes that emerge. This can help you gain clarity on what truly matters to you on a deeper level.

Remember, this exercise aims to shift your focus from the external to the internal, allowing you to identify the core desires and feelings that drive you. By becoming aware of what you truly seek internally, you can direct your energy toward cultivating those qualities within yourself, leading to a more authentic and fulfilling life.

Courage to Become Present, Get Clear, and Consciously Choose

Now that we have opened our eyes with previous chapters and become aware of the lies and all the layers of what we are hiding—such as trauma, images, and gender skin suits—we can start to become aware of what is true for us and break the unconscious cycle on the hamster wheel.

No school or company will tell us that: our awareness and what is true for us trumps everything.

The number one skill that is not on a pretty graph or alphabet soup degree is the courage to become aware and present. We're often taught the contrary: operate on autopilot, follow the crowd's choices, believe someone else has the answer, and fear making a wrong or bad choice.

I was taught by my Middle Eastern culture and immigrant status to put my head down and work hard, and that was the way to the illusion of success. Anyone else been sold that lie? No one ever told me to get clear on what it is I desire and value.

That feeling of being stuck or lost means we are disconnected from our purpose and our values. Are we aware of what we're choosing or taking what comes? Are we choosing or waiting for someone to choose for us?

> *"The number one skill that is not on a pretty graph or alphabet soup degree is the courage to become aware and present."*

Discovering our uniqueness and gifts involves internal factors such as these:

- **Self-Awareness:** Understanding our strengths, weaknesses, values, and passions
- **Authenticity:** Being true to ourselves and embracing our individuality
- **Personal Growth:** Continuously learning, developing skills, and exploring new potentials
- **Passion and Purpose:** Aligning our passions with a sense of meaning and contribution
- **Staying Present:** Expanding out, understanding, and managing emotions instead of reacting
- **Mindset:** Embracing a growth mindset and overcoming challenges
- **Gratitude:** Practicing appreciation for the positive aspects of our lives
- **Authentic Connections:** Building supportive relationships that celebrate our uniqueness

I observe too many extremely talented people I mentor and coach (including myself) get lost in the noise that is irrelevant to the future they desire to create. I literally watch thousands of people in the workplace unconsciously sacrifice their identity, values, and vision. Heck, most have no clue what they are choosing; they just "go with the flow" of whatever their bosses or companies hand them.

We think someone else or something else has the answer. We think, *Well, if they have a big title and more money, then they have power, and they must know more than me.* We think some degree or accreditation means something. We let statements like "they say do this" or "Sally/Bob/Joe did it that way and they're successful" run our lives and choose for us.

We change bend, staple, and mutilate (graphic but true) ourselves to make sure we are right, good, worthy in our bosses' and organizations' eyes. Don't believe me? Then why do we obsess that we got a "meets expectations" or "exceeded expectations" on our performance reviews when they are given by people we are not even sure fall in line with our values or goals. We seek validation from people who are not going where we are going.

Choosing from a place of awareness means making conscious choices based on being fully present and aware of the different possibilities available to us versus what we are sold and told as right, good, and appropriate. Choosing from a place of awareness takes acceptance of being judged and even rejected, not resisting and fighting it nor aligning and agreeing to it. It's neutrality.

Awareness is not about judgment or analysis to make the perfect and right choice

but rather about being in tune with our intuition and inner knowing. It involves being aware of the energy and the information that each choice carries, allowing us to make choices that are more aligned with our true desires and intentions.

Choosing from awareness also means being willing to let go of preconceived notions, societal conditioning, and external expectations. It encourages us to trust our own judgment and follow our own path, even if it may go against the grain or seem unconventional.

Examples of choosing from awareness include these:

- **Career Choices:** Be fully present and aware of your passions, interests, and skills when selecting a career path. Make conscious choices based on what resonates with you, rather than societal expectations or external pressures.

- **Relationships:** Stay aware of your needs, values, and boundaries in relationships. Listen to your intuition and make choices that honor your authentic self, rather than seeking validation or conforming to norms.

- **Personal Growth:** Be present and open to self-improvement opportunities. Make choices that support your growth by identifying and letting go of limiting beliefs, patterns, or behaviors.

- **Lifestyle Choices:** Consider what brings you joy, fulfillment, and well-being when making lifestyle decisions. Simplify your life, prioritize self-care, and engage in activities aligned with your passions and values.

- **Decision-Making:** Pause, tune into your intuition, and weigh the possibilities and consequences of your choices. Make everyday decisions from a place of awareness, aligning with your desires and intentions.

Remember, we all have the capacity to choose from awareness. Trust yourself, be present, and listen to your intuition. By doing so, you'll make choices that bring clarity, joy, and expansion to your life's journey.

> *"Awareness is also a muscle we build. It demands our presence, openness, and willingness to accept the information and insights available to us in every moment, even when they might not be what we initially desire."*

I'd like to stress that making choices from a place of awareness is an ongoing practice. It's not a one-time event but a lifestyle shift, and it often runs counter to our conditioning. Just as you wouldn't expect a single visit to the gym or a yoga class to bring lasting change, awareness follows the same principle—awareness is also a muscle we build. It demands our presence, openness, and willingness to accept the information and insights available to us in every moment, even when they might not be what we initially desire.

This process includes removing the metaphorical rose-colored glasses we often wear in our personal and professional relationships. It also entails acknowledging the genuine impact that conscious choices have when contrasted with reactive choices driven by fears like the fear of being alone in work or play.

Through this practice, we can create a life that is more authentic, aligned, and in harmony with our true selves.

Awareness and Choice in Relationships

Relationships come in various forms, and they have the power to either contribute to or limit our lives. Relationships encompass the support and love we receive from our family and friends, the connections we form with romantic partners, the collaborations we engage in with colleagues, or even our relationship with our company.

We have all thrown around the saying "You are the average of the 5 people you spend the most time with" without fully grasping what that means. We turn this concept into picking people who have the "image of success" and trying to mimic them. We look at someone we define as outwardly successful, idolize them, and seek to emulate them without fully understanding what we see behind the image. We then seek validation from these very people. I have met many miserable millionaires and depressed "successful" executives.

Think about it. If we choose people who we can control, or who can control us, we will never be pushed into looking at what is real and true for us. We will never be pushed into choosing greater.

These people are not actually contributing to the life we are capable of creating; they are actually limiting us by keeping us trapped in the reality that is true for them, which is also just an image.

Remember that it matters what the *right* people think of us, the ones who align with our values and our mission, whether it be in a personal or professional capacity. It matters that these people recognize us for who we really are and give us the space to expand and be fully ourselves.

Seeking validation from those who don't share our vision is like asking directions from someone who has never been to our destination. With our new and fast-changing world, has anyone really been to where we are going? Or are we following someone from an outdated path and journey that no longer works the same, without fully understanding how the journey is different for us?

We might lie to ourselves and call those who align and agree with us wonderful and brilliant and hold onto those people for dear life because they validate our autopilot—our status quo. These people are actually costing us our lives and the capabilities we have.

We might even unconsciously choose people who are limited enough for us to control. This happens in work relationships all the time, and if we are not "controllable" and don't follow the exact process and what has been done, we are *rejects* in the cogwheel of the corporate system. Then we turn around and say . . . why can't we be a more innovative culture?

What most people, leaders, and organizations do not realize is that when we do this, we don't take into account that what we are trying to create won't be any greater than what we have already created before. There is no growth—only comfort.

"What we are trying to create won't be any greater than what we have already created before."

Please read that at least 5 more times!

If we truly desire to create something greater, more amazing, and filled with bigger possibilities than what we have ever created, we must choose people who will not tolerate or choose from a perspective of autopilot and limitation but instead demand greater of not only themselves but also of us!

Look around at all the people with similar goals to you and consider how fast the world is changing. Then make a list of all the people you spend the most time with and ask, *Does this person contribute energy to my expansion, or are they contributing energy to my contraction, autopilot mindset, and limitation?*

Generally speaking, the autopilot unconscious program causes us to pick people who will never push us to go beyond our current limitations because it's uncomfortable. These people contribute to the ideal checkbox scene of normal and basic. Therefore, they will never push us to break out of our box of limitations. Instead, we need to choose people who will make us question everything we know, push us to be courageous, push us to get uncomfortable, and make us aware that we can create greater possibilities filled with joy, purpose, and growth.

It does not need to be this way. You can ask questions, expand your awareness, and have the courage to choose greater. Let's look at it!

Pen to Paper Homeplay: Tools and Exercises

1. List out the names of people and things that you spend a lot of time within the areas below:

   a. People you work with: Leaders, managers, direct reports, colleagues, project teams

   b. The organization you work for: Understanding their true values and beliefs by observing what they genuinely tolerate in practice, as opposed to what's presented in the marketing materials, employee handbook, and website

   c. Friendships

   d. Communities you are part of: Fitness, church, etc.

   e. Family members

   f. Your romantic partner

   g. You could also list things like your home, where you live, the courses or trainings you've signed up for, books, etc.

   h. Even the social media you are scrolling, the people you are following, and the content you are consuming

2. Go through each name and get their energy and ask these questions:

   a. Is this person (or thing) a contribution to the life you desire to create? Are they going where you desire to go?

      i. Are they contributing to your expansion, growth, courage, creativity, possibility, and everything you can be capable of creating? Or are they controlling you, limiting you, and keeping you on autopilot?

   b. Next to each name or thing, write E (for expansion) or L (for limitation).

   c. Next, ask if you can change the relationship and trust your knowing. Don't lie to yourself. You know. Trust what comes up.

   d. Ask if you are willing to lose this person or thing. If not, be aware that anything you are not willing to lose has full control over you.

3. Choose to have the courage to take action. Choice creates awareness and opens up the space for others to enter your life.

Below is an example of a worksheet and the tools:

People and Things	Assessment of Each Relationship Expansion (E) or Limitation (L)	Small Courageous Action Step
Work life		
Manager	(L)—Limiting	Have a discussion
Colleague		
Organization itself		
Values	(E)—Expansive	Lean into more opportunities
Demonstrated traits		
Partners/friends		
Close friend		
Romantic partner		
Content consumption		
Social media and who you follow and the content you consume		
Books		
Classes		

Choose your life. Seriously, stop waiting to be chosen! That's how we evolve. That's how we live a life of no regrets. That is how we stop "should having" all over ourselves. We need to get present with our values and choices.

Self-Loyalty and Accepting the Reasons, Seasons, and Lifetimes

As part of all this, we are often sold another myth called "loyalty." Especially in the workplace, we are encouraged to be loyal to the company, the person who hired you, or your relationships with coworkers or departments. Even if they are toxic.

Your first loyalty should be to you.

Society often instills in us the idea that loyalty means putting others before ourselves at all costs. However, it's important to remember that we cannot effectively support and be there for others if we neglect our own well-being and happiness. Prioritizing ourselves doesn't mean being selfish or disregarding the needs of others. It means acknowledging our worth, honoring our values, and caring for our physical, mental, and emotional needs. By doing so, we cultivate a strong foundation of self-love and self-respect, which allows us to show up authentically in our relationships and contribute meaningfully to the world.

I've misapplied this one. My "close friend" at the time was personally connected to a toxic leader who was fully aware that thousands on his team were being emotionally abused and manipulated by a sociopath who worked for him. Yet he chose to ignore it so he could get ahead. For years I stayed quiet because I was trying hard to stay loyal to both him and my friend. I finally realized one day my silence was actually acceptance and my loyalty was totally blind!

From there, I chose to step into my inner strength of using my voice to expose the years of emotional abuse thousands of people were enduring and get those whom I had blind loyalty toward fired!

It was one of the hardest choices of my life to walk away from what I called "friendship" at the time and choose my values and me. It was hard as hell to set fire and burn bridges I had spent years building. Yet I was clear on this: turning my head to the emotional abuse for money and a title was not part of my values.

The myth of "don't burn any bridges" is the biggest lie we base our careers and workplace around. Open your eyes. If there is toxicity and emotional abuse, and it's celebrated, your silence is not loyalty; it's self-sabotage.

> *"The myth of 'don't burn any bridges' is the biggest lie we base our careers and workplace around. Open your eyes. If there is toxicity and emotional abuse, and it's celebrated, your silence is not loyalty; it's self-sabotage."*

Looking back, my hardest choice many years ago was my best choice and allowed me to step into my power and help the many people I had left behind to have a chance at flourishing. To this day, that "leader" resents me and forbids his wife from contacting me, and she remains loyal to his wishes. Some people will leave this earth without the experience of true growth and freedom, and this is not wrong, but it is limiting.

Remember, *some bridges are meant to be burned down.* One of my coaches reminded me of this quote: "People come into our lives for a reason, a season, or a lifetime." Not all relationships are meant to be permanent, but they each serve a purpose in our personal growth and life journey.

We buy the program that it's wrong to put ourselves first, or we submit to the golden rule—*do unto others as you would for yourself* never meant choosing others above yourself. Embrace the idea that your first loyalty should be to you. True kindness to you is putting you and your desires first. Let go of any blind loyalty and choose to involve yourself with people who appreciate your authentic self.

"Some bridges are meant to be burned down."

Embrace the ebb and flow of relationships in your life, especially the ones in the workplace that are drilled into our heads to maintain forever at all costs. Cherish the lessons, joy, and love that each person brings, whether they are there for a reason, a season, or a lifetime. And remember, every interaction holds the potential to leave a lasting impact on your journey of personal growth and fulfillment. Even the bad ones that require a bridge to be burned down!

Becoming Aware and Clear on Your Values

Remember the perspective that when we are born, we arrive with no suitcases? We have no programs, points of view, no judgments, no fears of failing and not being good enough, no bills. Then slowly, we pick up beliefs and programs from our parents, family, schools, friends, from everyone and everywhere.

These beliefs and values may not be ours and might not be true for us, or they may evolve and change. If we do not continuously and consciously challenge and ask questions about what we have bought as real and true, we are carrying baggage that is not even ours and making choices in our lives based on someone else's beliefs.

Here are the limitations this creates in our lives:

- **Loss of Self and True Desires:** Without a firm grasp on our values, we risk losing our sense of self, compromising our long-term fulfillment, and allowing external influences to shape our thoughts and actions.

- **Caving into Immediate Pleasures:** Succumb to the allure of immediate gratification and pursue external rewards like money, promotions, and titles. It's easy to get caught up in the pursuit of external validation and instant gratification. The desire for money, promotions, and titles can be tempting, but it's important to consider whether these goals truly align with our long-term happiness and fulfillment.

- **Choosing for Others, Not Ourselves:** Operate based on the viewpoints of your parents, family, or societal expectations regarding work, finances, and hierarchical structures. Society and family often have certain expectations when it comes to work, finances, and hierarchical structures. However, it's crucial to question whether these expectations truly resonate with us. Each person has unique dreams, aspirations, and values.

- **Unconsciously Giving into Conventional Interpretations:** Understand that definitions and interpretations can be highly subjective. Take the time to delve into what specific concepts mean to you on a personal level. For instance, creativity can express itself in countless forms, and its definition can diverge from one individual to another. Embrace your distinct understanding of these concepts and allow them to influence your choices. If existing definitions and interpretations do not resonate with your authentic self, don't hesitate to question and challenge them.

For example, creativity can manifest in countless ways, and its definition may differ from person to person. Embrace your own understanding of these concepts and let them guide your actions. Don't be afraid to challenge existing interpretations if they don't align with your authentic self.

- **Selecting from Outdated Points of View:** Many viewpoints are extremely outdated, such as the ones I've highlighted in Chapter 1, like fearing that a gap in your résumé spells doom and that you are not good enough. If we were present, aware, clear, and confident with our values we would respond with:

  "Why would I choose to work in a place that doesn't recognize the value of the time I spent raising a child, exploring the world, or enhancing my education? I'm not interested in working at a place with these kinds of values."

Isn't this more empowering?

By recognizing these tendencies and consciously choosing your own values, resisting short-term temptations, following your own path, and embracing your unique interpretations, you empower yourself to live a more authentic and fulfilling life. Best career advice to follow: Don't ever attach yourself to a person, a place, a company, an organization, or a project. Attach yourself to a mission, a calling, a purpose only. That is how you keep your power and choices clear.[46] Remember, it's your journey, and you have the power to shape it according to your own truth.

> *"Best career advice to follow: Don't ever attach yourself to a person, a place, a company, an organization, or a project. Attach yourself to a mission, a calling, a purpose only. That is how you keep your power and choices clear."* [47]

Here are a few core values to think about: Everyone is different. You may desire a more structured environment that is not fast changing. You might lose your mind in that type of environment. Again, there is no right or wrong core value.

It's OK if your top core value is money. I get it. It was mine in my early 20s. It's critical to do this exercise at least once a year, if not every 3 to 6 months, because your values evolve, shift, and change. That is part of the human experience. So don't limit yourself by making this solid. It should be fluid and changing.

Pen to Paper Homeplay: Tools and Exercises

1. Consider the following and identify which, if any, of these values are central to you in your life at this moment. Be as honest with yourself as possible, and feel free to add additional values of your own.

Core Values Sample				
Creativity	Balance	Appreciation	Honor	Trust
Inclusivity	Boldness	Courage	Adventurous	Respect
Learning	Fun	Integrity	Growth mindset	Generosity
Flexibility	Compassion	Vulnerability	Communication	Structure
Awareness	Curiosity	Wealth	Expansive	Constant change
Mental wellness	Physical wellness	Emotional wellness	Gratitude	Kindness
Freedom	Caring	Family	Faith	Excellence
Belonging	Career	Cooperation	Contribution	Forgiveness
Confidence	Courage	Efficiency	Contentment	Kindness
Contentment	Integrity	Ethics	Financial Stability	Loyalty

Core Values Sample				
Gratitude	Humor	Transparency	Independence	Respect
Power	Pride	Simplicity	Recognition	Security
Success	Risk-taking	Spirituality	Reliability	Stewardship
Resourceful-ness	Present	Time	Serenity	Alignment

Remember, discovering your core values is a personal journey, and it takes time and self-exploration. Be patient with yourself, trust your intuition, and be willing to delve deep within to uncover what truly matters to you. Your core values will serve as a compass, guiding you in making choices that align with your authentic self and bring you a greater sense of fulfillment and purpose.

Living in alignment with our values means more than just professing them; it requires us to practice them actively. It entails ensuring that our intentions, words, thoughts, and behaviors are in harmony with our deeply held beliefs.

1. This chart allows you to assess how you perceive your alignment with each core value, your current actions or behaviors related to them, and the time you allocate to them in your weekly schedule. It can be a useful tool for self-reflection and goal setting to ensure you're dedicating time and effort to what truly matters to you.

Core Value	How I'm Showing Up	Time Spent (Daily/Weekly)
Health	Prioritizing fitness and a balanced diet	5 hours
Learning and growth	Actively seeking new knowledge and skills	10 hours
Family	Spending quality time with loved ones	15 hours
Creativity	Engaging in creative hobbies and projects	8 hours
Community	Volunteering and participating in local events	3 hours

Does the Workplace Actually Match Your Values?

"It's not hard to make decisions when you know what your core values are."

—Roy Disney

One of the most significant misconceptions we're told is the importance of "being a culture match," which forces us to buy into a list of company values on a website because we don't know our own. It's crucial to remember that value should flow both ways. Equally significant is contemplating what value your company brings to your life and if it's aligned.

For whatever reason, we buy into the misconception that we are the ones that constantly need to prove our value to the organization. Your time is a currency. Stop chasing the dangling carrot.

Assessing the gaps between your values and the organization's performance is crucial for making informed decisions about your professional path. By understanding these discrepancies, you gain valuable insights into how well the company aligns with your priorities.

Identifying areas where there are significant gaps allows you to evaluate whether the organization can provide the experiences, opportunities, and environment that are important to you. It helps you determine if the company's culture and practices are compatible with your values, enabling you to make more informed decisions about your career and job satisfaction. Evaluating these gaps empowers you to seek out opportunities that better align with your values, leading to a more fulfilling and rewarding professional journey.

Here is an example: list your values, then your score and priority, and then an assessment with reality. Below is an example of using the Values Alignment Scorecard that I leverage for people I coach.

My Value	Priority to Me (Scale 0 – 3)	My Organization's Performance (Scale 0 – 3)	Gap
Learning	2	0	2
Growth opportunities	3	0	3
Flexibility	2	2	0
Pay	2	1	1
Creativity time	1	2	1
Totals	10	5	7

Learning: This value is highly important to you, as indicated by the weight of 2. However, the organization currently has a performance rating of 0, resulting in a gap of 2. This indicates a significant misalignment between your value and the organization's performance in terms of learning opportunities.

Growth Opportunities: This value is given the highest priority, with a weight of 3. Unfortunately, the organization's performance in this area is also rated as 0, resulting in a gap of 3. This signifies a considerable discrepancy between your expectations and the organization's ability to provide growth opportunities.

Flexibility: The organization's performance aligns with your value for flexibility, as both have a rating of 2. Therefore, there is no gap in this aspect.

Pay: You consider pay to be moderately important, as indicated by a weight of 2. The organization's performance in terms of pay is rated as 1, resulting in a gap of 1. There is some misalignment between your value and the organization's current pay structure.

Creativity Time: Although creativity time is of lower priority to you (weight of 1), the organization performs well in this area with a rating of 2. Thus, there is no significant gap.

It is important to note that the "total" row reflects the cumulative gap across all values, which in this case amounts to 7. The higher the gap, the greater the misalignment between your values and the organization's performance. It is advisable to pay closer attention to the values with the highest gaps, such as learning and growth opportunities in this case, as these areas may require further evaluation and consideration.

Pen to Paper Homeplay: Tools and Exercises

Discovering your core values for each area of your life is a personal and introspective process. This is an honest and vulnerable exercise to gain clarity on what you desire to create. There is no right or wrong answer here again, just clarity.

Try to get as clear as possible on what a core value actually means for *you*.

For example, let's say growth is one of your core values.

You might be looking for something like this: "An environment that is committed to providing me with opportunities where I can learn, try different things, work with diverse people. They are interested in how I learn and thrive in my unique way and leverage my strengths. They are committed to hands-on experiences because I learn by doing, not by going to training."

If you list growth alone, it's vague and unclear to you and even more unclear if you are evaluating a boss, company, peers, or leader.

Here are some steps you can take to help you figure out your core values and how the organization you are working for aligns:

1. **Reflect on Your Experiences:** Take some time to reflect on your past experiences and moments when you felt most fulfilled, alive, and aligned with your true self. Ask these questions:

   - What values were present in those moments?
   - What principles did I honor?
   - What is true for me that is not true for anyone else?
   - If I was not being realistic, what would I choose from the heart?

- What part of my values is an image I desire to portray to show that I'm successful?

- If no one else existed or was watching, what would really make me happy?

2. **Identify What Matters Most:** Consider the areas of your life that are significant to you, such as relationships, career, health, personal growth, and spirituality. For each area, ask yourself what truly matters to you. What do you value the most in those aspects of your life? Is it honesty, connection, freedom, growth, or something else? Make a list of the values that come to mind.

3. **Ruthlessly Prioritize and Evaluate Your Values:** Once you have a list of values, prioritize them based on their importance to you. Align your actions with your values.

   Take a look at your current behaviors, choices, and actions in each area of your life. Are they aligned with your core values? If there are discrepancies, consider how you can make adjustments to align your actions with your values. What is it costing you? This may involve making conscious choices, setting boundaries, or seeking opportunities that are more in line with what you value.

4. **Make This a Conscious Practice and Habit:** Cultivate a practice of self-reflection and self-awareness to evaluate and refine your core values continuously. As you grow and evolve, your values may also evolve. Stay open to new insights and experiences that may shape your understanding of what you truly value in life.

Successfully determining whether or not your company's values align with your values starts by connecting or reconnecting with those very values. Take the time to do some deep self-reflection here. What is most important to you as an individual? How do you embody those values? How do you envision them manifesting in your life?

Remember, while some values may remain fixed throughout our lives, others will change, sometimes even from one season to the next. That's OK. The important thing is to stay in tune with who we are and who we are becoming. We must allow ourselves the flexibility to become different, more authentic versions of who we are.

Then once you have a firm handle on what your values are, you'll be better prepared to pursue them in every aspect of your life—especially at work. Don't be afraid to walk away from situations, companies, or roles that aren't in alignment with who you are or who you are becoming. If you have the courage to live in accordance with your values, you will experience greater harmony and fulfillment across the board.

CHAPTER 9

Perception Is Not Reality:
It's Just a Point of View

"When you judge others, it's really an indicator that you're judging yourself. 99.9% of the people that judge you or have opinions on you have no idea what's actually happening in your life. Same thing goes for when you judge them."

—Gary Vaynerchuk

"**M**ichelle, you need to change Bryan's review to a 'needs improvement' because 5 months ago, in that one meeting, he questioned our strategy, and he is not on board with where we're headed, and you need to coach him!" —*One of my many WTF moments in Corporate America.*

Yes, this demand was repeatedly made by a former individual I reported to, commonly known as "Chief." What's even more concerning is that 8 of my peers just sat there during the situation above, with nothing to say, deer in the headlights. I could feel the fear and heat rise from their bodies. I swear they would have crawled under a table if they could.

They sat there, frozen in place, and an eerie silence enveloped the room. Astonishingly, not a single voice dared to break the stillness, even though Bryan, the highest achiever on the team, had been the savior for each of them on numerous occasions.

Bryan was the embodiment of authenticity, guided by his values and boundaries and choosing not to engage in what most called "the game," in contrast to some of his colleagues. This principled stance made Bryan the target of the Chief's animosity.

When I shared the story with other executive members of the organization, they said, "Oh, he's just a bully that abuses people," like it was no big deal. The consistent "advice" I got from those that called themselves "leaders" in a multibillion-dollar organization was to not get involved and that he was protected by the head of human resources, and others who have raised the issue are no longer here.

This Chief was also excellent at putting on the show for his bosses; it was so bad that grown men old enough to be my father would tell me with tears in their eyes that they felt abused and scared but had no choice to leave because of their families. After leaving meetings with him, people would walk around like drugged zombies and even came up with jokes like, "Oh, did you get Chiefed today?" As you can imagine, I had sleepless nights over what to do.

We are given so much advice to take feedback. But it's so critical to see where the feedback is coming from, and oftentimes we are not taught that. People project their experiences, their past, their pain, their trauma onto us and we take it because we think they are in power because of some weird title and box. It's self-abuse and insanity on another level.

Remember, perception is not the same as reality; it's merely a point of view. So, while listening, let's also refrain from diminishing ourselves and recognize that our worth and value are not solely determined by someone else's perspective. It's about embracing empathy, understanding, and mutual respect while staying true to ourselves.

This is why the previous chapter is so critical. We must become present and aware of all our unconscious blind spots, all our unconscious programs, and all our points of view that do not belong to us. We must be super clear on our values and our strengths.

Get crystal clear so that when we are given "feedback," we know what is real for us versus what is being projected at us.

The Ugly Truth of What Happens behind Closed Doors

The ugly truth is that bad behavior happens more frequently than it should behind many organizations' closed doors. The stories thousands of clients I coach tell me would blow your mind. We are talking about people at large organizations responsible for many people's livelihoods.

The pressure to conform and meet predefined expectations can magically drain your courage to ask if things are real and true for you. We are so quick to make ourselves wrong and others right, who we perceive based on an image.

Courage is the willingness to embrace vulnerability, to let go of preconceived notions, and to be fully present in the reality of the situation. It involves asking ourselves important questions such as:

- What is true for me in this situation?
- What is actually true and happening here?
- What is happening with this person, and what might be their hidden agenda?
- What is their lens and where do they function from?

By honestly exploring these inquiries, we can better understand ourselves, the situation at hand, and the motivations of others involved. It takes courage to confront these questions and seek the truth, allowing us to navigate the complexities of relationships and interactions with greater clarity and authenticity.

We have been ingrained to accept sayings like "perception is reality" or "they are not a good culture fit." It's part of normal language and reality. But it's not! We give "feedback" based on our points of view and belief systems and make them gospel.

Could you imagine if we changed ourselves every time one of the 8 billion–plus people on the planet gave us feedback from their point of view? Crazy, right? But we do it all the time. We call people wrong and ask them to bend, staple, and morph themselves into a box that is not always real or true for them or relevant anymore. We do this to ourselves too! We do it to our kids.

The important thing to remember is that perception is *not* reality. It's just a point of view! It's not real unless you make it real.

The problem is that we all unconsciously do make it real. How often have you changed your style or behavior because a boss or coworker made you wrong and gave you feedback? Even the flip side of that, how often were you given "good" and "right" feedback, made it gold, and carried that around?

How many bosses and colleagues have you had in your career? Do you know that unconsciously you make micro-changes to yourself each time to fit in? All based on the right and wrong of someone else's point of view.

In corporate America, we dress a fish in a monkey suit and ask it to climb a tree. If the fish fails to climb the way other monkeys do, it's the fish's fault. Shaming the fish for its failure is considered good leadership.

"Everybody is a genius. But if you judge a fish by its ability to climb a tree, it will live its whole life believing that it is stupid." —Albert Einstein

Richard Branson

Richard Branson, CEO of Virgin and a neurodivergent leader with dyslexia, reminds us that everybody is a genius in their own wonderful way, and if it was left up to the school or corporate system, he would have been deemed a total failure.[48]

Many corporate environments and workplaces have made us lose sight of our bold, brilliant genius. We have forgotten what is true for us, our innate curiosity, courage, and creativity.

Awareness of Projections and Judgments

The more present and aware we are, the better we can see that many points of view are actually projections and judgments people make so they can be right and make us feel like we are wrong. It's usually not personal at all and it is unconscious. This is where it's critical we stay present and ask ourselves questions like: *"What is really going on here? Am I just making them uncomfortable about their choice, and they want me to be like them?"*

Most people do not know us. They don't know our backgrounds, our capabilities, what is in our minds and hearts. They have no idea what is happening inside us or behind closed doors and why we are the way we are.

What happens is we look at an image, a title, or a position of leadership power and think they are always right. We forget it's just a point of view from their backgrounds, experiences, and trauma. Usually, it has to do more with them and their point of view and journey than it does with us. It's critical that we do not take their point of view literally and make ourselves feel wrong or change ourselves. Ask questions instead.

Do you know what I later found out? The Chief had suffered a great deal of abuse from his father, and he chose to flex his power onto other people in his own insane way of healing his past. Obviously this does not work, and he basically passed on the abuse he received instead of choosing to end it. That was his point of view and what he was projecting. It had nothing to do with Bryan, me, or anyone in the room.

At the end of the day, though we may not have known his history at the time, both Bryan and I remained steadfast in our values and held our ground. We recognized that his judgment was flawed and influenced by his own past trauma, which distorted his perception. Neither Bryan nor I conformed to follow the crowd, even when it meant going against our peers and superiors.

Today, all of us are precisely where we belong, thanks to that pivotal decision and the path it paved for everyone. P.S. Bryan has risen to an executive position today.

Ways to Stop Diminishing Yourself and Others

Don't get me wrong, feedback is 100% imperative to learning and growth, but only feedback that is real and true for **you**. Not points of view that are from a fixed, finite perspective. That can become a limitation we create if we buy into the lie. The world is changing too fast not to be fluid. Fluidity is where creativity, growth, learning, and magic happen!

When getting and receiving feedback, here are a few questions to ask yourself before believing something as finite, accurate, and true.

Disclaimer: This is a knowing (awareness) exercise, not an intelligence test on whether you are right or wrong, so don't overanalyze.

1. **Is This True for Me or My Point of View?** Or did I buy it as mine from a name in a box (a.k.a. status) that is "above mine," the news, media, parents, friends, colleagues, the process, or the structure? You will find through this exercise that 90% of your "stuff" is not yours. You're unconsciously buying it as yours because of an old boss or a toxic culture you worked in 10 years ago. You are buying into an outdated process or structure handed to you. Ask if this is yours. *Is this true for me? Or is it a program I have bought into?*

2. **Is This Person a 360-Degree View of Who I Desire to Be?** Remember, point of view is all relative based on someone's view of the world and experiences. Not the title or résumé! Even with the best intentions, unless you are laser clear on your vision and values and trust *yourself*, no one, and

I mean no one, can give you the "right" feedback or view, no matter how successful they appear or how much someone cares for you. Only you know! Ask whether they demonstrate who you strive to be in what they advise you. How long ago were they successful at this? Would you take fitness advice from someone who has never exercised or been on a fitness journey? Or financial advice from someone who is broke?

3. **Is This Relevant to Where I Am Headed and What I Desire to Create?** We are taught to doubt and not trust ourselves at a very young age. We are programmed to think others know better or to look to society to tell us what to do and how to fit into the tribe. Here is a mind-blowing secret: no one knows what they are doing! You are unique and on a unique journey. These are extraordinary times that have never happened before. Every time we put our heads on the pillow, something changes somewhere in the world. Stop looking to others for feedback to morph yourself. Stop giving feedback that is from your lens only.

4. **What Is This Person's Point of View?** Ask yourself if their lens might be limited. What era were they raised in? Are they still active players in what they are giving you feedback on? What experiences do they have that might be different from yours?

5. **What Can This Person Hear?** We often go so fast to check a box and give or even receive feedback that we forget to ask what that person can actually hear. What is their point of view, and how do they see the world? Then ask if your feedback is even relevant. Should I deliver this? If so, how can I do it in an empowering way that does not diminish or make

them feel wrong? How can I give them space to choose if it's true for them and the future they desire to create?

No, I never changed the performance review; instead, I just took the anger and total rage from the Chief, who I had no idea had major narcissistic personality disorder. No, I never told Bryan because I asked myself the questions above, and he was one of the highest performers. I was in no way going to put doubt in his world or disempower and diminish his reality.

Un-Hiding Our Limiting Points of View about Ourselves

The perceptions and points of view of others are so detrimental to us if we are not clear on who we are. Yet what is even more detrimental are the hidden and unconscious points of view and perceptions we have about ourselves.

This is so critical because the life we end up creating will match the point of view of what we think we deserve!

It is critical to understand how our unconscious beliefs and points of view have a significant impact and can either support our ability to thrive and be creative or hinder our ability to be ourselves and choose what is true for us.

So many of us walk around in victim mode without realizing it. We say things like, "That is how it is," "Work is hard," "Money is hard," or "My boss is an ass." What we miss is that we are so powerful we end up creating all of it. As Dr. Dain Heer writes in *Being You, Changing the World*, "Your point of view creates your reality; reality does not create your point of view."

Ever notice when you want to buy a new black car of a certain model, all of a sudden you keep seeing that car in the streets? That's because all of your focus and view is placed on it, so you see it. That is how powerful we are!

This is a type of visualization technique many athletes use to focus on the end goal, crossing the finish line, getting the medal around their neck, that sense of accomplishment. They keep that focus when the 5:00 a.m. alarm goes off, and it's dark and cold and time for a 5-mile training run.

When I embarked on the challenge of running a marathon on the Great Wall of China, it was precisely this laser focus that enabled me to resist the temptation of hitting snooze when the alarm sounded early or to complete those grueling 16 training miles in scorching 102-degree weather. This focus was fueled by the vivid image of the finish line, my commitment to friends who joined me in this adventure, the act of registering for the race, and booking the tickets—all these factors combined to generate the momentum needed to keep going.

Here's the thing: I was never a natural athlete, I didn't play sports in school, and I was actually overweight growing up. One day, I changed my belief and point of view and decided, "I am an athlete." That's it. That simple. Change your belief, change your language and how you see yourself, and change your life.

99% of people underestimate their capability and power which creates a brick wall for creativity and growth in our lives. Our outdated corporate structures, processes, and societal pressures to check the boxes perpetuate these barriers. This is why we see innovation, overall employee sentiment, and general happiness at an all-time low. Our beliefs and points of view create our personal and professional lives and impact everyone connected to us.

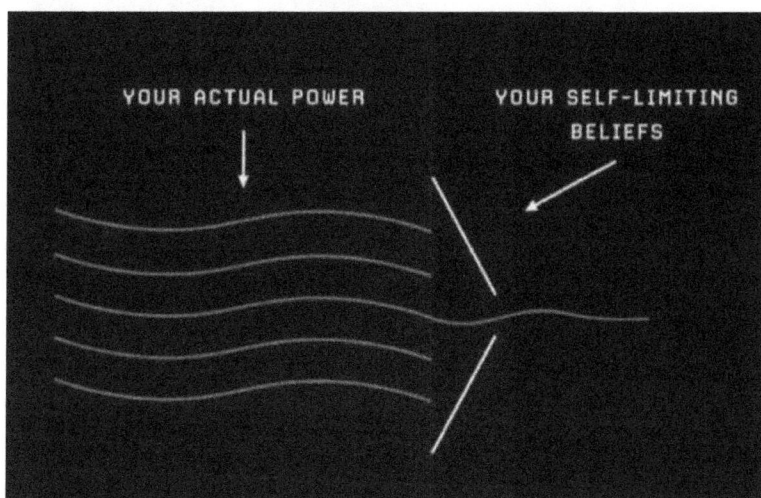

VELKO Academy[49]

Points of View and Beliefs We Keep Hidden from Ourselves

Here's where it becomes a mind cluster: what about our beliefs and points of view that keep us stuck and limited? We are functioning in this place from projections, judgments, assumptions, and conclusions. Sometimes these are on autopilot so much that we don't even realize we are doing it.

A simple example is when we message someone, and they don't respond. Or we see someone we know, and they don't smile at us. Do we make up stories about how they are ignoring us? Do we ask a question? Do we assume the worst? Do we think it's something we did or said? Do we fire off another email or message?

We don't realize this is stirring up something inside of us, not them. It's a point of view about ourselves! Do we feel ignored, abandoned, or unseen? If not caught in time, we go into reaction and judgment of ourselves, the situation, or the other person.

The only way to uncover our hidden points of view is to look at the places in our lives that are not showing up how we would like. Let's say you desire to become a manager at work and no matter how much you try, how much hard work you put in, you can't seem to break through. It's time to ask: what limiting point of view do you have about yourself?

> *"People treat us and look at us the way we see ourselves.*
> *If subconsciously we think deep down that we are*
> *unworthy, guess how others are going to see us?"*

In reality, people treat us and look at us the way we see ourselves. If subconsciously we think deep down that we are unworthy, guess how others are going to see us? If we don't look at our unconscious beliefs, we cannot change them. How do we know they are unconscious? Usually, it's all the things in our lives that we are having a hard time changing.

Hidden Glass Jars and Boxes We Create

It took me so long to see where in my life I was creating this. My image showed success, yet I could not break through what I used to call the "glass ceiling." I blamed someone or something (the company, the boss) until I realized that it was a glass box I had put myself into because of a core belief that I hid from even myself: the belief that I was not good enough.

This glass box I created when I was a kid I could never break away from. This glass box contained all my outdated beliefs about myself that I held subconsciously. Then I would replay these views repeatedly, renaming the characters and the story.

We are so powerful that once we believe something, we will loop it to make ourselves right!

This was a learned limitation I created that was no longer true or real. I did this with personal relationships, work relationships, and even my relationship with the companies I joined.

I call it a "glass box" because many of us, somewhere deep in our knowing, can see the limitless possibilities, yet we have a hard time stepping out. To start to look at your hidden points of view about yourself, you have to look at what is showing up in your life that you can't seem to change.

Let's take a big one for most—money.

Get vulnerable with yourself, and look at all your points of view of money. Is your belief that money is hard to make? That you need to work hard for money? That money is the root of all evil?

Or is it that money is easy, it's abundant, it's freedom? It comes and goes?

2 very different points of view. Now if you look at how money shows up for you in your life, I'm sure it matches those beliefs.

This goes for anything. Jobs, partners, a house you desire, travel—you name it! In life you will simply recreate the unconscious point of view you have about yourself.

Building a Powerful Point of View of You

Gary Douglas and Dr. Dain Heer, cofounders of Access Consciousness, emphasize the importance of building a relationship with oneself as the foundation for meaningful connections with others. This principle extends beyond romantic relationships and is relevant to friendships and workplace dynamics, as explored in their book *Divorceless Relationships*.

To build a powerful self-image, we must have a solid point of view about who we are. A stable, intimate relationship with ourselves is crucial. This is why looking in the mirror and being vulnerable can be so challenging.

We cannot achieve vulnerability with others without first being genuinely honest and vulnerable with ourselves. This includes embracing both our admirable qualities and those deep-rooted aspects we may feel extreme shame about.

Most people think vulnerability is sharing some personal detail about them at work or to someone they do not know. It's not. If you feel uncomfortable, it's usually a sign of vulnerability.

"If you feel uncomfortable, it's usually a sign of vulnerability."

If you skip this then you will easily give up your reality and make others greater than you so you can be validated by them. Why? Because if you are not connected with yourself and what is true for you, you will in a heartbeat give yourself up and make other people or things greater than you.

As you ponder on elements of intimacy concerning yourself, consider how you treat and talk to yourself. Then observe how others show up for you in these areas. Being honest with yourself is essential for developing this awareness. People will treat you the way you see and treat yourself. Ask yourself: Do you trust you? Do you honor you? Are you grateful for you?

If you begin hiding and not being intimate with the person in the mirror, you will deprive the world of the brilliance and uniqueness of you; we will all become robots.

1. **Trust:** Do you trust you and your knowing? Or are you always looking for others to have the answer and tell you what to do? Do you wear rose-colored glasses and try to "see the good" in everyone, or will you see things exactly as they

are, good, bad, ugly, and beautiful? True trust is seeing all of it and knowing that good people will choose bad things and vice versa.

2. **Honor:** Do you honor and respect yourself? Do you put your needs first? Do you voice what works for you? Or do you change and morph yourself to what others need from you?

3. **Gratitude:** Are you constantly judging yourself for your mistakes or what you should or could have done? Or are you in gratitude for your doing the best you did with tools you have or had?

4. **Allowance:** Do you allow things to be? Or do you want to control every outcome in the name of "the right thing"? Do you allow people to just be and let them choose when they are ready, even if what they choose will create suffering?

5. **Vulnerability:** Are you willing to truly un-hide and be seen? The good, the bad, all of you? Are you willing to lower all your walls and barriers and be radically honest with yourself?

Trust was always big for me as I was raised to see the best in everything. This is nothing but fake positivity. Trust what someone shows you. Trust is not believing everything is going to turn out all right just because we want it to; that is 100% blind faith.

If your boss is an insecure control freak, believe them first and they'll show you that. If they don't have your back once, believe that. If they don't give you opportunities to shine, trust that. As Maya Angelou said, "When someone shows you who they are, believe them the first time."

> ## WHEN SOMEONE SHOWS YOU WHO THEY ARE,
>
> ## BELIEVE THEM THE FIRST TIME.
>
> **MAYA ANGELOU**

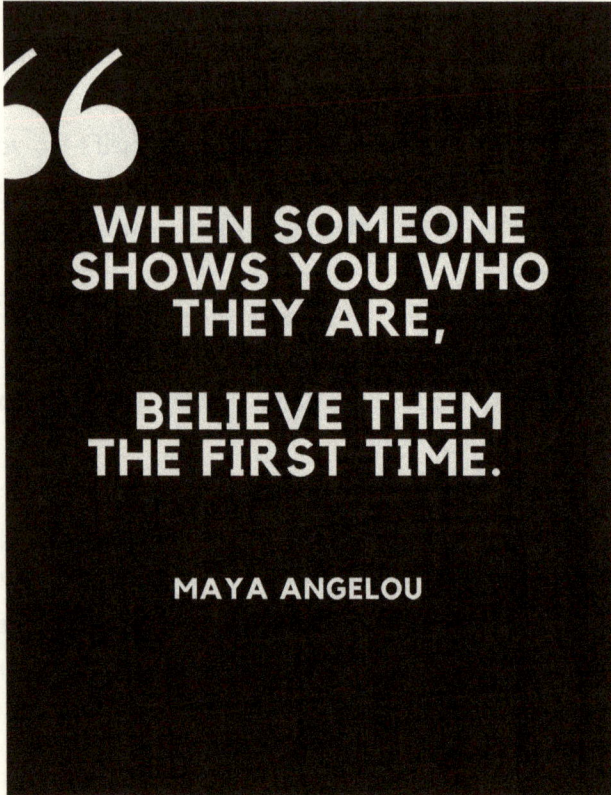

I realized I didn't trust myself or the universe when I went deep into this one. You might find the same as you go through this and truly get vulnerable and honest with yourself.

Organizations teach us to dishonor ourselves and buy into fake gratitude like, "You should be grateful you have a job in these tough economic times." Talk about a point of view someone else is projecting on you that is not true. The *do it at all costs, kill yourself, burn out all for the carrots and money* is how we dishonor ourselves and buy into someone else's construct. These are the key lessons to remember:

- Have the courage to look at your limiting points of view; you can lie to everyone else, but don't lie to yourself. Get brutally vulnerable with yourself. If you un-hide your limiting points of view, you can open the floodgates to your true power.

- In a world and corporate environment that is set up so you don't trust yourself and don't honor yourself, take steps to make sure you know what is true for you.

- Be grateful and lean into your strengths and abilities. Build those up and don't get stuck judging your perceived weakness. Even if you are getting feedback on top of feedback. Do not let the judgment win or shake your confidence.

Pen to Paper Homeplay: Tools and Exercises

1. **Make a List of Your Strengths across All Areas of Your Life.** List out all your transferable skills. This includes if you are a parent, an athlete, an overcomer of adversity, a soccer coach, etc. Build your awareness on how these can translate to your power in all areas of life.

2. **Witness and List Out Your Thoughts and Limited Beliefs.** Typically, this is in your subconscious and will show up in areas you cannot seem to change. Examples: money is hard work, I can't seem to get my team to be creative, I can't lose weight, there is not enough time, etc.

3. **Create a New Belief and Point of View to Counter the Items in Number 2.** Ask questions to change each one: What will it take to change this? What's one micro-step I can take this week? Is it time to change my environment? What am I avoiding or defending?

When you give up being you it's a slow process; little by little, every day, you give up your knowing and give up yourself. Just like the analogy of putting a frog in water and slowly turning the heat up until it boils to death. You will wake up one day and not even recognize yourself.

I ever so slowly and subtly changed myself to the point that I woke up one day standing in front of the mirror, tears running down my face as I no longer recognized who I was even looking at.

Choose to knock down the walls of your subconscious limited beliefs that hold you back. Please, choose to unleash your full power and potency and evolve our beautiful world.

It takes courage; it's uncomfortable; it's for the warriors committed to evolving our beautiful planet and creating a field of infinite possibilities beyond right and wrong.

So what is true for you? Choose to step into it.

CHAPTER 10

Leadership Is a Behavior, Not a Title: Unveiling the Conscious Leader in You

"A leader without a title is better than a title without the ability to lead."

—*Simon Sinek*

It's interesting how we often regard titles and images on organizational charts as more powerful than ourselves. It's like a psychological game where if someone's box is positioned above ours on a chart, there's a strange belief that they must know more than we do. It's similar to how children perceive adults as knowing more just because they're in bigger bodies.

This is one of the most absurd myths we buy into, and I certainly did as well.

Really step back and think of the insanity we are buying into. Our entire world has changed, and what got us here will not necessarily take us to the future. Yet we are buying into an idea that some outdated title or person has the answer.

We follow leaders who are no longer leaders. What is worse is sometimes we are following just an image of a leader—we are not always seeing reality. We see a picture, an office, a title on LinkedIn, a media post, and we think they *must* have it together. We lose our minds to read a "successful" person's book, to find out how they did it, etc.

What if what got them to where they are will no longer build a new future? What if they went to school, followed the rules, are miserably overweight, have hair falling out, are taking ten pills a day, are divorced, and are not talking to their kids?

That is often literally what we are emulating and making more powerful than us. Would you take financial advice from a broke person? Fitness advice from an overweight person? How about relationship advice from someone divorced twice, or not even in a relationship? Yet we do this in the workplace unconsciously, like it's normal.

What we often overlook is that many individuals have leadership potential, and in the new world order centered on networked teams, we all need to cultivate true leadership skills. It's important to recognize that just because we are good at our jobs that doesn't automatically mean we are prepared to be responsible for other people.

In many cases, organizations promote people based on their technical expertise, whether it's excelling as an engineer, a number cruncher, or a human resource analyst. The focus tends to be on how well they made widgets in their respective areas.

One of the biggest misconceptions is that leadership is just a title on an organizational chart, how many processes you create, or how many KPIs you execute. In reality, leadership is a behavior—the behavior of bravery. The uncomfortable courage to let go of what is no longer relevant and reimagine a new future.

As we transition to a world where networked teams play a central role, leadership skills are becoming increasingly essential for everyone.

New World Order: To Thrive Requires Behaving as a Leader

We're at a pivotal moment, and it's not just about the latest technology like generative AI.

The old-school leadership behaviors and "best practices" that used to work won't necessarily serve us in the future.

Leadership hinges on bold and courageous behaviors. These are in stark contrast to outdated, finite management behaviors that have been typically seen as entirely normal but will quickly become irrelevant.

Courageous leaders who think differently are preparing for a future never seen before through reimagination, not repetition of what worked in the past, and they will be the ones who are set up to thrive!

Companies like Allianz, Haier, Microsoft, and Nucor are setting the pace. They're transitioning from an industrial mindset of stability and profit to one of adaptability, focusing on the broader impact of their actions and transforming their industries.

The new approach is open, fluid, and inclusive, and it's all about delivering value to all stakeholders including employees, communities, and our planet.

The key shifts include long-term impact over profit, creating possibility over preservation, creating value through cocreation over competition and scarcity. Creating organizational structures that foster partnership and collaboration over command and hierarchy. Creating environments where work is executed through discovery and evolution instead of through control, and where leaders prioritize authenticity and wholeness over conformity and being the same.

> *"The question isn't whether the future is coming. It's whether you're ready for it. In order to pivot and prepare, we must all shift to becoming conscious human-centered leaders!"*

The question isn't whether the future is coming. It's whether you're ready for it. In order to pivot and prepare, we must all shift to becoming conscious human-centered leaders!" Conscious human-centered leadership is centered on inspiring everyone to be part of creating a greater possibility and future. Through self-awareness, empathy, and ethical responsibility, it avoids old judgments and traditional thinking, focusing instead on innovation and growth. Rejecting the "that's how we've always done it" approach, conscious leaders embrace integrity and inclusivity, fostering a collaborative environment where all stakeholders shape a sustainable and positive future. These skills are not necessarily technical in nature but are rather rooted in creativity, courage, and adaptability.

The easy part was becoming aware, taking the blinders off, and getting clear on what is real and what is a lie. As we get more clarity and awareness, the hard part is the day to day and choosing to break the habit of autopilot and to be a courageous leader instead of waiting for someone else to do it.

We're entering uncharted territory where the tried-and-true methods of the past won't light our way. What's needed is a new kind of leadership, one that ignites passion, sparks creativity, and builds a future filled with possibility. True leadership is questioning everything we know, both in life and in the business and organizational setting.

The future of conscious leadership includes these critical leadership shifts that can usher in sustainable, inclusive growth for both people and organizations:

- **Shift to Impact:** Moving from a sole emphasis on profits to creating a comprehensive impact for all stakeholders, embracing a mentality of potential rather than mere preservation.

- **Moving to Authenticity:** Transitioning from projecting a facade and an image to embodying authenticity and completeness. Leaders should remain mindful of the ripple effect of their behaviors, choices, and actions, considering long-term implications.

- **Increased Collaboration:** Evolving from a directive approach rooted in structured hierarchies to collaborative engagement within empowered networks, promoting partnership rather than relying on authority.

- **Discovery Mindset:** Shifting from a mindset of control based on predictability to one of evolution driven by rapid learning. Leaders must embrace a spirit of discovery rather than seeking absolute certainty.

- **Greater Cocreation:** Replacing the competitive drive for existing value with a focus on cocreating new value through reimagining possibilities and adopting an attitude of abundance rather than scarcity.

In this new era, leaders must be forward thinking and embrace change, fostering a culture that inspires everyone to contribute to a greater and more sustainable future, which means we must disrupt ourselves. Disrupt what we focus on, how we create value, how we show up.

Consider how these traditional leadership skills are evolving:

Traditional Mindset	New Mindset	Outdated Behavior	New World Behavior
Preservation	Possibility	Profit	Impact
Scarcity	Abundance	Competition	Cocreation
Authority	Partnership	Command	Collaboration
Certainty	Discovery	Control	Evolution
Conformity	Authenticity	Sameness	Uniqueness

> ## WHILE MANAGERS ARE OFTEN ABLE TO MAINTAIN A TEAM AT ITS CURRENT LEVEL,
>
> ## LEADERS ARE ABLE TO LIFT IT TO A HIGHER LEVEL THAN IT HAS EVER REACHED BEFORE.
>
> JOHN MAXWELL

To embark on this journey toward shaping the future, the initial steps are to:

1. Develop an awareness of the necessary mindset for future creation.
2. Make a conscious choice regarding how we wish to present ourselves.
3. Distinguish between those who align with our chosen approach and those who remain in the status quo, displaying unconscious management.
4. Decide on the environments and individuals with whom we invest our time and energy.

Raise the Bar, Know the Difference of Leadership

The question we must all ask ourselves and get super clear on regardless of our titles is this: *do I truly desire to be a manager or leader?*

I don't mean just in the workplace or within your given title, I mean in life. You could be a Fortune 500 CEO and still be a manager. You could be a developmental engineer with direct reports and be a powerful leader. You could be a stay-at-home mom or dad and be a leader. You could be a leader at 10 years old in elementary school.

As we navigate this new AI automation era, it's crucial to understand that the future of leadership relies on fearless actions. This is the opposite of outdated management behaviors, which will become irrelevant.

The harsh reality we face is that traditional management roles and tasks will be automated and become obsolete, leaving room to elevate behaviors to meet the complex demands of the future.

Changing employee expectations will further accelerate the need for more value-based behaviors and less administration.

With this in mind, I'll ask again: do you want to be a manager or a leader? There is no right or wrong answer. There is just clarity. Clarity on what we desire to be and who we are actually being. Whether it's a choice you are making as a behavior in your life or if you are actually in a position with a title.

If you genuinely don't desire to be a leader, you should seriously step down, as your decisions are impacting people. If you are choosing leadership to feel powerful and present an image, stop here and go back to Chapter 3.

Here are some differences between a manager and a leader to reflect on and become aware of:

- **Question Everything:** Managers take an order from the top and kick the can down the road. Leaders question everything, seek to disrupt the myth of normal, and are driven to change the future. The top can be at a corporation, on the soccer field, or meeting with a principal who says your child is a misfit because they learn differently.

- **Inquisitive Behaviors:** Managers check a box, but leaders get curious about what's in the box and if what's in it even makes sense. It's like the call center agent you get once in a blue moon who says, "You are right. This process doesn't make sense, so let me see what I can do." I've had this experience and told the agent, "Do you know you are a leader?" She was stunned and thrilled.

- **Turn Off Autopilot:** Managers are unconscious and are quick to judge and come to a conclusion; leaders are ruthlessly in the present moment and not on autopilot. They are curious and ask as many questions as they can.

- **Lean into Fears:** Managers have the mindset of "that's just the way it is; I don't have the power to change it." Leaders themselves are fearful and uncomfortable and do it anyway.

The planet is under a universal transformation. Quite literally, the molecules in the galaxy are in constant flux and motion, their changes unpredictable. In light of this perspective, let's contemplate why we engage in the following actions:

- Choosing to follow someone or make them the only source with an answer.
- Calling people experts and making them kings or queens.
- Taking a back seat to life and our futures and trusting that someone with a made-up title knows more than we do.
- Sticking our heads in the sand and letting so-called VPs, CEOs, heads of departments—who have been programmed from the industrial revolution and cookie-cutter school with behaviors, mindsets, and leadership styles that are from the assembly line—dictate our future.

Why? Because it is scary to choose on our own. It's so scary that we want someone else to tell us even if it limits us. We buy into these lies:

- They have 15 years of experience. (But at what, the assembly line?)
- They have an MBA, so they must know more. (Seriously, they read about outdated business practices, took a test, and passed; is this relevant? Plus, remember, the education structure is also a business.)

- There is no way I have the answer, and if I choose and I'm wrong, then I'll just blame someone (culture, company, leader).

In a world where people are pursuing employment at popular technology companies, the true pursuit should be finding the right leader. This leader will not only shape your future but also embody your values.

We often fall for the well-branded and marketed company that has reached the "best place to work for," when in reality those titles are often bought, skewed, and relative and are not an accurate representation of your values. Or we go with, "Well, they say company ABC is such a great company." But who are "they" exactly?

Here is the biggest lesson of all: Don't buy the hype. Choose wisely the leader you will be working for. You will not be working for the company; you will be working for that leader.

We also need to normalize asking, "Who is the leader you work for?" not "What company do you work for?"

I have had about 20 bosses and have led over 300 people in my career. I have noticed that I am at my best both in behavior and mindset, when leading a team, when I have an open, growth-mindset, compassionate leader above me. Other times, I've worked for a fixed-mindset, checkbox-focused inauthentic leader, and that impacted my career and growth and how I showed up as a leader. This is because behaviors are contagious.

Leaders make the culture—period, end of story. Leaders can make your energy expand and help you grow, or they can limit and shrink you.

You should actively seek out and directly request sponsorship from these leaders, rather than just seeking their mentorship. Demonstrate your value to them and ask if they would be willing to endorse and advocate for you when you're not present. It's crucial to carefully consider who you approach for sponsorship and ensure they possess the capability to do so.

Pen to Paper Homeplay: Tools and Exercises

Take time to reflect on the following questions:

1. Honestly and vulnerably look at yourself. Where do you spend most of your time? How do you show up and behave?

2. Look at the leader you report to or who you interact with the most—which behaviors do they exhibit?

3. If you behave in ways you don't desire to, are you being influenced by a person with a title and a box above you, and who behaves as a manager?

Then watch the TED Talk "To Get Ahead at Work, Get a Sponsor" by Carla Harris. Stay present, ask questions, and choose wisely.

Leadership Behaviors That Are Expansive	Manager Behaviors That Are Limiting
Inspires	Directs
Empowers	Controls
Collaborates	Dictates
Listens	Commands
Supports	Micromanages
Develops	Maintains
Innovates	Sticks to the status quo
Communicates	Instructs

Leadership Behaviors That Are Expansive	Manager Behaviors That Are Limiting
Builds trust	Fosters fear
Sets an example	Demands compliance
Recognizes achievements	Criticizes mistakes
Focuses on long-term goals	Focuses on short-term metrics
Embraces innovation	Prefers to be an order taker
Curious and open to learning	Resistant to change and new ideas
Courageous in taking risks	Prefers to stay within their comfort zone
Self-aware and present	Distracted and detached

Curious Questions Build Awareness

We talked in the previous chapter about building our awareness and making sure the people, places, and things we are choosing are aligned with where we are headed and with our values.

The only way to get to this is by asking questions.

Here are questions to know if the leader we will be working for is aligned with us. We can also use these questions to determine if a current leader is aligned with us, or if it is time to move on.

We can ask these during an interview, before working with someone, or in one-on-one meetings to assess leadership qualities:

1. How do you inspire and motivate your team members?

2. Can you provide an example of when you empowered your team to take ownership and make decisions?

3. How do you encourage collaboration and foster a sense of teamwork?

4. How do you approach listening to your team members and valuing their input?

5. How do you support the growth and development of your team members?

6. Can you share an example of how you have fostered innovation within your team or organization?

7. How do you communicate with your team members to ensure clarity and alignment?

8. How do you build trust among your team members and establish a culture of trustworthiness?

9. Can you describe a situation in which you set an example for your team to follow?

10. How do you recognize and celebrate the achievements and successes of your team members?

11. What percentage of time does the team spend on creativity and innovating versus on operations and running the company?

12. Get an idea of what is important to them: Ask, If I looked at your calendar, where do you spend most of your time at work? People spend most of their time on what they value. If I looked at your bank account, I could tell what you value based on where you spend your money.

13. Metrics drive behaviors: Ask, What metrics and measurements do you measure on? What metrics and measurements are the team measured on? If the metrics are vague, ask more questions about whether they are quality, volume, or

quantity based. If it's quality, then ask what the key qualities are measured on.

14. Ask them what their top 5 core values are personally, and their top 5 professionally. (If they are a deer in the headlights, you might want to give them this book!)

15. Find out their personality by asking where they spend their personal time. Depending on your life stage, you may want to look for someone who is more laid back and family oriented. You may desire someone who is growth oriented and always reading, listening to podcasts, attending leadership events. There is no right or wrong answer, just awareness.

16. Ask what their relationship is with their peers. What is their relationship with the leadership team? What works and what can be improved?

Additionally, these are questions we can ask ourselves when evaluating someone's leadership abilities if we already work for them:

1. Do they inspire and motivate me through their words and actions?

2. Do they empower others and encourage them to take initiative?

3. Are they collaborative and open to diverse perspectives?

4. Do they actively listen and value input from others?

5. Do they support my growth and development?

6. Are they open to new ideas and willing to take calculated risks?

7. Do they communicate effectively and ensure clarity in their instructions and expectations?

8. Do they foster a sense of trust and create a positive work environment?

9. Do they lead by example and demonstrate the behaviors they expect from others?

10. Do they recognize and appreciate achievements and successes?

11. Do I feel like I'm growing with them?

12. Do they have relationships with key individuals in the organization?

13. What is their reputation?

14. Do they take risks and have courage?

Remember, these questions are meant to guide our assessment and help us determine if someone possesses the leadership qualities we value.

The Biggest Question That Supersedes All Questions

Do they have an infinite or a finite mindset?

Simon Sinek's book *The Infinite Game* explores how adopting an infinite mindset can help leaders and organizations achieve long-term success. Infinite mindset leaders prioritize long-term goals, ongoing improvement, and creating sustainable success. They focus on collaboration, innovation, and adaptability.

On the other hand, finite mindset leaders have a short-term perspective, prioritize immediate wins, and often prioritize beating competitors. Infinite mindset leaders foster strong relationships, empower their teams, and aim for overall long-term success. In contrast, finite mindset leaders may focus on short-term gains and individual achievements.

The key difference lies in their mindset and approach to leadership. Infinite mindset leaders have a broader and more sustainable perspective. In contrast, finite mindset leaders prioritize short-term wins without considering the long-term implications.

Naturally, leaders from finite and infinite mindsets will approach the same issues quite differently. Consider the following:

Area	Finite Leadership Mindset	Infinite Leadership Mindset
Purpose	To win, beat competitors, and achieve short-term goals	To sustainably advance a cause or idea over the long term
Focus	Internal goals and metrics	External context and adapting to change
Mindset	Fixed, with an emphasis on controlling outcomes	Growth oriented, with an emphasis on learning and adaptability
Time horizon	Short term	Long term
Collaboration	Minimal collaboration outside of own organization	Collaboration and partnerships to advance the common cause
Risk	Risk-averse, focused on avoiding failure	Risk-tolerant, willing to take calculated risks to advance the cause
Communication	Emphasis on communicating success and achievements	Emphasis on sharing learning, failures, and adapting to change

Area	Finite Leadership Mindset	Infinite Leadership Mindset
Competition	Emphasis on beating competitors and winning	Emphasis on improving oneself and advancing the cause

Ask yourself, your leaders, and anyone you're in relationship with open-ended questions to understand which mindset they function from. Try to ask for examples and situations. It's important to note that leaders may exhibit characteristics of both mindsets at different times or in different situations, and that the most effective leaders are able to balance both mindsets as appropriate in a situation.

Choosing to Be a Conscious Human-Centered Leader

A human-centered conscious leader means prioritizing the well-being and growth of individuals while leading with being present and aware of this current reality. It involves recognizing the value and potential in each person and actively seeking to create a positive impact on their lives for the long term.

It also means playing an active role in hacking the autopilot programs and system and shifting to questioning and challenging the automatic thought patterns, beliefs, and behaviors we may have adopted without conscious awareness. It involves becoming more mindful and aware of our thoughts, emotions, and actions.

By breaking the programs, we can better understand ourselves and the world around us. This allows us to question societal norms, cultural conditioning, and personal biases that may limit our perspective or hinder personal growth.

We open ourselves up to new possibilities and expand our consciousness. We become more aware of the interconnectedness of everything, recognizing that our thoughts, actions, and choices have ripple effects not only in our own lives but also in the lives of others and the larger world.

As human-centered conscious leaders, we focus on fostering an inclusive and supportive work environment where everyone feels valued, respected, and empowered. We prioritize open communication, empathy, and active listening to understand the needs and perspectives of our team members.

This leadership approach also involves self-awareness and personal growth. It requires reflecting on our own values, beliefs, and behaviors, and making conscious choices that align with our principles. By continuously learning and developing ourselves, we set an example for others to follow and inspire them to do the same.

Being a human-centered conscious leader goes beyond just achieving business goals. It means recognizing each individual's inherent worth and potential, and striving to create an environment where they can thrive personally and professionally. It involves making decisions considering the greater good and the impact on the well-being of people, communities, and the planet.

Ultimately, choosing to be a human-centered conscious leader is a commitment to leading with compassion, empathy, and a genuine desire to make a positive difference in the lives of others. It's about recognizing that leadership is not just about authority and power but also serving and uplifting others to reach their full potential.

I will repeat this again and again. The cornerstone for unlocking your potential lies in understanding the *why*, which is meticulously detailed in Chapters 1 and 2. Without the audacity and courage to delve introspectively into your own trauma, identity, and the various myths and misconceptions you've embraced as reality, as elaborated in Chapters 3 through 7, we cannot construct a stable foundation. Only by comprehending this can we utilize the principles delineated in these final chapters.

Below are a few examples of the behaviors and actions associated with becoming a human-centered conscious leader:

Behavior	Action
Self-awareness	Reflect on values, beliefs, strengths, and areas for growth
Empathy and compassion	Actively seek to understand and connect with others, show care and concern
Active listening	Give full attention, suspend judgment, and validate others' experiences
People-centric mindset	Prioritize each individual's growth, development, and fulfillment
Accountability and feedback	Take responsibility, seek feedback, and embrace constructive criticism
Embracing diverse perspectives	Include people from different backgrounds and value diverse viewpoints
Avoiding echo chambers	Encourage open dialogue, challenge assumptions, and foster psychological safety
Continuous learning and growth	Prioritize personal development, challenge biases, and embrace a growth mindset

Behavior	Action
Building a future-oriented culture	Balance short-term metrics with long-term vision and purpose
Valuing relationships and collaboration	Cultivate positive relationships and collaborate with peers and leadership
Being self-aware and present	Practice self-awareness, active listening, and empathizing with others

The top 4 foundational choices to make to enable all of the behaviors and characteristics above are these:

1. Become Aware!

We can change anything we become aware of. We have to become ruthlessly present and pause and engage objectively. Why? Neuroscience has shown that 90% of what we do is unconscious; we don't know we are doing it. We go to the people we are comfortable with, and we promote the people we know.

A study conducted by MIT revealed that, when presented with otherwise identical résumés, candidates with names typically perceived as white received 50% more interview callbacks.

Set reminders—write a sticky note on your monitor, set an alarm, put it on your phone's lock screen.

2. Get Curious! Ask Questions!

Questions open a world of possibilities and conclusions, and judgments do not. Why? We are all wired for known comfort, and we want to be right.

Our assumptions and conclusions often stem from our personal experiences and perspectives, and this self-reflection extends to ourselves as well. It's remarkable how a single question can have the power to transform everything!

When we came to the US, I did not speak English. Couple that with the trauma I had experienced, and I became shy and introverted. I couldn't even ask for ketchup at the McDonald's counter. If you asked me to speak in a meeting in front of 5 people, I felt like I was going to vomit and die.

I had a leader that asked me a question. He asked me where I grew up. We got to a series of more questions. Although I had an inner confidence buried deep, I was outwardly shy because of my experiences. He then asked: how would you feel about leading the next team meeting? That little question led me to present at multiple meetings, give town hall presentations, present complex topics to the board, and eventually give keynotes, TED Talks, and write this book.

I hear people say all the time that they want to change the world or leave a legacy. Cool. Ask a question! One question makes people feel seen and cared for. One question can change a person's day. One question can change the trajectory of a person's entire life, like it did mine.

3. Ask, Is This Even My Point of View?

Or did I buy it as mine from news, media, parents, friends? You will find through this exercise that 80% of your "stuff" is not yours. You're buying it as yours because of an old boss, a toxic culture you worked in 10 years ago. Keep in mind as I said before—as babies, we come here with nothing! A clear slate. And we think, *Whoa, how do they do it in this weird place called earth?* Then we start collecting points of view like luggage. Ask, *Is this mine, or is it a program I have bought into?*

4. Build Compassion Muscle. Expand Your View. Get Out of the Box.

Read books you normally would not read. Listen to a podcast where your initial reaction is *meh*. Have a cup of coffee with someone who is from another country or speaks another language. Visit a country that isn't popular on Instagram or Facebook. Instead of a cruise, go on a tour with a local and understand the history and experiences of the local culture. I promise it will change your view. Ask questions you normally would not, like, "Where are you from?" or "How was the experience?" or "What do you do when you are not working?"

We can choose to get to know people—the whole person, not just their title and what they do at work. We will uncover aspects of people that will make them feel included and unique.

These all work together. If we stay present and aware, we can be curious and courageous enough to ask a question and challenge our outdated points of view and beliefs, and then naturally we will expand our lenses, build our muscles of compassion and empathy, and get out of our boxes.

When we dare to become uncomfortable and get off autopilot, we step into true leadership that contributes to changing our world and future.

Consciously Regain the Creativity We Had as Kids

As Brené Brown teaches us, "There is no such thing as creative people and non-creative people. There are only people who use their creativity and people who don't." To consciously regain the creativity we had as kids, we need to summon the courage to behave differently and embrace more of our authentic selves, just as we did when we were our younger, more creative selves.

Non-Creative Behavior Is Learned and Can Be Unlearned!

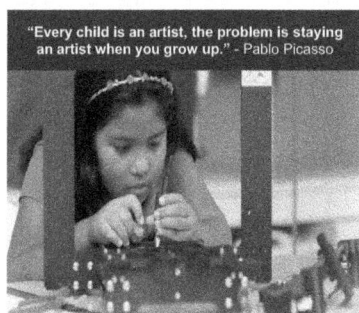

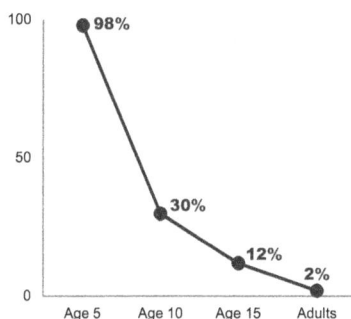

"Every child is an artist, the problem is staying an artist when you grow up." - Pablo Picasso

100 — 98%
50
30%
12%
2%
0
Age 5   Age 10   Age 15   Adults

Source: George Land and Beth Jarman, Breakpoint and Beyond: Mastering the Future Today

If you research the most innovative companies or leaders in the world, you will find key behaviors and traits, and what is interesting is all of the qualities they touch on is what we once naturally had as children.[50]

Here they are:

1. **Connect the Dots:** What did you do when you were little and creating? I watch my 7-year-old niece Lana create; she'll take glitter, glue, crayons, and Legos and connect everything together. She's a true creative genius, finding unique ways to bring different elements together and make something special. Her imaginative spirit is truly inspiring! She connects every dot possible. We all once had that!

2. **Embrace the "Why":** It's fascinating to think about how we used to be filled with wonder and ask a million "whys" as children. When did we stop questioning things like why the sky is blue? Embracing that childlike curiosity can bring a sense of awe and discovery back into our lives. So let's reignite that spirit of curiosity and start asking those "whys" once again!

3. **Discover through Empathic Observing:** As kids, we had this incredible ability to discover and learn through empathic observing. We would keenly observe the world around us, paying attention to the smallest details and immersing ourselves in the experiences of others. It allowed us to understand and connect with different perspectives, fostering a deeper sense of empathy. By tapping into that childlike quality of empathic observing, we can rekindle our curiosity and gain valuable insights that lead to greater understanding and growth.

4. **Experiment, Fail, Learn, Repeat:** As kids, we fearlessly approached new things, watching, observing, and seeing how they worked. Even if we fell off our bikes, getting bruises and bleeding, we didn't care because we were determined to try again and learn from our experiences. That resilience and willingness to embrace failure as part of the learning process is something we can bring back into our lives.

Companies like Apple, Tesla, Airbnb, eBay, PayPal, Uber, and Amazon came to life by connecting the dots and building upon existing innovations. Amazon, for example, didn't invent e-commerce or the supply chain. Still, they brilliantly connected the dots between these 2 existing concepts and focused on improving customer needs. They found a way to make online shopping convenient, efficient, and customer centric.

Similarly, Uber questioned the traditional expensive taxi model and asked why it couldn't be more accessible and affordable. Steve Jobs observed his daughter using a clunky, big Walkman and saw an opportunity to create something better, which eventually led to the development of the iPod. These companies exemplify the power of connecting existing ideas, observing customer needs, and innovating to provide improved solutions. It's about identifying opportunities and finding creative ways to address them, rather than inventing entirely new concepts.

Like when we were kids, connecting the dots and being innovative is all about embracing our natural curiosity, fearlessness, and creativity. As children, we had this innate ability to see possibilities, ask questions, and combine different ideas without being bound by conventional thinking.

We weren't afraid to try new things, make mistakes, and learn from them, and as adults, we can tap into that childlike mindset and regain the qualities that made us such natural innovators. By staying curious, observing the world around us, and being open to making connections, we can discover unique solutions and approaches to problems. Embracing a playful and adventurous attitude allows us to think outside the box, take risks, and explore uncharted territories.

So let's bring back that childlike wonder and creativity, and approach life with the same excitement and eagerness to explore and connect the dots. By doing so, we can unlock our inner innovator and positively impact the world around us.

Imagine if each of us had the courage to authentically express who we are and inspired others to do the same.

CHAPTER 11

Fear Is a Reaction, Courage Is a Choice: Embracing the Power of Bravery

"She's very quiet in class, won't make eye contact, and hides in the playground alone during recess. She's also not understanding English very well. We're not sure what to do, but we might have to hold her back."

—*My preschool teacher to my mother*

Our caveman brains are hardwired to prioritize survival, which manifests as an instinctual aversion to pain and discomfort. This fear-based response was vital for our ancestors in avoiding immediate threats, such as predators. In today's world, the threats we encounter are generally less life threatening but more psychologically complex.

Fear is often our instinctive response to unfamiliar situations, even those that could ultimately benefit us. It's crucial to acknowledge that in most everyday circumstances, fear is exaggerated and can be disguised as growth.

The antidote to fear lies in vulnerability, a concept rooted in the Latin word *vulnerare*, meaning "to wound." Vulnerability entails courageously exposing our wounds and shedding light on the hidden corners harboring shame, judgment, trauma, and abandonment.

As we discussed in Chapter 4, the silent epidemic of trauma often triggers subconscious reactions, such as unfounded fears and self-judgment. It's essential to understand that these fears, deeply ingrained in our human psyche, encompass a range of emotions, including fear of death, failure, rejection, the unknown, and loss.

These fears are frequently underpinned by psychological elements stemming from a desire for approval and love or the need for acceptance and connection. These fears are fundamentally linked to our longing for belonging, security, and self-preservation.

To navigate the complexities of the human experience, it's imperative to become aware of, understand, and address these fears, rather than constantly reacting to them.

Growing up as an immigrant, my fear of rejection led me to remain invisible in a new culture. Overcoming this fear involved taking small steps to find my voice, ultimately leading to giving a TED Talk and speaking vulnerably in various public settings.

A valuable lesson I learned is that fear and excitement can sometimes feel remarkably similar—the racing heart, sweating, and quickened breathing. In moments of anxiety, ask yourself, "Am I scared or excited?" Then, take a small step forward and embrace it. I now call this sensation "SCARECITED!"

I've observed that the more willing we are to be authentic and seen, the more we inspire others to do the same, particularly in professional and corporate environments where many conceal their true selves to fit in.

This is a vital skill and tool to equip yourself with within the corporate environment, which often operates on a foundation of fear. Without presence and awareness, you risk becoming entangled as a cog in the wheel of the machinery.

As mentioned in Chapter 1, various aspects of the corporate world, such as HR protocols, salary ranges, performance metrics, and the stigma associated with employment gaps in a résumé, are intentionally crafted to trigger fear responses.

In such an environment, breaking free from reactive patterns and self-limiting behavior becomes even more imperative.

If you sift through the misconceptions highlighted in Chapter 1, it becomes evident that the system is designed to exploit our unconscious fears, many of which are groundless. To illustrate this, consider the insurance industry, a trillion-dollar sector primarily focused on capitalizing on our fears and uncertainties.

The corporate structure is organized to keep us in a perpetual state of concern about performance reviews, meeting expectations, promotion prospects, and fitting into the corporate culture. These fears can be crippling and hinder personal growth and fulfillment. It's essential to acknowledge this construct and actively strive to discern what is genuine and authentic.

Fear Is an Unconscious Reaction Designed to Control Us

If we are not present, fear is a reaction that limits our lives, potentials, and possibilities. Courage to become aware and stare fear in the face and choose to change it is something we all have the power to choose.

Fear is a natural reaction that often stems from our need to be in control, seek structure, and maintain a sense of security. It triggers our instinct to run, hide, avoid, defend, or resist.

Our unconscious programs, also known as deeply ingrained patterns of thinking and behavior, play a significant role in shaping our reactions. These programs are often formed through our past experiences, conditioning, and beliefs without us consciously realizing it. They act as automatic filters through which we perceive and interpret the world around us.

If we are not present, we end up recreating our entire lives based on a "fear" that is no longer even present or relevant. We allow it to distract us from creating our lives in the present.

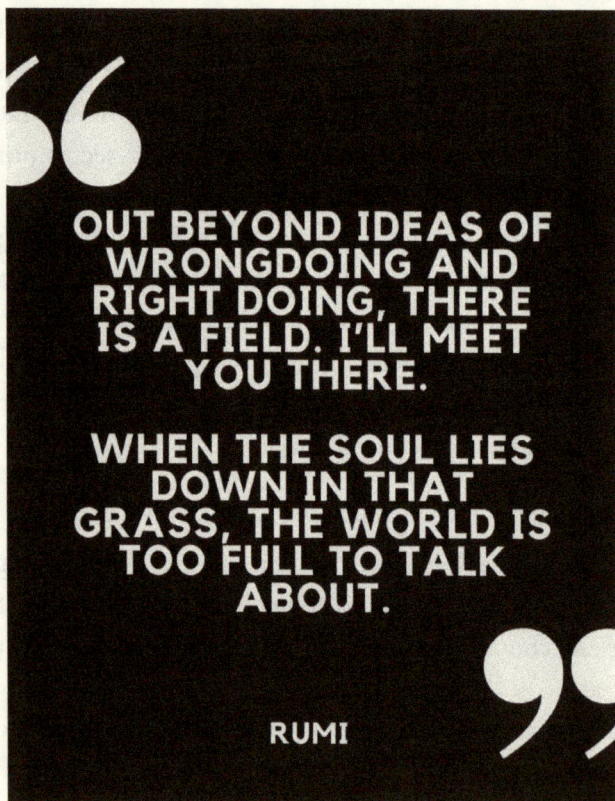

> OUT BEYOND IDEAS OF WRONGDOING AND RIGHT DOING, THERE IS A FIELD. I'LL MEET YOU THERE.
>
> WHEN THE SOUL LIES DOWN IN THAT GRASS, THE WORLD IS TOO FULL TO TALK ABOUT.
>
> RUMI

Recognizing that many emotions are rooted in fear can be a helpful step in understanding and addressing them. Jealousy, for example, often stems from a fear of not being good enough or of losing something or someone important to us. It's a common human experience to compare ourselves to others and worry about our own worth or abilities.

Other emotions that we react to, like anger, judgment, over-thinking, and self-doubt, can also be linked to underlying fears. Anger can stem from a fear of injustice or a perceived threat to our well-being. Judgment can arise from a fear of being judged our-selves or from a fear of the unknown. Overthinking can be driven by a fear of making mistakes or facing negative consequences. Self-doubt often originates from a fear of failure or rejection.

By identifying the underlying fears, we can develop self-aware-ness, self-compassion, and strategies to overcome or manage those fears.

Here is a list of common, unconscious reactions to fear:

- Anger
- Judgment
- Overthinking
- Procrastination
- Anxiety
- Guilt

- Shame
- Frustration
- Sadness
- Resentment
- Jealousy
- Defensiveness

- Self-doubt
- Perfectionism
- Avoidance
- Nervousness
- Impatience
- Irritation

Fear Is Actually Our Unwillingness to Be Out of Control

Fear represents the deep-seated human desire to control our world. Back in the caveman days our ancestors relied on fear to inform them of oncoming danger. They used it to interpret the presence of a nearby predator or to sense the signs of an oncoming natural disaster. In the modern world we have translated fear into our unwillingness to be out of control. It can show up as modern-day fears:

- "Will my boss think I'm an idiot and fire me?"
- "Will my wife find someone better?"
- "What will they think of me?"

Translation these into needing control:

- "I want to control what people think of me."
- "I want to control my wife so that she doesn't leave."
- "I want to control how I am seen or how much I am seen."

The last one is a big one. We often blame others for not seeing us, yet how much do we unconsciously actually control being seen? How much do we unconsciously put our walls and barriers up and hide ourselves because it's more comfortable? Then we blame others for not seeing us. We create these catch-22 situations so we can be right again about not being seen and replay childhood stories in adult bodies.

Then, we unconsciously pull in people and situations that will make us right—"See, I'm not seen again," or "See, they excluded me again."

I'm not saying the environment doesn't need to be "psychologically safe" to allow the space for us to un-hide and show up. Yet we are as usual swinging the pendulum to the extreme, based on the latest trendy research that places the focus on someone else and something else. The only way we can truly change things is through the person in the mirror.

Imagine the world we would have if everything was a journey in accountability and looking in the mirror and asking, "How am I creating this?" "What can I change?" "What different choice can I make here?"

Build awareness of your fears and things you are trying to control. Control and fear are distractions that keep us from moving ahead and creating possibilities.

Even though I had a crazy journey, I was so scared of losing stability again that I chose at one time to stay for ten years at a job I wasn't happy with and in a relationship for eleven years that wasn't working. I was desperately controlling the narrative, creating a false sense of comfort and limiting myself. We all do this in at least one area of our lives. Why? To fit in. To seem normal.

We then take advice from people who have the same fears. Here is a really big secret: people are afraid that if we choose to let go of our fears, be out of control, un-hide, and choose for ourselves, then they will have to look in the mirror at their own choices. Their own autopilot choices. Their own unhappiness. Of course, this is not conscious (well, not all the time). It includes our parents, friends, and partners.

We buy into a false sense of control to manage our fears. This is why we choose limitation. We have to look at everyone in our life and ask if they are actually contributing to our creating greater or to our need to control and fears. Is this boss, colleague, organization, friend, or partner adding to my expansion or to my contraction and limitation?

The need for control is often a by-product of fear and creates major limitations. It's often reflected in behaviors such as micromanaging, aggression, being overly nice and agreeable, perfectionism, exclusion of others, linear thinking, status quo mindsets, and more. These behaviors can be our biggest fears in disguise.

In the past, I struggled with speaking publicly and being seen—as in really being seen for all of me. It was a childhood program I picked up. This resulted in my exerting excessive perfectionism.

Humans possess an inherent addiction to control, which can be limiting as it often leads to unconscious efforts to evade judgment, rejection, conformity to predefined norms, and failure. The reality is that most of these fears are unfounded and untrue. We make them up! Ironically, we make them up to control ourselves or be controlled. Yes, to be controlled. Why?

So we can predict the future, even if it means limiting our growth and capabilities.

The need for control is a fundamental human need that enables us to navigate the world around us. This need can become overwhelming at times and manifest in various behaviors that can negatively affect our lives. There are deep-seated fears that frequently underlie the need for control. Below are points on how courageous leaders overcome them, with tools and questions you can use to become more aware of them. These principles apply not just to the workplace but also to personal life and relationships.

Additional common fears that underlie our desire for control, whether it's self-control or being controlled by others, include:

- **Fear of Failure:** Perfectionism and the need to always be good, right, and celebrated or to avoid disappointing anyone. The fear of making mistakes or not meeting expectations can lead to a need to control details, other people's perceptions of you, or your image to ensure success. This often stems from childhood, where you felt unseen unless you achieved perfect grades, excelled in athletics, and attended the perfect college.

- **Fear of Losing Power or Influence:** We are conditioned as a society to present an image to the outside world (titles, salary, spouse, and 2.5 kids). We believe that this image is our identity. Losing control over a situation, group, or our image can lead to the feeling of losing everything and everyone and shattering everything we imaged up—hence, the need to control.

- **Fear of Vulnerability:** In almost everyone vulnerability triggers and masks the deep-rooted fear of exposing their wounds. In the workplace, for example, the "mask of masculinity" for men and the facade of faux allyship for women act as defense mechanisms that mask deeper feelings of shame and abandonment. This becomes particularly pronounced in emotionally restrictive corporate settings. Here, the fear of vulnerability intensifies and manifests in control-oriented behaviors which makes them think they are protected by a false shield while perpetuating a cycle that keeps them emotionally walled off and the connection and creativity out.

- **Fear of Uncertainty:** We remain in workplaces that no longer support our growth, or with partners, bosses, and personal relationships that are mundane and ordinary so that we feel safe and keep our lives predictable. Fearing the unknown can lead to our need for control to create a sense of stability, so we remain in places and with people who don't support our growth, simply so we can have what we call "certainty."

- **Fear of Judgment and Rejection:** We are hardwired to be part of a tribe, and we frequently give into the false fear of rejection. Therefore, simply to fit in, we give into things that are projected onto us and are not true for us. What we often do not realize is that by doing this we are actually rejecting ourselves from possibilities.

Pen to Paper Homeplay: Tools and Exercises

We all have hidden fears that we often conceal. What's yours? If you believe you don't have any, the limitations or walls that seem to constantly appear in your life and that you are unable to change may be your starting point for self-awareness.

The antidote to fear and to making a real change in our lives is becoming very aware of our actions and having compassion for ourselves and others. It also takes courage to face and overcome the hidden fears that often hold us back from creating the future we want.

To start today, try the following:

1. **Identify and Address Underlying Fears:** Through self-reflection, recognize and acknowledge the fears that drive the need for control.

2. **Develop Self-Awareness:** Practice observing thoughts and behaviors and recognize when the need for control arises.

3. **Build Trust:** Trust yourself and others and become comfortable relinquishing control when appropriate.

4. **Seek Feedback:** Actively seek feedback and constructive criticism from others. Know when something is true versus when something is actually judgment from someone trying to control you.

5. **Embrace Vulnerability:** Dip your toe into becoming more comfortable being vulnerable and admitting mistakes.

Here are some tools you can use to help you in the moment or during reflection:

1. **Pause:** When you feel the need to control, ask yourself these questions:

a. What is my biggest fear here? Ask it 5 times to get to the actual deep fear. The acknowledgment of it will be the first step to setting you free.

b. What just got triggered? How old am I being? When you notice a trigger, take a moment to consider what's causing it. Reflect on how old you feel in that moment and think about which age from your childhood you might be reenacting. Try to pinpoint when you've experienced similar feelings before.

c. How can I reframe this fear and story into a positive one? (For example, vulnerability is a sign of strength, not weakness.)

2. **Pause:** When you feel controlled by someone or something, ask yourself:

a. What is their biggest fear here? Try to walk a mile in their shoes from their perspective.

b. What just got triggered in them? If someone else appears triggered, take a moment to consider what might have caused their reaction. Reflect on how old they might feel in that moment.

c. Can I help them change this? Is there space to talk to them? If there is no space to talk to them, just let it go and don't take it personal or be controlled by it.

Remember, true control and power come from challenging your thoughts, beliefs, behaviors, choices, responses, values, and goals.

Don't let fears, limitations, or childhood programs hold you back. By identifying and addressing your underlying fears, practicing self-awareness, building trust with yourself and others, seeking feedback, and embracing vulnerability, you can overcome the need for control and become a more effective and compassionate leader.

Become Aware of Our Autopilot Programs

Becoming aware of these unconscious programs is the first step toward managing and transforming our reactions. It allows us to question the validity of our automatic responses and explore alternative perspectives. Constantly running away, hiding, or avoiding our reactions such as fear can limit our personal growth and prevent us from realizing our full potential.

Awareness is indeed the first step to facing any reaction. When we become aware of our fears, we gain insight into the thoughts, emotions, and sensations associated with them. This self-awareness allows us to identify and acknowledge the specific fears that are holding us back or causing distress.

By bringing our fears into conscious awareness, we create an opportunity to examine them more closely. We can explore the root causes of our fears, understand how they manifest in our lives, and recognize their impact on our well-being and choices.

Awareness also helps us recognize patterns or triggers contributing to our fears. It allows us to observe how fear affects our thoughts, behaviors, and relationships. With this understanding, we can start challenging and reframing our fearful beliefs, gradually shifting our perspective and reducing the hold fear has on us.

We can only change what we have the courage to look at, become aware of, and face head on. Here are some steps to build awareness:

1. **Reflect:** Take time to think about your thoughts, emotions, and behaviors.
2. **Be Present:** Practice mindfulness to observe your experiences without judgment.

3. **Journal:** Write down your thoughts, fears, and experiences.

4. **Seek Feedback:** Ask trusted individuals for their insights on your patterns.

5. **Educate Yourself:** Read and learn about self-awareness and personal growth.

Looking at fears takes warrior-status courage and is not by any means easy. This is why most of us avoid looking at this in our lives. Or we defend our choices. But remember, anything we avoid or defend keeps us comfortably stuck and numb and limits our awareness and ability to change it, and this ultimately keeps us from reaching our true capacity to thrive.

True Confidence Is Having Courage to Not Buy Fear as Real

I'd like now to return to a question we discussed at the beginning of this book: *How hard can it be to go up to the counter at McDonald's and ask for ketchup? The answer might depend on how confident you are in English.*

How confident are you with anything unknown? How willing are you to learn? How willing are you to put yourself out there to be seen? To be vulnerable and expose your wounds? How willing are you to use your voice? How willing are you to be judged? To be rejected?

True confidence is feeling fear and leaning in, not buying the distraction as real and moving forward anyway!

Sometimes trauma can leave people irreversibly damaged. Other times trauma can inadvertently fuel a fire to impact your world and make a difference in the lives of others. The key is to recognize it, let the story go, and then ask questions. OK, this was my experience, now I am aware, and what can I choose? How can I change this? What small step can I take tomorrow?

Building confidence is like strengthening a muscle. You cannot step out of fear once a year and think you will build up your confidence. That is like thinking you can work out once and be lean and fit. It requires consistent effort, failure, looking stupid, practicing, and repeating the cycle over and over.

When we choose courage over fear, we step outside our comfort zones and challenge ourselves to grow. We learn to navigate through uncertainty, take risks, and embrace new experiences.

I'm an athlete, and I can tell you any new athletics I took on (in the gym, running, cycling, yoga, swimming, etc.), was uncomfortable. You will look stupid at first! You will fail! You will be judged! The voice that says *you're not good enough* can come back and take you back to old wounds. Yet each time we face our fears and choose courage, our confidence grows stronger.

As a child it felt like death to me to even walk up to a McDonald's counter and cut in front of the line and loudly ask, "Can I please have some ketchup?" Literal death! My English was terrible, and I had already decided I was doomed to be forever shy. As we discussed in the trauma chapter, I carried my childhood wounds of escaping a war, having machine guns in my face, into a McDonald's, as silly as it sounds.

I would have that same feeling of death and shyness as an adult in my interactions. I looked tall, strong, attractive, and confident as an adult, yet inside I walked around as a scared little girl afraid to ask for ketchup.

How many of us have a moment from our childhoods that we are replaying as adults? Can you be vulnerable and look at moments in your childhood or past that have the same story or energy tied to them that you might be replaying as an adult?

For me, it was facing what I called "shyness" that was actually the "lack of willingness to be seen." I could have sat there and wondered *why me*, but instead I made a choice to change it. I chose to have the courage to un-hide me.

As I embarked on my journey, I decided to make the choice to take incremental steps to break this cycle. I realized this limitation would not work if I desired to thrive in the workplace.

So I made a list and asked questions:

1. What are all the small, possible choices and actions I could take to begin to break this?

2. What would my life look like in 5 to 10 years if I didn't choose this?

3. What would my life look like in 5 to 10 years if I did choose this?

4. What is the absolute worst that would happen if I took these steps and failed?

Real confidence involves making a myriad of small choices. It requires being our authentic selves and welcoming judgment, even if it leads to short-term discomfort.

Creating confidence also involves taking small steps toward personal growth while embracing vulnerability and self-acceptance, as well as being willing to risk judgment, rejection, and loss as part of the equation. True confidence is created when we trust that the leaps we take, regardless of the outcome, set us up for the future we desire to create.[51]

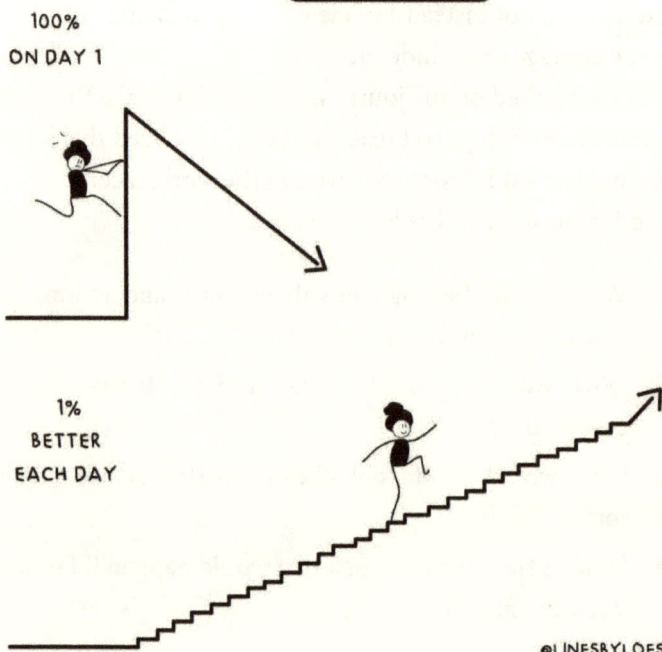

NEW HABITS

100%
ON DAY 1

1%
BETTER
EACH DAY

@LINESBYLOES

Taking Incremental Steps to Being Seen

I was into sports and fitness, so I decided it was safe for me to try new things having to do with athletics. I started taking spin classes, which I had never tried. I became pretty good at and asked the instructor how she became a teacher. I had no idea at the time, but she was the fitness manager at my local gym and invited me to become certified and teach at the gym. My small action led to even bigger action.

The universe shows up for us when we choose to change things and take action. This entire thing that may seem small over weeks and months ended up elevating my confidence by 1% at each step. It melted 1% of my shyness and fears, and I un-hid a tiny part of me.

I found 99 more of these little challenges that took weeks and months and in some cases years to get to 90% confidence level. I say 90% because I don't think we ever fully get to 100%. I failed and looked pretty stupid along the way, and I was looked at funny and judged. I fell, I cried, I felt exhausted, I gave myself time to rest and recover, and then I chose to keep going.

Learn to follow your own path. As I progressed and figured out that I needed to get better at speaking up and being seen, everyone shared what they did and what I should do. Going to speaking classes or training sounded boring and like an untrue path for me. Fitness and teaching spin classes was one choice that helped me build my confidence muscle to go from having the fear to ask for ketchup at a McDonald's counter to being able to give keynotes and TED Talks.

I had the realization that when it came to sports, fitness, and athletics I was really good at setting a goal or vision, taking small steps, learning and adjusting and repeating. So I transferred that to my willingness to be seen and heard.

When we set a vision or goal we must allow it to expand, morph, and change into something we never expected. We almost have to believe in this thing we used to believe in as children called *magic*!

I never set out to do a TED Talk; all I set out to do was break my limitation and fear of using my voice and being seen. All I set out to do was be heard in meetings and at work.

At the time I had no idea what TED even was. I literally said to the person asking me, "Who is Ted and why does he want to talk to me?" (FYI, TED stands for Technology, Entertainment, and Design.)

She said they wanted me to talk about technology in front of about 500 people. Before I could answer, she added that it would be recorded on YouTube as well.

There was the death and vomit sensation I mentioned. I felt like Ketchup Girl all over again. My reaction was *no way*, yet in that moment I chose to pause.

I made a conscious choice to remain in the moment, realizing that this was a chance to embrace something bigger and shatter my comfort zone to a degree I had never before considered or requested from the universe. I softly whispered, "Sure . . ." and suddenly, a new vision and goal emerged, one that I had no clue how to approach. I had approximately 4 months to prepare, even though I was clueless about the path forward.

In my initial approach to the presentation, I followed the standard corporate protocol, complete with a well-structured script and PowerPoint, relying on the frameworks endorsed by many costly experts.

The TED team's response, however, was enlightening. They encouraged me to engage with people on a human level rather than treating them as mere cogs in the corporate machinery. This lesson was invaluable and mirrors the insights I share in this book.

When we converse naturally, we don't rigidly insert emotions or stick to a formulaic structure; we go with the flow. We speak like humans not like robots.

What we often overlook is that we have been programmed to hide behind established conventions or corporate jargon specific to our industries. It's essential not to operate on autopilot based on what may have worked for others. Instead, present as a genuine human being!

Learn from what works for you; do not go into autopilot and use what works for others. Mix and match modalities and read into what is unique for you. Remember Bruce Lee's words: "Adapt what is useful, reject what is useless, and add what is specifically your own."

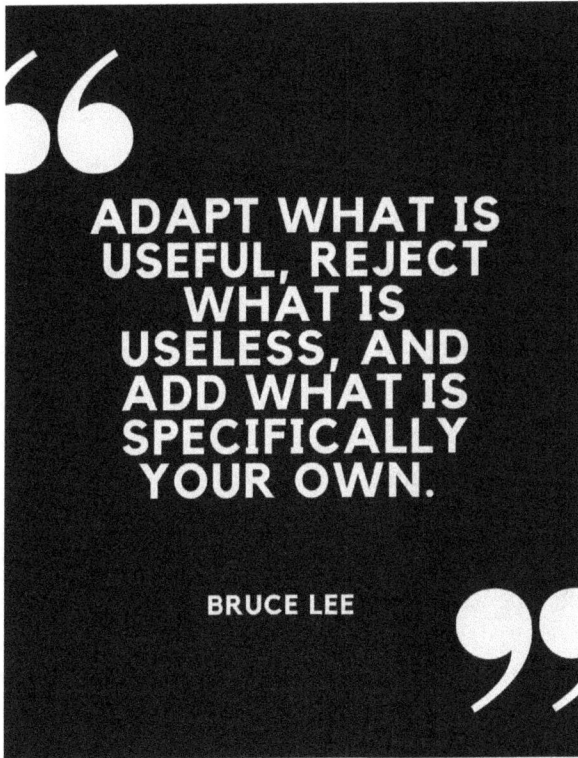

> **ADAPT WHAT IS USEFUL, REJECT WHAT IS USELESS, AND ADD WHAT IS SPECIFICALLY YOUR OWN.**
>
> BRUCE LEE

The pathway to genuine connection with others is through being the vulnerable you, not an image of you. Whether in personal relationships or professional settings, the crux of impactful interaction lies in your willingness to be seen and heard for who you truly are.

Sure, some won't like you, some will judge you and reject you, and yet that is how you know you are being more of you!

Embracing vulnerability to be truly seen and heard starts with self-compassion, acknowledging that you're human and imperfect. Counterbalance negative thoughts with affirming beliefs that align with your true worth. Accept that universal approval isn't the end goal; authentic self-expression is. Finally, celebrate each little instance in which you manage to be vulnerable, as this builds both confidence and resilience, paving the way for more genuine connections.

Trust Yourself! No One Is Going Where You Are

We often seek validation from others when making decisions, but it's important to consider if their perspectives align with your unique experiences, path, vision, and desires. Building confidence begins with trusting yourself. This involves believing in your abilities, making decisions with conviction, and recognizing your worthiness.

To build confidence and get comfortable with being seen, honor yourself by acknowledging your inherent worth and strengths. Your differences!

Make a demand and a commitment and take incremental steps to build confidence:

1. **Step Outside Your Comfort Zone:** Identify very small challenges and gradually expand your boundaries. It could be as simple as speaking to someone in the grocery store line to be seen and see and acknowledge them.

2. **Get Creative and Ask Questions:** Identify areas in your life where you can start with familiar tasks, such as coaching your child's soccer league.

3. **Set Achievable Goals:** Break larger goals into manageable steps to build confidence and momentum. Don't make your

goal something that is too far out of reach; for example, when I had the vision of running a marathon someday, I set my targets and goals around first running a 5k and worked up from there.

4. **Embrace Failure as a Learning Opportunity:** View set-backs as valuable lessons and adjust your approach accordingly. Whatever you do, don't waste time in self-judgment and pity. Find the nugget of wisdom in what you learned and quickly move on.

5. **Practice Self-Compassion:** Treat yourself with kindness and celebrate your strengths and accomplishments. Talk to the 7-year-old in you.

6. **Surround Yourself with Positive Influences:** Seek support from those who believe in you and inspire you. Stay away from those that judge or say things like, "That's crazy, why are you doing that?" Trust me—those with similar big goals have zero interest in demeaning yours.

7. **Visualize Success:** Imagine yourself confidently overcoming obstacles and achieving your goals.

Be patient, celebrate small victories, and maintain a positive mindset. Many that know me today would say my confidence, determination, and heart stand out as my strengths. They only see the tip of the iceberg; they do not know the tears, the struggles, the pain, the fear, the doubt, the paralyzing self-critical judgment. The sheer terror in trying to speak up and use my voice. I'm living proof it can be done.

We can all choose to come out of hiding, stand in our power, and use our voices to not only change the deck of cards we were dealt but to inspire others to do the same. To do this requires us to (you guessed it) become present and aware.

So remember, fear is a reaction, courage is a choice, and confidence is a muscle that grows when we actively confront our fears and embrace the unknown. Through this process, we can develop true inner strength and achieve personal growth.

From Shyness to Strength and Resilience

As an immigrant who landed in a country where I did not fit in or belong, I was bullied and went through severe trauma that put me in a place of extreme shyness and made me scared of practically my own shadow. In that moment I had to choose. Choose to see the world from a lens of possibility or from one of cruelty and unkindness and limitations.

I opted for possibility! Overcoming obstacles and adopting an abundant mindset instead of succumbing to scarcity requires significant strength and resilience. Sometimes, all it takes is one individual who recognizes our potential and has faith in us to ignite a positive transformation.

It also taught me that, by persisting and taking one more step, out of a hundred people who may judge and reject you, one person can step in and change your life. In my case, it was a leader who had the courage to pose a question: "You are so intelligent, wise, and strong—how can I help you break your shyness and use your voice?"

I literally about dropped out of my chair when he said that. He opened space for me to share with him what I had never told anyone. That I had severe trauma and self-doubt. He said, "Cool, let's create small opportunities to change that."

He would turn to me in meetings, ask my thoughts, and give me the floor. He had me take 5 minutes in his presentation to present just one slide. He created small moments of confidence for me.

His one question changed the entire trajectory my life. It's one of the reasons you are reading this book.

More importantly, he taught me how to keep doing this for myself and how to do it for others. Interestingly, one part of your life can create confidence in the other. So start in your personal life and then let it build into the workplace. Here are some things you can try:

- **Focus on Strengths:** Identify and develop your strengths to boost confidence in your abilities.

- **Learn New Skills:** Acquiring new skills fosters a sense of accomplishment and belief in your capabilities.

- **Practice Positive Self-Talk:** Remind yourself of strengths and achievements, reframing negative thoughts.

- **Persevere:** Keep going despite judgment or rejection to build courage and attract supportive people.

- **Draw Inspiration from Others:** Learn from inspiring stories and role models to enhance your own courage.

- **Support Others:** Create confidence-building moments for those who struggle, inspiring positive change.

- **Remember:** your experiences shape you; sharing your story and taking courageous steps can inspire others.

The following are some key lessons I hope you will take with you:

- **Observe Your Thoughts:** Journal them and read out loud what you are saying to yourself. Ask: When did I buy this belief? From whom did I buy this from? Am I in an environment that breeds this? Is this really true for me? Identify a counter belief. Like "I will use my voice every day," or "I am confident."

- **Trust Your Own Knowing:** Stop looking to parents, society, bosses, friends to help you choose. Most people are just projecting onto you their own choices.

- **Fear Is a Need to Control Something:** It takes courage to truly recognize that we have control over very little. What people think of us, our identity, even death.

- **Celebrate Your Discomfort:** Make a list of all the micro-moments of discomfort you leaned into. Write out how you felt physically, mentally, and emotionally. What did you learn? How can you apply it to the next discomfort?

- **Take a Very Small Micro-Step:** Get creative. Ask: What would be a fun or creative way to lean into this fear of control?

- **Become Aware of Your Actions:** The action you took from being present versus on autopilot reacting. Celebrate it and take another one. Even if it wasn't perfect.

Pen to Paper Homeplay: Tools and Exercises

Get vulnerable with yourself and consider one fear you have. What is a micro-step you can take to help you get closer to accomplishing your big fear? Maybe it's one of these:

Fear Example	Courageous Micro-Step Example
Public speaking	Present in a meeting with 3 people
Being a leader	Coach your daughter's soccer team
Writing a book	Write a blog article

Hacking just one fear and false sense of control can change your life! Just like it did mine.

Courage to Use Your Voice

Have you ever felt the knot of fear tightening in your stomach when it comes to speaking up, especially in the workplace? It's a common experience. We often hold back, staying silent and invisible, afraid of the consequences.

But remember the title of this chapter: fear is just a reaction, and courage is a choice we can make.

Many people may not realize that every single one of us possesses the power to effect change. It all comes down to a choice.

This choice necessitates the courage to embrace discomfort, accept judgment, and even face rejection. It involves the bravery to be fully present, use our voices, and carefully select our words. Most of us shy away from this because we've been sold the idea that conformity—reciting the same phrases and adhering to norms—is the path to success and happiness.

When you do muster the courage, it's essential to believe in your own power. You must deliver your ideas or challenging questions with confidence and clarity rather than a soft tone or from a place of fear, doubt, or shame, which often manifests in phrases like "maybe," "I'm sorry," or "I don't know, but perhaps we should try X." Conversely, using anger and resistance with a chip on your shoulder can also be counterproductive.

In either extreme, when you deliver your message this way, it becomes challenging for others to truly hear you.

This I had to learn the hard way. It has nothing to do with gender, as many people will lead you to believe; it has to do with what you think of yourself, your courage to be seen, and the energy and language you use.

> # DAILY REMINDER
>
> ## IT ONLY TAKES ONE VOICE, AT THE RIGHT PITCH, TO START AN AVALANCHE.
>
> ### DIANNA HARDY

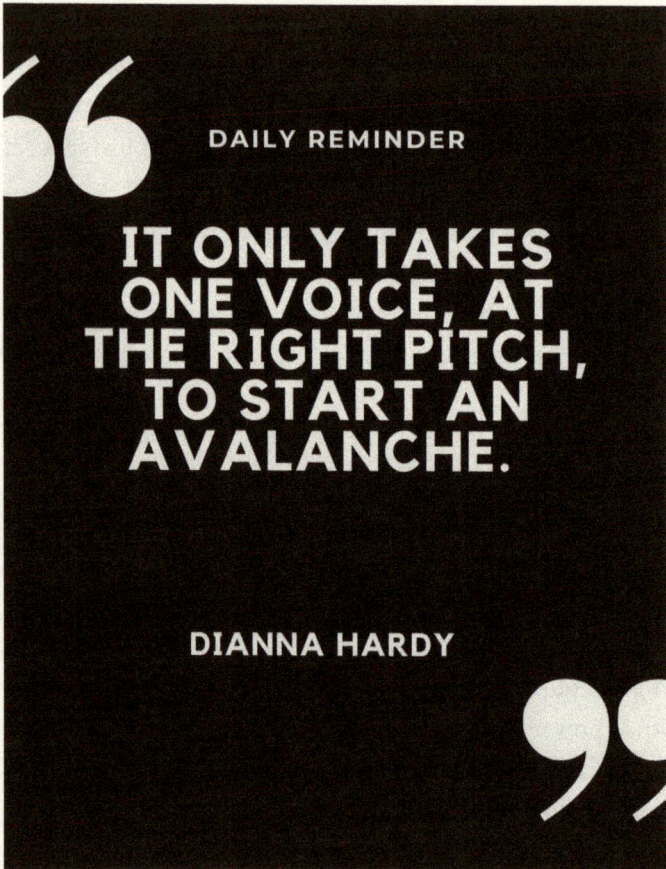

Once you've developed more self-confidence and trust in your own power, here are some tips to guide you in using your voice effectively:

- **Be Mindful of Body Language:** Stand tall, maintain an open posture, and make eye contact to convey confidence and assertiveness.

- **Develop Vocal Presence:** Speak with clarity, conviction, and a confident tone to ensure your message is impactful.

- **Release the Need for Approval:** Focus on expressing yourself genuinely without seeking universal likability.

- **Improve Delivery:** Pay attention to your physical actions, vocal elements, and language to enhance how your message is received.

- **Build Strategic Relationships:** Cultivate connections with influential colleagues who appreciate your ideas and can support your voice.

- **Use Deliberate Language:** Avoid filtering language, filler words, and softening phrases, to deliver your message directly and concisely.

- **Recognize the Power of Words:** Words have the ability to build trust, inspire loyalty, and lead effectively in both personal and professional realms. Be conscious of the impact and potential for miscommunication. When you repeat something enough, to yourself or aloud, it sooner or later will take hold not only in your own psyche but to all who hear you saying it.

There are several common words that can energetically disempower us and limit us in our thinking and actions. Throughout history many consciousness teachers and philosophers taught that thoughts become words, and words cast a spell of action into reality. It's true.

Here are a few examples. This one is from Access Consciousness:

- **"But":** This word can negate or discount previous statements, limiting our ability to see alternatives or possibilities.

- **"Why":** Excessive use of "why" can keep us stuck in analysis and prevent us from taking action.

- **"Try"**: Saying we'll "try" to do something implies a lack of commitment or belief in our ability to accomplish it.

- **"Can't"**: This word implies impossibility or a lack of capability, shutting down possibilities and limiting our potential.

- **"Should"**: Using "should" often imposes external expectations or judgments on ourselves or others, creating guilt or feelings of inadequacy.

- **"Never"**: When we use the word "never," we create a sense of absolute impossibility or permanence, closing off options and limiting our belief in what is achievable.

- **"Want"**: Solely focusing on what we "want" can create a sense of lack or dissatisfaction in the present moment, keeping us in a state of desire rather than taking action or appreciating what we already have.

Being mindful of these words and their impact can help us choose more empowering language that opens up possibilities, fosters growth, and supports a positive mindset.

Ask and Voice What You Desire

In the workplace context, it is crucial to understand that no one will read your mind and automatically provide you with the things you desire or deserve. It requires you to take the initiative, lean in, and have the courage to use your voice and ask for what you want. It may seem intimidating at first, but it is an essential skill to develop to achieve your goals and progress in your career.

When you voice your desires and express what you want, you open up opportunities for yourself. By articulating your needs, you allow others to understand your aspirations and help you achieve them. It's important to remember that asking for what you want does not guarantee immediate success but sets the foundation for progress.

It's important to acknowledge that hearing a "no" response should not discourage you. A no doesn't necessarily mean a permanent rejection. It could simply mean "not right now" or "I don't currently have the courage or power to fulfill your request." It might also signal that you need to improve your value or find more effective ways to communicate your desires.

By using your voice and being open about your ambitions, you are taking an active role in shaping your career path. It demonstrates confidence, assertiveness, and a willingness to pursue opportunities. Don't let fear hold you back from voicing your desires. Remember that it's better to ask and be told no than to never ask at all and miss out on potential growth and advancement.

Ultimately, the workplace is a dynamic environment where progress is often driven by those who are willing to step forward and assert themselves. By using your voice to express your desires and aspirations, you can create a path toward professional fulfillment and maximize your potential for success.

Give Up Resistance, Reaction, Alignment, and Agreement

There may be some of you, like me, who always had some level of awareness about the corporate environment and the list of lies and misconceptions, and to counteract it you decided to resist, react, and even fight like I did. Or maybe you are just starting to realize that you aligned and agreed with all of this and bought it all as true.

The true goal is neutrality to all of it. In other words, becoming so aware that none of it bothers you. When we talk about not resisting, not reacting, not fighting, and not aligning or agreeing, we delve into the realm of nonattachment.

As Carl Jung wrote, "What you resist not only persists but will grow in size." Resisting means pushing against or forcefully eliminating what we find challenging. Instead of expending energy in resistance, we can adopt an attitude of acceptance, acknowledging the reality of the situation without judgment or resistance.

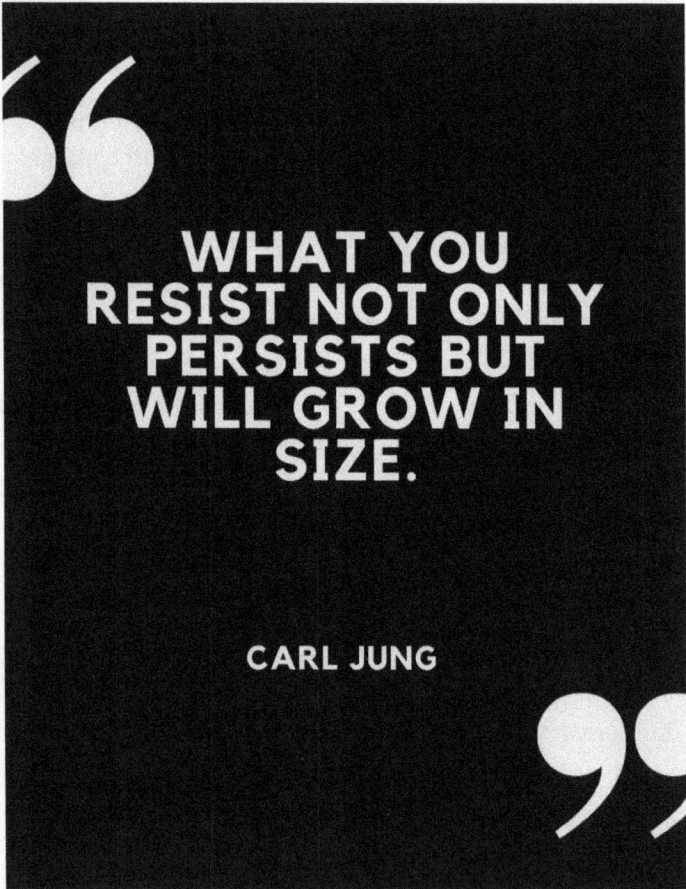

> **WHAT YOU RESIST NOT ONLY PERSISTS BUT WILL GROW IN SIZE.**
>
> **CARL JUNG**

Not reacting involves stepping back from impulsive or knee-jerk responses. It means observing our emotions, thoughts, and impulses without immediately acting upon them. By cultivating a sense of mindfulness and self-awareness, we can choose more deliberate and constructive responses.

Not aligning with everyone signifies the importance of maintaining an independent perspective and not blindly conforming to others' opinions or beliefs. It encourages critical thinking, questioning, and respectfully expressing differing viewpoints. By doing so, we can foster intellectual growth, innovation, and the potential for finding more well-rounded solutions.

By letting go of resistance, impulsive reactions, and the need for agreement, we can cultivate inner peace, better navigate conflicts, and foster personal and collective growth. It's a reminder that sometimes the most powerful response lies in finding harmony, understanding, and accepting things as they are while maintaining our individuality and authenticity.

True Courage Is Knowing When to Walk Away

Now that we know fear is a reaction and courage is a choice we make, we must also be willing to walk away from things we have outgrown. We often find comfort in the familiar, even if it holds us back and limits our potential. Stepping away from what we know can be unsettling because it means relinquishing control and venturing into the unknown. But growth and personal evolution require us to let go of the old and embrace the new.

Leaving behind what we have outgrown takes more courage than staying put. It means acknowledging that more awaits us beyond our comfort zones. It means challenging ourselves to push past our limitations and embrace the uncertainty accompanying growth.

While it may be daunting, it's essential to recognize that staying in situations that no longer align with our values, goals, or personal growth can stifle our potential and hinder our progress. By having the courage to walk away from what no longer serves us, we create space for new opportunities, experiences, and personal transformation.

Here are some short steps we can take to embrace the courage to walk away from things we have outgrown:

1. **Reflect on Your Values:** Take a moment to identify your core values and assess whether the situation or circumstance aligns with them. If it no longer resonates with who you are and what you believe in, it may be a sign that it's time to move on.

2. **Evaluate Your Growth and Progress:** Reflect on your personal and professional growth within the current situation. Consider whether you have reached a plateau or if there are limited opportunities for further development. If you feel stagnant or unchallenged, it may indicate that it's time to seek new challenges elsewhere.

3. **Trust Your Intuition:** Listen to your inner voice and trust your instincts. If you have a persistent feeling that it's time to move on, honor that intuition. Sometimes, our gut feelings provide valuable guidance, even if they seem intimidating at first.

4. **Seek Support:** Reach out to trusted friends, mentors, or colleagues for their perspectives and advice. Discuss your concerns and fears with someone who can offer objective insights and support your decision-making process.

5. **Create a Plan:** Develop a plan for your transition. Consider your financial stability, career prospects, and any necessary preparations before making a move. A clear road map can help alleviate some of the fear and uncertainty of walking away.

6. **Take Small Steps:** Take small steps toward your desired change. This could include updating your résumé, networking with professionals in your desired field, or seeking additional training or education. Breaking down the process into manageable tasks can make it feel less overwhelming.

7. **Embrace the Unknown:** Remember that growth and personal development often require stepping into the unknown. Embrace the uncertainty and view it as an opportunity for new experiences and possibilities. Trust in your ability to adapt and navigate through change.

8. **Celebrate Your Courage:** Recognize and celebrate the courage it takes to walk away from what no longer serves you. Acknowledge your bravery and resilience as you embrace new beginnings and the potential for personal and professional fulfillment.

By taking these short steps, we can gradually build the courage to let go of what holds us back and create space for growth, happiness, and self-fulfillment.

Just remember: fear is a natural reaction, but we have the courage to choose differently in the workplace. By becoming aware of our programmed reactions and embracing vulnerability, we can incrementally build our confidence. It's about choosing our own path, trusting ourselves, and using our voice to advocate for our desires and values. True courage lies in knowing our values, using our voice, and knowing when to let go. With courage, we can overcome fear, be seen and heard, and create a workplace where our authentic selves thrive.

CONCLUSION

Integrating Lessons:
Journey to Total Freedom

*W*e spend so much of our lives in a program and on autopilot, not realizing what is true for us or what we desire as our legacy. We forget that big fancy titles in corporations, owning cars and homes, and all the other status symbols we collect are not a legacy.

Being all of you in a world that is trying to shove you in a box is a legacy!

Shrinking ourselves into a box of conformity goes against any legacy. We are teaching our children that being a martyr and selling our souls and beings is more important that being real. Is that the role model and evolution we desire to leave behind?

Breaking free from the corporate box requires the courage to not fit in and to reignite our innate creativity, curiosity, and passion.

Throughout this book, we have explored the outdated limitations and lies that we have imposed on ourselves and all the lies we have bought as true. In our journey, we have learned the importance of looking within and unmasking ourselves, confronting our traumas, celebrating our inner immigrant, and embracing our uniqueness. By confidently celebrating our differences and challenging toxic masculinity and femininity in the workplace, we reclaim our power and realign with our true values and desires.

We have also discovered that perception is not reality; it is merely a point of view. By reframing our self-perception and recognizing the hidden conscious leader within us, we tap into our true potential. Fear may be a reaction, but we must embrace courage and be seen and heard with confidence.

Let us remember that breaking free is not easy. It requires ongoing self-reflection, resilience, and a commitment to personal growth. But by daring to step outside the confines of the lies, myths, and norms, we unlock a world of possibility, fulfillment, and genuine success.

May this book serve as a guide and catalyst for your journey toward breaking free, unmasking your true self, and reigniting the creativity, curiosity, and passion that were slowly burned out of you.

Embrace the courage to not fit in, and may your path be one of authenticity, fulfillment, and the unwavering pursuit of your true potential.

My journey has had many ups, downs, tears, bruises, laughter, and adventure. I don't regret any of it, as it allowed me to step into the path of consciousness and become the true essence of the courageous and creative little girl that was always there.

As a final reminder, I close with what I started: the letter to little me. I give you one last final homeplay:

Pen to Paper Homeplay: Tools and Exercises

- Write a letter to little you. What would you say?
- Print out a picture of you and look at it while you write the letter.
- Have the courage to frame it along with your picture as a reminder every day to step into your power!

Here is mine again. I hope it will spark transformation in your life the way it did in mine.

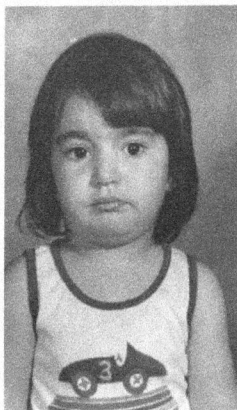

Dear Michelle Mehrnoosh Bazargan,

Hello, sweet, beautiful warrior. First of all, thank you for choosing to come to this weird planet. I know it seems like a strange land. I know you are highly sensitive and can "feel" everyone and everything and are a bit confused on what to do with the gift of being highly aware, having a 6th sense, and being an extreme empath and feeling so wrong.

You have been given a gift to see possibilities everywhere you go. This is why you look at people and desire to heal them and gift them everything you know they can have. You see their being and their souls and know they can be capable of creating anything they desire.

Please know that your awareness, your sensitivity, your passion, and your lens that anything and everything is possible in this abundant world is a strength, not a weakness.

You are different, you are here to create magic. You are powerful. Because of this, people may choose to be scared of you and scared that you can see them. The real them. The infinite being in them that is choosing to shrink and settle. They will hate that you see what they are capable of even though they are choosing limitation and lack for themselves.

They will judge you, fight you, abuse you, hurt you, shrink you, reject you, and try to tell you that you are wrong and to turn off your "light." It's a lie, it's not true. No matter how much you change and morph yourself, you will be seen as "too much" or "not enough." You will be too fat, too fit, too ugly, too pretty, too smart, too dumb, too tall . . .

Please don't change who you are, please don't lose you into the darkness of judgment. Whatever you do, please don't change your name to be accepted. Changing your name will become the beginning of hiding and masking your light, which is the essence of your real name. *Mehrnoosh* dates back to centuries of Persian origin, translated to mean "eternal light" or "everlasting light."

Mehr means "sun" or "love," and *noosh* translates to "eternal" or "everlasting." This name is quite poetic in its meaning and is reflective of the richness of Persian linguistic and cultural nuances.

You will eventually enter the corporate and workplace environment; you will be exposed to survival and lack mindsets and see outdated structures and methods that has turned many people into unconscious robots. You will see this right away and make it your job to save people and open their eyes to greater possibilities. You won't understand why they choose this life. You will try to convince them that the world is an abundant and big place, that there is so much to go around and it's not worth it to hate others for positions, titles, and money. They will hate you for it while secretly wishing they had your courage.

Don't separate, resist, react, or go into defense and fight. Definitely don't align and agree with them and make them right or prove them wrong. That will only give them more power and control over you. Don't step into their darkness. Keep your light and your power—it's the true essence of you.

I will write you a book and leave it for you. Please read it over and over! Don't buy the lies. Don't hide and mask up; it may feel good temporarily, yet it will come back to try to destroy you. Most of all, build your awareness, ask questions of everything and everyone. Use the tools in this book. Take absolutely nothing at face value.

Trust you, honor you, and be grateful for you. No one knows what they are doing or what is "true" for you; they are not you. Only you know, so don't pretend you don't. Don't make anyone else more important or powerful than you. They will try to convince you they have "more experience" and know more. It's a facade, and you are radically different.

You will most likely spend most of your time building a career in the business world or interacting with people in the workplace in some capacity. Make sure your career is aligned with who you are and what you desire to create in this world as your own legacy, not what is forced upon you.

True warrior status and legacy is not fitting in and not conforming; it's having the courage to be you and choose you. The rest is a lie. Have fun and laugh a lot!

Shine your light bright and inspire others to do the same. Now go have some ice cream and look up at the sky. It's filled with infinite possibilities and magic.

Love you to the moon!

I am who I am. My real name means "eternal light," and I am a proud, strong, compassionate, and courageous Iranian American who knows that accents, pain, failing, learning, grit, curiosity, and resilience are all signs of courage.

What if one person (you) choosing to be more of you inspired others to be and do the same, and that is how we evolved and changed the world? Never forget Rumi's words: "You are not a drop in the ocean. You are the entire ocean in a drop."

We all have the power to be a ripple of change. That is how we evolve our beautiful planet and leave it better for our children and future generations. What can I do? I am just one person—said 8+ billion people. Imagine if all of us took one very small step the drops can turn into a tsunami of change.

Please go back, reread, leverage the tools, and commit to one or a few!

"What can I do? I am just one person—said 8+ billion people."

I hope I have inspired you and empowered you to have the courage to become aware and take back your curiosity, passion, creativity, and compassion. That is something a machine, a robot, or artificial intelligence will never replace.

COURAGE TO CHOOSE
We thrive when we're free to be ourselves

Connection
Confidence
Creativity

Scan For Resources
and to Connect

RESOURCES   www.michellebazargan.com

Acknowledgments

I've made many unconventional, challenging choices on my journey. Writing a book stands among the top three toughest endeav-
ors I've completed, fostering a level of mental, emotional, and
spiritual growth that I did not think was possible. It lays bare your
blind spots, confronts perfectionism, tests patience, and exposes
layers of vulnerability and self-empathy versus self-judgment. It
forces you to become more aware and present. As an ex-hardcore
athlete, I thought, *How hard could this be? Focus, practice discipline,
fail, get some bruises, get up* . . . Nope, far more challenging than
that.

None of this journey would have been conceivable without the
unwavering support of my incredible family—my mother, Mehran-
giz Bazargan; my sister, Farnoosh Black; my brother-in-law, Aaron
Black; and my incredibly inspirational niece, Lana Azadeh Black.
My father, Mohsen Bazargan, who now has dementia and won't
know I published this book, taught me and always would say, "Faith
and patience, Mehrnoosh Jan" ("my dear" in Farsi) and "Never, ever
accept a NO from someone. There is always a way to your goals and
dreams—always."

The overwhelming support and encouragement I have received
from remarkable individuals, including close friends, family spanning distances, mentors, and the entire book-writing community,

have been instrumental. To all who crossed paths with me, whether for five minutes or countless hours, your uplifting presence carried me through the highs and lows, self-doubts, and moments of panic.

I'm forever transformed by and deeply grateful for everyone who has been a part of my life and this profound experience. Let's create a different possibility for our collective future.

Love and gratitude,
Mehrnoosh

Endnotes

1. https://libquotes.com/charlie-chaplin/quote/lby8f9f

2. https://hbr.org/2013/05/creating-the-best-workplace-on-earth

3. https://www.forbes.com/sites/forbesleadershipforum/2013/11/13/heres-to-the-death-of-microsofts-rank-and-yank/?sh=73aee874777b

4. https://pingboard.com/org-charts/evolution-org-charts

5. https://hbr.org/2013/05/creating-the-best-workplace-on-earth and https://www.mckinsey.com/capabilities/people-and-organizational-performance/our-insights/new-leadership-for-a-new-era-of-thriving-organizations

6. https://www.forbes.com/sites/grantfreeland/2020/10/06/great-leaders-realize-they-dont-even-know-what-they-dont-know/?sh=2ae665b76c41

7. https://www.theatlantic.com/health/archive/2020/02/most-annoying-corporate-buzzwords/606748/

8. https://blog.hptbydts.com/people-leave-managers-not-companies

9. https://hbr.org/2023/02/how-important-is-a-college-degree-compared-to-experience

10. https://www.businessinsider.com/microsoft-hr-layoffs-not-your-friend-former-vp-chris-williams-2022-7?r=US&IR=T

11. https://www.bbc.com/worklife/article/20220720-the-case-for-job-hopping

12. https://www.huddleup.ai/blog/performance-management/why-annual-performance-reviews-are-outdated/

13. file:///Users/michellebazargan/Downloads/state-of-the-global-workplace-2023-download.pdf

14. https://www.zippia.com/advice/burnout-statistics/

15. Dr. Nicole LePera known as the "Holistic Psychologist"

16. Dr. Joe Dispenza explains in his research from his book *Breaking the Habit of Being Yourself: How to Lose Your Mind and Create a New One*

17. https://eightify.app/summary/personal-development/transform-your-mindset-for-success-dr-joe-dispenza-s-brainwashing-techniques

18. *Breaking the Habit of Being Yourself* by Dr. Joe Dispenza

19. https://eightify.app/summary/personal-development/transform-your-mindset-for-success-dr-joe-dispenza-s-brainwashing-techniques

20. https://www.istockphoto.com/account/download/individual/credits

21. *The Deepest Well: Healing the Long-Term Effects of Childhood Adversity* by Nadine Burke Harris, M.D.

22. *The Body Keeps the Score: Brain, Mind, and Body in the Healing of Trauma* by Bessel van der Kolk, M.D.

23. *What Happened to You? Conversations on Trauma, Resilience, and Healing* by Oprah Winfrey and Dr. Bruce Perry

24. *The Myth of Normal: Trauma, Illness, and Healing in a Toxic Culture* by Daniel Maté and Gabor Maté

25. *It Didn't Start with You* by Mark Wolynn

26. *Complex PTSD: From Surviving to Thriving: A Guide and Map for Recovering from Childhood Trauma* by Pete Walker

27. *Daring Greatly: How the Courage to Be Vulnerable Transforms the Way We Live, Love, Parent, and Lead* (New York: Avery, 2012) and *Rising Strong: How the Ability to Reset Transforms the Way We Live, Love, Parent, and Lead* (New York: Spiegel & Grau, 2015) by Brené Brown

28. *A Little Book About Trauma-Informed Workplaces* by Nathan Gerbrandt, Randy Grieser, Vicki Enns

29. *Managing Trauma in the Workplace: Supporting Workers and Organisations* by Noreen Tehrani

30. https://www.global-psychotrauma.net/global-prevalence-of-trauma

31. https://hbr.org/2016/07/the-family-dynamics-we-grew-up-with-shape-how-we-work

32. ttps://hbr.org/2017/04/if-humble-people-make-the-best-leaders-why-do-we-fall-for-charismatic-narcissists

33. https://www.ncbi.nlm.nih.gov/pmc/articles/PMC9301298/

34. https://newsroom.haas.berkeley.edu/research/how-narcissistic-leaders-infect-their-organizations-culture/

35. https://www.ncbi.nlm.nih.gov/pmc/articles/PMC9301298/, https://newsroom.haas.berkeley.edu/research/how-narcissistic-leaders-infect-their-organizations-culture/, and https://hbr.org/2017/04/if-humble-people-make-the-best-leaders-why-do-we-fall-for-charismatic-narcissists

36. *The Biology of Belief: Unleashing the Power of Consciousness, Matter, and Miracles* by Bruce H. Lipton, PhD

37. *The Field: The Quest for the Secret Force of the Universe* by Lynne McTaggart

38. *The Namesake* by Jhumpa Lahiri

39. *The Book of Unknown Americans* by Cristina Henríquez

40. *Behold the Dreamers* by Imbolo Mbue

41. *Exit West* by Mohsin Hamid

42. https://web.pdx.edu/~mev/PS%20399%20WIN%202020/Derks%20et%20al_Queen%20Bee.pdf

43. https://www.forbes.com/sites/forbescoachescouncil/2020/01/21/why-women-dont-always-support-other-women/?sh=14ab81b73b05

44. https://headsupguys.org/suicide-stats-men/

45. *The Desire Map Experience: A Guide to Creating Goals with Soul* by Danielle LaPorte

46. Modified from https://www.pinterest.com/pin/best-career-advice-that-i-can-give-dont-ever-attach-yourself-to-a-person-a-place-a-company-an-organization-or-a-project-attach-yourself-to-a-mission-a-ca--187673509464120953/

47. https://www.pinterest.com/pin/best-career-advice-that-i-can-give-dont-ever-attach-yourself-to-a-person-a-place-a-company-an-organization-or-a-project-attach-yourself-to-a-mission-a-ca--187673509464120953/

48. Richard Branson Virgin Atlantic https://www.virgin.com/branson-family/richard-branson-blog/everybody-is-a-genius-in-their-own-wonderful-way?utm_medium=social&utm_source=linkedin&utm_author=richard

49. https://www.facebook.com/VeoAcademy/photos/a.4271554 90812179/1970936129767433/?type=3

50. *The Innovator's DNA, Updated, with a New Preface: Mastering the Five Skills of Disruptive Innovators* by Jeff Dyer, Hal Gregersen, et al. | Jun 4, 2019

51. https://www.linesbyloes.com